May this book bless your family with more peace, harmony & happiness now and forever!

Love,
B.

I BELIEVE IN YOU + ALL THAT YOU DO TO MAKE YOUR KIDS DREAMS COME TRUE!

HERE'S TO YOUR PARENTING SUCCESS!

CHEERS,
Thomas Liotta

Learn to Speak Kid

Your whole world will change as you gain harmony and cooperation with your kids! You can even take the "*dis*" out of child *dis*ruptive behavior *dis*orders like ADHD and oppositional defiant *dis*order.

For speaking inquiries, permission requests and bulk order purchase options, contact support@creatingchampionsforlife.com.

Creating Champions For Life
Bonnie & Thomas Liotta
701 5th Ave. STE 4200
Seattle WA 98104
CreatingChampionsForLife.com

Artwork and Design by Angela Domet

DEDICATION

I dedicate the contents of this book to my teachers, coaches, leaders, mentors, families, students and friends for their unconditional love and valuable world of experiences that allowed the perfect environment for this knowledge to manifest within me.

I acknowledge the one woman in my life who made this book finally available for the rest of the world to see and use. She is the *Apple to my Pie*, so I made her my wife, BONNIE LIOTTA. Because of her, the vision of empowering all the world's parents has come true!

This book contains the experience of more than 15,000 hours, 2,000 children and over 800 families with parents who usually began with an attitude of
"Please, fix my kid!"

Contents

Publisher's Preface

This book contains the experience of more than 15,000 hours, 2,000 children and over 800 families who usually began with an attitude of "Please, fix my kid!" However, there was a sheer desire to create healing, unity and empowerment within all families worldwide.

Here, you have an entire philosophy on successfully raising confident, productive and appreciative children in the 21st century! It has even been proven to remove the "DIS" from disruptive childhood behavior disorders. This information has been organized so that, when fully implemented, it will bring riches to your life in terms of happiness, peace and productivity. This book describes how to achieve the best results with your children and precisely how to do it!

It presents complete instructions on always getting the best behavior, creating the best relationships and receiving the most cooperation from your child, children and or teen every day of the year.

It will provide you with all of the necessary tools and the perfect system of self-analysis, readily disclosing what has prevented you from successfully interacting with your child in the past.

It describes the formula Thomas C. Liotta used perfectly to create successful circumstances and positive results with more than 800 families. He witnessed over 2,000 children take ownership of their lives, develop successful personality characteristics and improve their self-image. With these children, there was a dramatic increase in personal productivity, behavior and school grades. This philosophy works with every child in every situation.

You may have a wonderful family unit and do not need all the information in this book or the complete *Learn to Speak Kid Self-Study Course*. Still, you may need one idea, chart or suggestion that will allow you to add another dimension of positivity for you and your child. Somewhere within these pages are the answers you seek to solve the issues you may have with your child.

This book was inspired by Bonnie Liotta, a single mom raising four children. When Thomas began to share some of his wisdom, knowledge and personal child-rearing philosophies with her. They worked! She knew that every parent in the world deserved this information!

In this book, *Learn to Speak Kid*, 12 principles of child-rearing provide information essential for every parent choosing to see their child set up for the most success possible in their life, now and forever! When applied correctly, the information you read in this book will guarantee success for your child, your family unit and you as an individual. The research and applied application of gathering this information, before this book was written and before the book could be an idea conceived to be written, is an estimated 15,000 hours over 15 years with more than 2,000 children.

The knowledge in this book is not and has not been duplicated anywhere because the philosophy was initially created out of personal necessity and existed only in the mind of the philosopher Thomas C. Liotta.

Riches can be described through financial materials, but not all riches come from money. For most people, a core achievement is to find peace, attain freedom and create harmonious relationships with loved ones. They also need to understand that true peace of mind is only recognizable and measurable in terms of spirituality.

In the last couple of decades, the family unit has become recognizably divided; many parents find themselves in situations they do not yet know how to deal with. All who read, understand and APPLY the 12 principles of the *Learn to Speak Kid* formula will create and enjoy peace in the home, have authentic joyful relationships with their children and watch their offspring create success in their lives beyond their wildest imaginations.

Here, you have the necessary tools, strategies and power to lead your family toward cooperation, fun and peace that is measurable only spiritually.

Little Tommy and His Dad (Tommy II and Tommy I)

Author's Preface
Thomas C. Liotta

In the late summer of 1989, I found myself searching for meaning in my life. I was looking for more. One day I felt an energy flowing inside me that I had never experienced before. I found myself being drawn outside, towards the driveway, until I ended up at my pickup truck. When I arrived at my truck, I got into the driver's seat and started to drive. About an hour later, I found myself parked in the parking lot of a Taekwondo martial arts school which is something I certainly did not plan. I felt then, and am positive today, that I was led there; I was meant to be there for reasons far larger than myself. I walked into the school and introduced myself. I told the master the story I just told you and registered for class.

What inspired me the most was when I learned that you could go up the rankings as a student, where you began as a white belt and moved up the rankings through 12 colors, all the way up to a black belt. Here, I found a path that allowed me the opportunity to improve, grow and expand myself to a higher standard of life: a life of excellence mentally, physically and spiritually.

I worked hard and earned my black belt in 1994, five years into my personal development journey. At this point, I was offered the opportunity to teach white belts. This allowed my students to move up the same path of excellence I had experienced, as they were being led by me, similar to a father and son passing on skills, life lessons and discipline from generation to generation. This felt wonderful to me.

I found myself being a role model, an example of possibilities to other students. I was showing them what was possible for them to grow mentally, physically and spiritually. Throughout the next three years, I developed my teaching expertise to teach and train beginner, intermediate and advanced students. The coolest part about this is that once you follow the path from white belt to black belt, you can never go through that path again yourself. Like riding a bike, once you know how to ride, you can never "not know." When you guide someone else, you experience the journey again through their eyes, emotions and experiences, allowing me to renew my training repeatedly. To me, I wasn't just their teacher. I felt that I was on a mission to carry on traditions, and at the same time, I found myself building deeper stronger friendships with the students. The connections were very strong because our bonds were created through mutual learning experiences, like a subculture or a family unit.

In 1997, my teacher asked three black belts to come into his office. I was one of them. He said he had to leave the school to return to Korea and asked if one of us would like to take over and run the school. I don't know why, so you can't ask me that, but instantly, I said, "Yes." I don't even know where the words came from. I cared so much about the school, the students and the path of excellence that I was overcome with a definite decision.

At this point, I discovered the business side of things when it came to running a martial arts school. The business side meant that there needed to be cash flow, and cash flow came from new and existing students taking higher-ranking belt tests. The school's landlord does not care how many students you have or how long it takes for your students to move up the rankings; they want their rent every month and, they want it on time. There was a fee associated with every belt test, and often students were forced to test and pass without being ready because the school needed the money. These tests are what keep the lights on in most Dojos.

When I took over the school, I had a full-time job to support myself and cover the difference. I could run my school without any income. I could pour my heart into the students. I noticed that many students were three, four or five belts into a 12-belt system, and they still could not tie their belts. They would ask their mom or dad to tie their belts at tournaments. In martial arts, there should be some signs of personal responsibility as you move up the ranks of excellence to black belt. The ability to tie your belt should be one of them!

I had an integrity issue with this. I believed that if the student could not tie their belt, they should not have a status any higher than a beginning belt, which, for the most part, is considered a white belt. I began to add more and more curriculum to the belt levels to represent what I had learned while studying in Korea. This basic concept of integrity seemed to be diluted or washed out as schools became more and more commercial. This fact was truly disturbing to me. I began a quest to find out about government grants and foundation money so I could run the school based on the children's character development rather than the pocketbook of the business. This would later introduce an incredible opportunity to many children whose moms or dads could not afford for them to come.

I was on a mission to help children experience their path to excellence. I set my mindset on how to make the school work and create a positive experience for everyone. It became the first martial arts school in Washington State to become a martial arts after-school program. Finally, parents in our community could have a constructive alternative to regular daycare. During this process, I met many single moms who would have loved to have their children attend, but they received subsidies for daycare and could not afford any alternative. That began the quest of getting the school to become a state-licensed childcare center that teaches martial arts.

As pioneers, we were the first school to implement a martial arts after-school program and the first fully licensed martial arts daycare center. As a prerequisite, the director of the program (myself) was required to have a minimum of a two-year degree in early childhood development from a credible institution. My school worked with elementary and school-aged children, so I completed both two-year programs. I will always remember the first day of orientation; it was hilarious when I walked in (the only male) and was told I was in the wrong place!

We ended up with all the funding we needed to provide uniforms, a games room and field trips for the children. We began to receive many registrations for the after-school program.

I never wanted to see the look on a child's face when they did everything right to earn a logo uniform of the third-ranking belt of orange, but couldn't get one because Mom didn't have an extra $100. Here's little Timmy, who has earned his belt and uniform, but with a cost of $200 and no money available to pay for it. Little Timmy would understand this as "I'm not worth it." This injustice became my driving force. Everybody thought it was strange and would comment, "If they can't afford it, just send them to daycare." But, I had a mission to bring joy to these children.

I began working with many of my students' parents. They were mostly single moms with one to four children. I saw good-hearted single moms working to make things go well for their children while using parenting techniques that worked against them. My main driving force to succeed was to provide what I knew would be lifelong skills that their children would have forever, to do so affordably and to see smiles on all of the children's faces.

Through this mission, I was honorably invited into many families as a family member, role model or father figure to these children. Even though I do not have a child of my own, I feel that I have raised thousands of children. I learned detailed things about them from watching them turn obstacles into opportunities with character development training.

I'm not here to *sell* you on listening to me over someone else. You would listen to me because I have been through the trenches and I discovered simple techniques that worked to achieve desired results with school-aged kids — *every time.* Just like lowering the temperature of water will create ice every time, when you create the right environment, ask the right questions and find out what is important to the child, you get the desired results. These are time-tested and mother-approved techniques.

I discovered something incredible about kids. When the environment is correct, children behave beautifully. I wanted the school's teachings to last forever in their hearts. I wanted it to mean something. I didn't want my school to be a place that would take our students' money and not care what they learned. Sadly, I saw that happening in many other schools.

Children could participate in the program and as soon as they began to show characteristics of self-control at home, at school and in Taekwondo, they would be eligible to test for yellow belt. Not until then. The children would know that their devotion to cooperation and engaging in learning earned them the privilege to test.

I loved observing children taking ownership of what their bodies could do. They began to say things like "I am in control of my body and my actions." They began to release excuses of why things didn't happen or didn't get completed. They began to *take responsibility* for basics such as folding their uniform and tying their belt. I enjoyed how children would begin to automatically do things for their parents and teachers by being asked only once.

This was why their parents wanted them to come to do martial arts in the first place, to learn self-discipline. It did not feel good in my heart to advertise "Learn Self-Discipline" and then see that they had not yet learned it after a year. I love watching children be able to focus on tasks and finish them in a timely manner, which many of the parents I worked with did not think was possible for their children. They were wrong.

When the children first came to me, they complained, blamed and acted out. Parents asked me, "Can you fix my child?" Within a very short period, I could take the entire class, these same children, to the fire station for a field trip and be welcomed with open arms because the kids showed self-control, responsibility, self-discipline and focus.

I *Learned to Speak Kid* to help us care for one hundred-plus children in our after-school and all-day summer camp programs. Any parent can handle a responsible, self-disciplined child with self-control. What if you had 100 children like that? You could go to a movie theatre and have fun! And we did. You could take them all to a Mariners baseball game and have all the children stay safe, happy and well-behaved. And we did that, too. You could take them on an overnight trip to the Museum of Flight and leave the museum cleaner than when you arrived. We did that as well! I had fun witnessing improved behavior, self-confidence and overall happiness. I saw children who developed self-discipline, responsibility and gratitude.

After being *ridiculed* and *violently opposed,* my program was *accepted by self-evidence* in 2004 when the Creating Champions For Life Character Development Program was nominated and inducted into the Martial Arts Hall of Fame for the Most Creative School Program

Award. We were the first fully licensed martial arts daycare and after-school program for kids and teens.

In 2009, a large corporation bought the property and vacated everyone off the premises. They destroyed the building. The children were moved to other programs. It hurt my soul. It was then that I continued my personal development journey, attending seminars and workshops around the world, including China, Korea and Egypt, to improve myself even more.

Significant Turning Point in the Future of Parenting...

While on that journey, I found myself in the Bahamas on a personal development cruise ship in January 2011. There, I met Bonnie Harrison. One thing led to another, and through collaboration with her, I had an opportunity to meet her four children in May of 2011. I immediately observed how she fell into the same category as the hundreds of families I worked with at my martial arts school. She was a single parent who appeared to make decisions so her children would feel happy rather than teach them life skills that would serve them for the rest of their lives. I watched her raise her children on a *welfare system* of give, give and give. I have never forced my knowledge on anyone, but when I observed Bonnie giving her children things to make them happy, I had to say something.

You see, I know that when you continually give things to your children, you have to continue giving them more and more to create the illusion of love. She was filling her bucket with water that was being siphoned out by her four children faster than she could fill it. This would include energy, money and time. When it came to a simple example of "Mom, can I?" she would always answer, "Yes." However, when her children would ask me for something, I would say, "Sure, I would love for you to play on my phone. What would you like to trade for it?" At first, they would look at me funny. It was like they just ate a sour candy. "What? Trade? Earn?"

The first example of this special language Bonnie observed was when her children cleaned her car so they could play a game on my cell phone. The children were excited. She asked them to come inside, and they said, "We can't come in yet. We are not done cleaning the car." That was a shock to Bonnie. She asked me, "What the heck did you just say to my kids? I couldn't get them to do that if I paid them."

I used a simple technique I taught my students in my martial arts daycare center. I learned what the children wanted and gave it to them in a trade. I understood that they appreciate it more when they work for it.

At that point, Bonnie had the same experience that the families I had worked with several years before also experienced. She said, "You are doing something magical and whatever you are doing, it works!" I remember Bonnie telling her friends "If I didn't see it for myself, I would never have believed it."

Bonnie began to ask more and more questions. "What do you answer when they say this...?" "You took how many children to the bowling alley? I can't take my kids anywhere because all they do is want more."

We stayed in contact as often as possible about this, and I began to coach her to help her create a new environment in her home. The more she implemented the strategies, the more success she began to experience. Like many other single parents, she felt that this was so valuable she would pay any amount of money to have this knowledge. As a successful entrepreneur, success coach and inspirational speaker, she knew in her heart if this worked for her four children, she had to share it with others, including YOU. She asked me, "Do you know how many other moms out there would love to know just some of this information?"

What a great moment. Bonnie felt that this knowledge must be shared with other parents around the world. She knew that bringing this information would be the saving grace for moms, dads and children everywhere.

Bonnie and I were married in the spring of 2012. And that began the journey we are now on. Guiding and showing moms, dads, teachers and children how to create harmony, peace and cooperation has become our life purpose and mission.

I am grateful to have you on this journey with us.

Creating Champions For Life...
Any parent can handle a responsible, self-disciplined child with self-control.

Author's Preface
Bonnie Liotta

How excited were you when you discovered you would be a parent for the first time? What kind of emotions did you experience throughout the gestational period of your pregnancy or adoption process? Do you remember how much instant love you felt for that unborn child?

Whether you are a mother or a father, we have all been there. You would have the perfect child and parent differently than your parents did. Have you ever heard yourself say, "I am never going to be like my mom or dad!" And then you found yourself saying and doing the exact thing you did not want to duplicate? Through all the emotions, the anticipation and the excitement, the day comes and the new baby arrives in your world.

Wow! The pain of labor immediately disappears. The room goes quiet. You lay your eyes on the most beautiful creature you have ever had the pleasure of laying your eyes upon. An overwhelming feeling of absolute joy hits your soul like a sledgehammer, but with the softness of Cupid's arrow. It's a love that you have never felt before. You decide that this baby, your child, will want for nothing. You have already decided that your child will have a better life than you had when you were a child. They would wear the nicest clothes, have the nicest things and always be safe and secure. You would parent so well that your children would be different from the other children. They would be polite and well-behaved and would not need to rebel.

I know we all do this, or at least most of us do this. Am I right? We look forward to them taking their first steps and saying their first words. What happens then? We begin to hear, "Mom, Mom, Mom, Mom, Mom, Mom, Mom, Mom, Dad, Mom, Mom," and we wonder who taught them how to talk! Are you with me on this?

In a day and age when babies seem to be born with cell phones in their hands and the knowledge of how to log on to the computer, making sure that they feel loved has become our number one priority. This is the first time in history that parents have thought this way. So, what the hell do we do with our kids now?

It seems the more you give to your children, the less appreciative they are: the more you do for them, the more depressed they become. Do you notice this, too? If you didn't, you will notice it now.

What is wrong with our children?

We are at a very critical time in this world. There has been a dramatic rise in childhood depression, youth suicides, drug overdoses and school shootings.

It's time to do something!

I raised my four children as a single mom. Like you, I always wanted to be a great, best and magnificent parent. And I thought I was. I have always worked extremely hard, ensuring my children had everything they needed. I read parenting books and followed all of the techniques (well, some of the techniques) to the letter. One of the techniques I used often was consistent time-outs. I stuck to my guns when they were toddlers and well into their childhood.

On December 24th, 2008, at 7:00 am, I remember my three-year-old son, Zachary, had a temper tantrum in Walmart. We were in the line to pay, but I wouldn't get him a chocolate bar. Right then, I put him in a time-out until he was done. It was a very long 30 minutes. I thought it worked because he never again had another temper tantrum in public. However, I would handle the situation completely differently today! I didn't know any better. The repercussions of my actions did not appear immediately, but would show up years later. I would have argued with anyone that I was right about sticking to my guns. I will tell you right now: time-outs work when they are young, but pretty soon, they are bigger, older and striving for independence. Punishment is a short-term solution at best. Humiliating my three-year-old in Walmart was a mistake.

I witnessed Thomas use some new approaches with my children and any child he came in contact with. I saw amazing positive transformations. It was then I became determined to share this information with the world!

I saw my 13-year-old son, who was refusing to get up and go to school, get up and go to school every day by his own choice. All of a sudden, he liked school! It is now 18 months later, and he still gets up on his own, gets ready for his day and is at school on time every day.

I saw my 12-year-old daughter go from "If you loved me, you would pay for my cell phone!" to getting herself a paper route, taking it very seriously and generating the plan to make her own money. She is learning that receiving nice things in this world takes:

1. A Goal
2. A Plan
3. Taking Action
4. Perseverance

Even better than that, she and my children were all developing a solution oriented mindset.

I saw my 10-year-old daughter, Jennie, go from always talking about how people are mean to her and how no one likes her to "Hey, Mom! Do you know who is awesome?" "Who is awesome, Jennie?" "I am!"

To me, that is what it means to be rich in life. To look in the mirror and know that you are awesome. Jennie never had that before.

I witnessed my seven-year-old son, Zachary, go from two and eight-hour-long temper tantrums daily to solving issues and moving onward with a positive happy attitude in less than five minutes. I heard Zachary say, "I like myself."

Before meeting Thomas that didn't happen.

When I left my first husband, the love of my life was my oldest son, Jacob, who was six then. Although I moved on from the marriage to offer my kids a better life (I was fighting for my life spiritually, mentally and physically), my son hated me. I believe some of him still hates me today because of this decision.

The first time I heard him say, "I want to kill myself" was when he was seven years old! That was mortifying. He was very mean, rude and disrespectful to me, which just got worse as he got older. He was depressed and failing in school. I have discovered that his father has said horrifying messages to him about me throughout his entire life. Having Jacob treat me this way at such a young age felt like someone had his or her strong hands around my heart, and it ached. I had no idea what to do. My other two babies were too young to understand anything that was going on. Jennie was two and Kyra was four.

When I didn't know what to do, I would "put it on ignore." I thought these issues would go away when my children got older and that I would be able to communicate with them and be cool with them. I put many things on ignore while searching for success, my quest for freedom, independence and the chance to offer a better life to my children. I felt I had to offer them a better life than I had when I was young. Have you ever thought that before?

I still advocate for my fight for freedom. I choose to be an example to my children by showing them what it takes for them to reach their dreams. I no longer put issues on ignore. You can create solutions easily, elegantly and effortlessly when you have the correct tools, strategies and power to lead your family toward cooperation, fun and peace.

I know that you are busy; we are all busy in today's age. I worked in my business and spent all my free time with my children. I would take them swimming, to the park, and for walks in our River Valley. I would watch movies with them and tuck them in at night with a story. We had a birthday party every birthday (and it seems like there have been a million of them). I bought them whatever they wanted. We also had the opportunity to visit Disneyland and Mexico and we drove across Canada.

During this time, I ran a very large successful business. I continued to cook meals, clean the house and clean their rooms; I did everything for them. I would ask them to pick up their toys, which they did sometimes. I always allowed them to dress themselves and choose their hairstyles. Beyond that, I did everything. EVERYTHING!

Time seemed to disappear. Suddenly, my children were six, nine and 11; one had just turned 13. It seemed like a time warp. It was as if I was in the movie, *Back to the Future*, with Michael J. Fox. Hit a button, and BOOM! Fast forward five years. Three out of four of my kids were placed in a "strategies" class at school; my six-year-old began to bully other kids; my nine-year-old daughter complained that everyone was mean to her and that she didn't feel well every day; my 11 and 13-year-old, especially my 13-year-old, Jacob, began to show big time bad attitudes.

Jacob began sleeping in and then would not attend school. He would lie around the house. I was a single mom. My son was bigger than me, and he was deciding whether he was going to attend school or not. He was diagnosed with ADHD (attention deficit hyperactivity disorder) when he was in grade three. The doctor prescribed a drug called *Concerta*. It was supposed to slow him down during the day. That way, he could sit still in his chair and pay attention during school. Then, it would be out of his system by supper time. Okay, no harm, no foul.

 After two months of being on this drug, Jacob had a panic attack when he thought he was out of pills. I immediately threw the pills away and began to study nutrition. There is a chapter on nutrition in this book to get you started, but Thomas and I highly recommend researching and reading the ingredient labels when you buy groceries.

When I would discuss this with other people, I would hear things like "Well, their dad had ADHD, and he was prescribed medication, so it's in his genes." I passed it off as normal. My 13-year-old son's attitude was passed off as teenage rebellion.

My six-year-old son's story was that he was just not as smart as the other kids (although I never agreed with that). This bothered him so much that he ended up having a temper tantrum at school. He threw all the chairs around; they had to evacuate the room. I knew there was a problem. The only thing I knew how to do was to love him. I began to cater to him even more, but this did not help; he seemed to worsen. I began to accept this as the *youngest child syndrome*.

My nine-year-old daughter's depression was passed off as *middle child syndrome*. Do you see where I'm going with this? It was NOT normal! I had been duped. And so have YOU!

I would go to the mall or grocery store and witness terrible twos, horrific threes, snotty, unappreciative, pre-teen girls and rebellious teenage boys. This is all acceptable, well, maybe not acceptable, but it is considered normal in our society and many societies worldwide.

This is not how I imagined my life as a parent. I imagined that I would be such a cool, fantastic and loving parent that my kids would have no reason to rebel. Boy, was I naïve!

xxx

I was tired. I had candles burning on both ends. I found myself nagging, yelling, or just saying nothing at all. When I would take them anywhere, they would fight with each other, nag me in the car, and tattle on each other. This turned all of our family events into nightmares.

So, where did that leave me? I became very successful in business but was worn out as a parent. I couldn't keep a partner in my life. My house was a mess. And my kids were unappreciative, lazy, spoiled brats (or that's what I thought). I had given up as a parent and was looking forward to grandchildren.

I have been on a mission to help people accept and discover their greatness for nearly two decades. Thomas has been on the same mission, just using a different vehicle. We were both survivors from broken homes and self-limiting beliefs.

The Beginning...

When we met, Thomas and I quickly became friends and spent many hours on the phone. He heard the commotion in the background, yet he never said anything about my parenting or kids. Based on our conversations regarding coaching and training people, I knew he was brilliant. Every time I hung up the phone with him, it seemed like I was smarter.

Seeing that we shared a passion for helping people create positive change in their lives, I invited Thomas to develop a series of seminars in Canada.

Until this point, I knew that, like me, he had invested more than $100,000 in his self-education. Still, I had no idea he had earned two child development degrees at Highline Community College and Green River Community College. I was also unaware that he had owned and operated a martial arts after-school program and that over 2,000 children participated.

I thought that Thomas and I made our connection to help transform the lives of adults as we worked together to host events around the country. However, during the first week he stayed with my family, I noticed that my kids responded very well to him. They seemed happier and more helpful when they were around him. We pulled into the driveway one day, and my two youngest children, Zachary and Jennie, were with us.

I have already described my kids to you, so you know what I am about to tell you was completely unexpected. We pulled into the driveway. Thomas and I opened the vehicle doors to get out, but I did not hear anything from the kids. QUIET. I turned around to look in the backseat. Zachary and Jennie were tidying, organizing and wiping down the vehicle's interior. Wow! I looked at Thomas and asked, "What did you do to my kids?"

They were cleaning the truck *without* being asked AND having fun doing it! Thomas asked me, "If I saw that you have the ability to fill your bucket with greatness but that there are holes in your bucket and you are losing a lot of unnecessary energy, would you want me to tell you about it?" I sucked up my ego and answered, "Absolutely!"

Thomas started coaching me as a parent. When he went back to the USA that following weekend, I often called him to ask questions about dealing with certain situations with my kids. *What do I do when they do this? What do I say when they say that? How do I get my teenager to go to school without a war every morning?*

He would give me an answer. I would take notes and execute his plan. What he was telling me seemed simple enough, but what he was telling me to do was effective sometimes and not effective other times. I did not have this book to read, the audio to listen to, the videos to watch, or the Quick Study Guides to follow, so I easily made mistakes.

Implementing this new approach is like learning to speak a new language. Using the wrong accent can change the meaning of what you are saying; that's what I was doing. But, I could see a definite improvement nonetheless. My son Jacob began to go to school. He even told me one afternoon, "I did not want to get up this morning, but I thought about it and decided I had enough time to make the bus." I believe he experienced self-discipline for the first time in his short life. The good news is that it is now a year later, and he gets up every morning, goes to school and gets good grades! In fact, good grades are more important to him now than they are to me.

 Since I invested my time in *Learn to Speak Kid*, I have seen Zachary, Jennie and Jacob be released from any ADHD label at their schools. Zachary has developed enough self-control and self-discipline to focus on his schoolwork. Now, we get along in harmony

as we work together as a team. He does what he is asked to do by being asked only once. He is a true gentleman at home and in public.

My now 13-year-old daughter, Jennie, has gone from victim to victor. She knows how to set goals, persevere and earn everything she receives in life. She walks around the house saying, "You know who is awesome? ME!" No one will bully her anymore! She has also improved her self-confidence so much that she went from a strategies class with ADHD to a mainstream grade eight class! Earlier this year, they sent us a letter stating that she does not qualify for special needs funding. Yay!

Kyra, who is now 15, is more helpful. She gets straight *As* in school. When she did not make it onto the cheer team in the fall, she could persevere, practice and make success happen when she tried out again in the spring. Our relationship is closer than ever. She tells me everything about her day at school the minute she walks in the door. This is an incredible feeling.

Jacob is 16 today. He is learning that everything in life is not just handed to him. He has a job, goes to school daily, and helps around the house with a positive mental attitude. We can go for a car ride for family outings or be together at home and experience peace. I mean true peace.

I told Thomas, "We must make this a program for parents. Kids will be healed, taken off medication, and taught real-life skills. Parents need to get their hands on the information that YOU have in YOUR head. I know that it will be life-changing, not only for children but also for parents!" He answered, "Yeah, someday, when we have time."

I left it alone for about six months.

However, when I saw my entire home transform from chaos into an organized, clean home, and it wasn't done by me, I noticed everything was peaceful and quiet. No yelling. No fighting. No miscommunication. I knew that the *Learn to Speak Kid* program was the *magic pill* for parents everywhere around the globe.

The Day that Changed Everything...

After an hour of prayer, I called Thomas one morning and told him, "God just told me to give everything we've got to *Creating Champions For Life*." He responded with an inner knowing, "Okay." We had many projects we were passionate about, but we made a decision right then and there to put everything on hold.

And so it began—our journey that has brought you here.

We had no idea what it would look like or the sacrifices that we would make in the coming years to bring this philosophy of truth to the world. However, we knew we were committed, and we did and continue to do whatever it takes to make parenting with empowerment a reality for families worldwide.

During this time, I had joint custody. Their dad did not choose to engage with this new philosophy. When the children were with me, I could bring out the champion after a few solid days, but as soon as they were back in the environment of laziness, they returned to being victims. I am telling you this now: when you find that it works sometimes and then doesn't at other times, know that it is all in your delivery.

The outcome you have with your children is completely up to YOU! By truly engaging in this *Creating Champions For Life* philosophy, you will learn to speak a language that will prepare your kids for success. You will learn how to *guide* your child's behavior instead of utilizing the traditional fear-based punishment that has been misused since the beginning of time. Your children will learn to be resourceful, independent and successful at whatever THEY choose to create in life. You will witness your children develop stronger self-esteem. You will learn techniques and strategies to help you create a winning environment, understand what your kids are saying, and learn how to motivate them into immediate action.

It is an amazing feeling to watch your children create success in their lives on their own. It is an incredible feeling for them to have the opportunity to rise to be the true champions they are. Congratulations on embarking on a journey that will be a major turning point for you and your children.

This will create a team environment in your home, self-esteem for your child, and happiness for you all. It is a win-win for everyone. This is not just a book, but a mission and cause.

Thomas and I are now married. Our house is spotless (and I never have to take a cleaning day), our relationship is amazing, our business is booming, and we have seen my kids positively transform beyond what my wildest imagination conceived was possible.

This is the answer for parenting in the 21st century! If just a percentage of parents, teachers and caregivers begin to implement the *Creating Champions For Life* philosophy, positive change will be achieved throughout the world.

Introduction

The pain I feel in my heart right now is hard to describe. My heart feels heavy. It's like someone has their hands wrapped around it and squeezing it tight with a pulsating motion. That is the feeling associated with my love for my children, combined with the frustration associated with always wanting the best for them but also balance and peace for myself.

I have created the experiences I have with my children. I unknowingly overcompensated and made decisions for my kids that I believed would make them happy. I did not take those opportunities to teach them life skills. I can't turn back the clock now nor would I want to. Without my experiences, I would never have learned this amazing language. I now have to pay the price for my past decisions with my children, and I have a burning desire in my heart to help all parents, especially single moms, make the right decisions for themselves and their children. I have decided to right the wrongs I have done so that my children can be more successful.

I understand and realize that if this change is going to happen for my children and myself, it is up to me to make it happen. Logically, I know that the feeling of pain associated with my children comes at times when I am thinking about what I am going through, with thoughts of loss, fear and limitations. As an inspirational speaker who has studied success principles for nearly two decades, I know to always focus on the end result.

When I alter my thinking and look at what is being created, I realize that it is the *journey* that counts. Today's events are not the end but the beginning of a new start, a new future, and a broken cycle of dysfunction.

This journey, our journey, will be worth something as our story helps you and other families see that there is a much simpler, more elegant and more empowering way to raise your children than what most of us have been taught. There is hope for a brighter future of family unity.

You are about to discover information written on these pages that you will not find in any other parenting book. There is always time to make things right.

The purpose of writing this book and developing the *Learn to Speak Kid* self-study course for parents is to help guide and create peace within the family unit and help the next generation become solution-oriented, confident and productive.

No matter what you are currently experiencing, your children have a strong desire to please you and to achieve. When the correct environment has been established, all children are a pleasure to be around. As you become more involved, you will see your child advance in all areas of his or her life.

You will see a sad child become happy, an unappreciative child become appreciative, and an unhelpful child become helpful. You will see a weak child become strong, disrespect turn into respect, and your child become solution oriented. You will see a dramatic overall improvement in your child's character.

It's like this: if there is a polar opposite to everything, and there is, what if the polar opposite of your child's faults came to life?

You are in the right place at the right time and reading the right message to make a huge positive impact on and with your family. This book will rock your world, and, like me, you will want every parent on the face of this planet to receive a copy. We are with YOU!

Congratulations on taking YOUR first step to *Creating Champions For Life*! I pray you are aware that it is just the beginning of a new empowering parenting journey. As you know, just like earning a diploma or learning how to drive a car, it doesn't happen by reading a book once. It *takes time* and *consistently focused effort.* We are here to help you and lead you for as much and as long as it takes to make a difference for YOU.

And So YOUR Journey Begins...

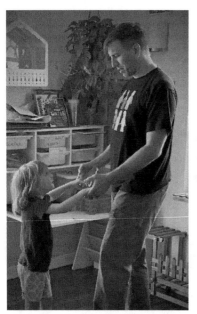

2

Chapter 1

Know Your Role as a Parent

~ My job is to give my child life skills so when he or she leaves me, he or she will have all the resources and ability to succeed at whatever they choose. ~
Thomas C. Liotta

Bonnie: Over the last several years, we, as a society, have witnessed a dramatic increase in childhood depression, teenage suicide, drug overdose and school gun shootings. ADHD has become a household name, and blatant disrespect has been accepted as normal adolescent behavior. Parents have lost or are losing control of their children. If your children are carrying cell phones, raiding the refrigerator whenever they choose, and playing on their own video machines, you are heading toward trouble, frustration and disappointment. Whether you agree with these statements or not at this moment, it is the truth. It's happening in homes all over the world.

The question is: how and why this is happening? Furthermore, is there anything you can do to make a change, break the pattern, and become a major part of a master plan to create a positive difference in the world when you **Know Your Role as a Parent**? I am happy to tell you the answer is a resounding "YES!" There is a magical language that you can learn when you have the right perspective. You are at the right place at the right time and reading the right book to change the momentum with your children. You can help them create successful habits that will serve them for the rest of their lives now and for all future generations.

It breaks my heart when I see a father load the truck for a family vacation, cook all the meals, and be in charge of virtually everything while his teenagers goof off, play video games and complain about how hungry they are.

It breaks my heart when I watch a fairly new mother yell at her toddler in the grocery store, "Stop it! You are embarrassing me!" while she continues to text on her cell phone while her toddler continues to cry harder.

It breaks my heart when I watch a mother constantly nag at her child, "Come here. Stop that. Get over here. That is bad. Do you want a time-out?" as the child continues to do what he is doing. It's like she doesn't even exist.

And it breaks my heart to see mothers and fathers everywhere bend over backward for their children to end up with unappreciative, disrespectful and unproductive teenagers who eventually become adults.

I know firsthand. I have created it. I have experienced it. However, I have taken control back as a parent. I know that you can do it, too. It's time to discover and truly come to **Know Your Role as a Parent**.

Do you understand that this is the first generation in the history of mankind when a parent's usual number one priority is to make sure their children are happy and feel loved? Society expects a good mom to spend money on her kids. It's in your "*good parent's*" job description to drive them everywhere they choose to go. We've been led to believe that somehow by overcompensating for our children, it will be returned with gratitude and love. Really? As you read these words, are you feeling an emotion telling you something is off the mark?

There seems to be a competition to buy the best homes, acquire the best cars and take the best vacations. Have you ever heard the term "Competing with the Joneses?"

Parenting has taken on a competition of its own over the last 50 years or so. Even low income families are buying their children cell phones, computers and a hundred and some channels on satellite TV. It's as if today's children are born with technology rights. Here's a shocker for you: they're not!

I know that Thomas may say something that hits home for you. You will know because you will either firmly agree or firmly disagree with him. At the end of this chapter, change will be YOUR choice. As a mom, I encourage you to keep an open mind to the fact that you don't know what you don't know yet. Remember, your mind is like a parachute. It works best when it's open. Read the entire chapter, perhaps more than once, and decide which side of the fence you land on.

Thomas: It is time for us as a society and for you as the reader to take control as a parent. You do this when you **Know Your Role as a Parent.** Have you ever taken a moment to map out your job description as a parent?

We always do that with our job or career: "I'm a dentist; I drill and fill. I have a secretary. She answers the phones, schedules appointments and keeps my files in order."

Nine times out of 10, when we encounter a scenario where things are not working correctly as parents, it's easy to come up with all sorts of ideas about what's not working. As you explore this chapter, you will reclaim your power as a parent by discovering what your job is.

Most people have very superficial answers when asked, "**What is Your Role as a Parent?**" "Ummm...I want the best for my kids?" "Ummm...I want them to be happy?" Notice the uncertainty in the answers? I've heard it many times, and if this was your first response, tell me, how's that working for you?

Where did you learn to parent your children? Of course, you learned to parent from your parents. That's it! And your parents learned to parent from their parents. It's time to dig deep, understand, and maybe even permit yourself to Know Your Role as a Parent for the very first time. Once you begin implementing the actions with this subject, many things will fall right into place for you and your family.

Consider this further:

What is your job or role as a parent?
What are you taking control of?
What are you taking ownership of?

Some people started off having babies because they had low self-esteem. They wanted to love and be loved. If this was true, they satisfied that one desire at the beginning of their child's life. Or better yet: "Everybody else is doing it." Or maybe even your parents pressured you: "Well, it's time for you to get married and raise a family." After about a year or two, you satisfied that requirement. It's done. Now, what do you do? See how it goes?

Just like a successful business will have a plan, a successful family unit will have a plan. Over the next several chapters, I will help you craft and develop **Your Role as a Parent**, take ownership of it, and create your job description.

If you would like your kids to have more, just be happy and things like that, well, you're done. Congratulations! I even had one mom tell me she would like her name or her genes passed on. Once the kid is born, you've satisfied that primary directive. "What would you like now?" Blank. It was almost like you could hear, "Ribbit. Ribbit," as if a frog was in the background. It got really quiet.

Take a moment to not think of yourself as a parent. Think of yourself as a *human being* responsible for children who will become adults someday. Soon. It is extremely irresponsible to raise children without an *exit plan*. This statement may strike you as odd if you have never looked at it in this fashion before. Think about it.

Does this make sense?

You must have an *exit strategy* when you plan to teach, coach or raise children. If you quantify yourself as a parent, what will happen when your children get ready to leave at ages 16 to 21? You'll fall into a condition called empty nest syndrome. It's essential to nip that in the bud right now.

You are a great *human being*. You're not "just a parent." Make sure you don't label yourself as "just a parent" because when your children leave, oh, my gosh, life will cease to exist. You'll have some turmoil inside that will manifest for you later in life. You'll thank me in 20 years for that one.

Let's examine what's going on. *You are feeding your kids fish.* You are *giving* them everything they need, usually everything they desire. You put them into a schooling system at age three, four or five and they will remain in it until age 18 and beyond.

Now, you will research appropriate developmental stages for different age groups in certain blocks of time. You'll learn that there is a breakdown of each stage of life, ages zero to two, two to four, five to eight, nine to 12, 13 to 17, and 18 plus, each of which has certain criteria of its own. There is so much massive growth in the first two years that you should almost research *monthly* milestones.

It's similar to the process of driving a car. You start in first gear. Then, you go to second, third and fourth gear until you finally get to the fifth gear. Do you see how there's a sequence of events that you build on to achieve full speed? Begin with the first gear. Begin to think about and craft the life skills you choose for your children to learn as they grow. Your job or role as a parent is to teach your children the skills to become a *fisherman*, not just feed them fish. Feeding them fish means you are always doing something for them, buying them stuff, and taking ownership of THEIR personal responsibilities.

If you cease to exist when your child reaches the age of 18 and they are on their own, how successful will he or she be?

Based on what you've learned about kids, I know this sounds a little harsh to some of you. It's not your job as a parent to make your kids happy. It's not your job to give them things, to make them love you, or to win the contest between separated or divorced parents. Many parents today will unintentionally make decisions for their children to make them happy.

That said, you will now take the time to write out your job description. Your job as a parent (or as a human being having offspring) is to ensure that your child has the life skills to be successful so that when they are automatically separated from you, they can walk away having all the life skills to succeed.

This separation automatically triggers around age 13 — ready or not. A biological chemical is released inside the child's brain to separate the child from their mother and father. You can't stop this process. And why would you want to? Right?

I know that this makes perfect sense to you. Yes? Teach your kids social skills when they're young. Teach them what it means to develop self-control. Show them what responsibility looks like. Your child can learn life skills like self-discipline. This means they do what they're supposed to do by only having to be asked once.

For example, decide today to teach your child the life skill of *focus*. "I keep my attention on the task at hand."

Speed is another life skill you can teach your child.

Speed: *"I create swiftness in my actions while maintaining focus."*

The previous life skills are missing when your child has been diagnosed with a child disruptive behavior disorder like ADHD and ODD (oppositional defiant disorder). When you medicate your child, you are altering their behavior without any effort from your child. Therefore, they will miss these necessary life skills and neural pathways for the rest of their lives. Take the time to help them develop new habits, skills and neural pathways.

Here's an example of the life skill of *speed*: Let's say it takes them 20 minutes to make their bed right now. By showing them how to be more efficient and with consistent practice, they can conquer it in 15 minutes, then in 10 minutes and in five minutes. Eventually, they will be so efficient that they will get up and BOOM! It's done within a minute.

It's just like standing up and walking when your child was younger. You will find that life as a parent is amazing when you **Know Your Role** is to teach those life skills.

When you begin to teach your children life skills, you may hear them complain. This is normal, especially if your children are past the age of three or four when you are reading this book. They are used to you being responsible for their lives and doing *everything* for them. At this point, your child will have no idea that he or she can earn more on his or her own.

Please understand that their **complaints** will all come down to two things:

1. Your child *doesn't know how* to complete a task.
2. Your child *doesn't want to* complete a task.

For example, you might tell your child (We will teach you later how to disguise your dictations), "Make your bed."

Then, if you see that it didn't get made, you need to ask yourself, "Did I sincerely take the time to teach them exactly *how to make the bed to my standards*?"

Before reading this book, it is likely that if they left it long enough, you would go in and make it for them. However, nine times out of 10, the child has never been intentionally taught. Well, maybe you showed them once. "Here, throw this here. Do it like this. See, it's a piece of cake." You made the bed, and then you walked away. Right?

So, when they don't make their bed, or they don't clean up their dishes from now on, *your job* is to take a breath and ask yourself a couple of questions:

1. Did I SHOW them how to do this job correctly?
2. Are they just being lazy?

"Which one of these two must I engage with for this circumstance?"

What's the best way to teach a child life skills? Teaching them to make the bed means **showing** them step-by-step how to do it to YOUR standards. Then, you **watch them** actually do it. Continue the process until they've gotten proficient at it and can do it **on their own.**

Now, you have satisfied them having the life skill of making their bed. Does it take you a day to do that? Maybe. Does it take you a week? Maybe. It might even take you a month. But, think about this: if you're not going to do it now, when will you show them? This example is just one of the many life skills that your child needs to become an independent, cooperative, responsible and successful member of society when they "leave the nest."

Once that life skill has been taught, you've eliminated one of the two reasons the bed was not made properly. If they don't know how, SHOW them. Now that you know they know how, it's because they don't want to do it. I will show you how to solve this issue in upcoming chapters. For now, it's important to **Know Your Role as a Parent.**

"I will help my child develop life skills that will make them cooperative, capable, happy and productive in whatever they choose to do in life."

Your children will naturally gravitate towards whatever they like to do. You can fight them or GUIDE them elegantly. Which sounds better to you?

What other skills do you choose to have your children learn? Have you ever written out a list of the top 10 skills you want your child to be able to do, and when asked to do it once, it's done?

Start your list now.

Let me use another example. Let's say you're an employee, and your boss didn't show you how he wanted you to format a letter. Then, he yelled at you when the letter didn't look how he wanted it. Is it because you *didn't know how,* OR is it that you *didn't want to* format it to his liking?

That's what it comes down to for your children. You'll show them how to make their bed. You may want to show them how to clear the table. The next lesson would be to show your child how to put their dishes into the dishwasher after rinsing them off. Show them how to put their bike away correctly. Make sure it goes in the right spot. That way, it will be safe and out of the way. Show them how to put their clothes away in drawers, among many other skills. You must take the time to show these life skills to your children.

Do it once, and it's done for the rest of your life.

Neglect to show, and they'll develop habits that won't serve them for the rest of their life.

Too often we bark orders at our children, thinking they'll eventually wake up knowing how to make the bed to our standards. "Put your clothes away!" "Clean your room!" "Did you actually vacuum?" "Yes, I did!"

In the next chapter, **Parent's Brain vs. Kid's Brain,** I'll explain how to bridge the communication gap further. Right now, it's imperative for you to discover what is important for you and your children. Once you discover what's important, you need to document key "must haves."

Begin to create a game plan.

During the first two years, your baby will have certain milestones that should be achieved. There will be strategies you can use to help your baby develop confidence, strength and thought patterns. When your baby is about one to two, you can begin to empower their newfound independence rather than fight it. By age five to eight, it's critical to your child's future success to begin an authentic transition to more independence. What are some basic things that you want them to be able to do?

Make that list now!

When a child is between the ages of nine and 12, they can accomplish even more successful actions on their own. Most families have a household chore list set up. This list could include, but is not limited to, vacuuming, cleaning, doing the dishes, tidying their rooms and doing their homework. It makes sense to set it out systematically. What life skills have you personally researched so that you can create a checklist?

Parents have been led to believe that children are supposed to learn this stuff eventually, by some "magic." I don't know if you were born with an instruction manual; I know I didn't come with one when I was born. I'm sure my mom would have loved to have one for me!

So, where did we learn how to parent?

Simple, we learned to parent from our parents who learned from their parents. Then, we parent our children the best we can with what we know. Like most families with parents who wanted the best for their offspring, you might have had a stubborn dad or a stubborn mom. "Git 'er done!" "Just do it!" "I showed you once; what the hell's wrong with you?"

We bring many things to the table that have been passed down through the generations. You have a decision to make. Either accept things the way they are and keep the same cycle of dysfunction moving forward, or break the cycle and make a decision now to prepare your child for the real world. "You know what? My child will have this list of things down pat by age 18 and that's my job!"

You are still reading, so I assume you have decided to break the cycle of dysfunction. Congratulations!

What are a few basic life skills your children should have by the time they are 18 outside the norm of *cleaning your room, doing your homework and picking up your socks*?

Let's look at some common sense skills:

1. Communication
2. Writing
3. Social
4. Respect for others
5. Negotiating
6. Budgeting
7. Putting gas in a car
8. Etc…forever and ever

You get the point. Yes?

As you know, and I know, kids will always take the point of least resistance. Heck, you and I did. "Go ahead and get this." "Go do that." "Go vacuum." And they say, "Well, where's the vacuum?" See, they are still asking you to do things for them. When you do, you are unknowingly and unintentionally crippling them by *feeding them fish* rather than *teaching them to be a fisherman,* and where they can get their own fish eventually without you.

Chances are that your children have been classically conditioned. You did so much for them because you love them. "Oh, let me get that for you." "Let me get this for you." "Oh, you're going to write; let me sharpen your pencil for you." "Here's a nice pen and paper for you."

Would you agree that it would be a great idea to experience a transition eventually? You feed them fish to get them started in life. It's vital that you wean them off as soon as possible. The less you do for your kids to find the missing vacuum cleaner, for example, the faster they will automatically engage in a *solution oriented mindset* on their own.

Now, they won't ask you where it is; they'll find it themselves. Your kids will feel so good about themselves when they begin to figure things out on their own. In a later chapter, they will learn how to EARN their own things.

When you do everything for your child, they may feel that they are not smart enough or good enough to do things independently. Yes, we are even referring to a two-year-old who CAN pick up their toys and put them away. If they can take them out — it's time to SHOW them they can also put them away.

Do you want a self-reliant, confident, young adult who would say, "I was just asked a question. I researched and found the answer on my own." You're preparing your child for LIFE. An employer is looking for a self-reliant and independent worker. They're looking for an employee who can follow directions, have the power and resources to find the answers, and get the job done. They don't want to hear good *stories*. Are you beginning to see the importance of teaching life skills?

Therefore, if you want your child to be successful, whether as an entrepreneur or an employee, they must still be solution oriented. Even more so as entrepreneurs. Entrepreneurs have to create an environment in which other people can be employed. If they're not resourceful, oh, my gosh, they will never be successful. Even if you were to buy a franchise, you would still have to be able to research certain things independently.

So, let's make that big list of life skills. I wouldn't be doing my job correctly if I laid out everything for you here. I'd be a hypocrite! I would contradict what I am teaching you to instill in your children. So, what does your list look like?

I'll guarantee you that your list will not be the same as mine or anybody else's. Please understand that your list is perfect for you. So, when the time comes, and your child comes up to that age of 18, you can be completely happy with what they have been able to develop with great success.

Either way, when your child becomes an adult, you know you have developed them. You trained them. Anything they produce is a 100% direct correlation to how much you engage in taking ownership of **Your Role as a Parent**!

It doesn't mean you are right or wrong or good or bad. Just understand that you create their training for them. You have them for 18 years. You have plenty of time. Now, either you *don't know how* to or *don't want to* teach them. Now that you are reading this, you **do know how**. That's what makes this so much fun.

It's time to plan, organize and do something directive. How many of us had a parent who said: "You're going to play a musical instrument!" "Eh, do I have to?" "Yes." Or, "You're going to go out and play a certain sport, you're going to get involved with a social group, you're going to get involved with some Girl Scouts, Cub Scouts, or some kind of organization that promotes social interaction"?

At first, your child will probably resist and may need to be encouraged to do the new actions. Once they learn those skills, they will possess them for the rest of their lives. That's why showing, practicing and showing some more is imperative.

Do you have your new job description? What is your job as a mom or dad, or a couple, or however you wish to label it? If you haven't put this book down to write it all out yet, now is the best time to do so.

"My job is to give my child life skills so that when they leave me, they will have all the resources and ability to succeed at whatever they choose."

Repetition is one of the keys to success, and as you get this, you will exclaim, "WOW! This is a job. This is real! I am a producer; I'm making something happen. I'm a co-creator!" Once this awareness sets in and you have accepted it as truth, create your job description and write down your expectations of your children.

Be crystal clear.

Begin to break your schedule down into different categories. Focus on each day and week with things that are essential to you. For example, you need to leave the house at 7:30 am to take the kids to school so you can get to work on time; what needs to happen for that to take place?

You can create a systematic way to have lots of fun as you do this. How awesome is that? You can expect and believe your children to have their own responsibilities along the way. Have some fun SHOWING your children how to do everything you need them to do, step-by-step. This makes a lot of sense. Right? Yes, it does!

This chapter is to get you to do something. It's to inspire you to know that you are absolutely correct with what you choose to do. If you skip this part and don't write out your plan, the next time your child does something you dislike, you have no basis to complain about it. You don't like what they did? Well, you didn't give them any clear directions to learn or to know what to do.

Guess what?

This book was not written to fix children. It was written for you to gain the necessary parenting knowledge to GUIDE your kids with life skills rather than using traditional punishment techniques like time-outs, spankings and groundings. In **Creating a Champion**, there's always an apprenticeship program.

When you learn a trade anywhere in the world, whether carpentry, plumbing or architecture, it doesn't matter what, you'll have a senior and a junior. In parenting, the junior is the child and the senior is the mom or dad. They work together to transfer life skills so the child can eventually do the job 100% on their own. One can read and become aware.

Know that it takes time and much repetition to create authentic change.

You will have questions as you go through this transition. When you email us with questions about your child's behavior, nine times out of 10, you will already know the answer. Did you write out your job description? Do you even know what a mom or a dad is supposed to do? "Oh, I haven't done that yet." Good! Nothing else matters until you get that done. The job won't have direction until then.

Imagine working for somebody. When you show up for work and ask, "Hey, what do we do today?" "Um...yeah, we'll let you know, but just go ahead and start doing something." So, you are at work, and you're looking around. "Okay, um, well, I'll get on the computer and send some emails. I'll organize some papers over here." Anything you do, you're bound to get chastised for later. "What are you doing?" "Don't touch that." See how confusing that would be? That's the same way children do not understand what they are supposed to learn when we tell them what **NOT** to do.

Let them still play and be kids, of course. There's a whole gamut of things that you would love for your child to learn. Once they do, they'll always be able to complete tasks on their own. Think of yourself as the CEO of your family. Your kids are your trainees.

What are the minimum requirements for a parent or guardian raising children?

With all that being said, here is a vital point. The notion that kids are self-entitled to receive things is an illusion. You can research to understand the legal laws in your area. I worked with **Child Protective Services** for many years while running an after-school program. **Child Protective Services** could not protect children until they lacked one of these three things: basic shelter, clothes that fit, or minimum food.

Now, that doesn't mean a five-bedroom house, right? With lavish everything? That means a place for them to sleep. They have to have some kind of clothes on them; that doesn't mean they are designer this or designer that. Do they even have to match? I know you're nodding with your head, but the answer in your heart is no. Am I right? You also must provide them with something to eat. Does that mean it has to be nutritional? No. Does it have to taste good? No.

Your three minimum requirements as a mom or dad are to provide shelter, put clothes on their back, and feed them something. Everything else is considered a benefit or a privilege that the child must *learn to earn*. If you choose to keep feeding them fish and give them all kinds of lavish things, guess what? You had better plan on doing that for the rest of your life. They didn't acquire the life skills to sustain the necessary responsibilities to create that same lifestyle on their own.

If you cannot provide it for them anymore, they usually begin whining, "Why can't I have a cell phone?" "Why are you taking that away?" "Why can't I have designer clothes?" "Why can't I have this electronic gadget?" Stay with me, and continue to read this book, chapter by chapter, principle by principle. You will begin to understand how you can encourage them to *earn* what they want beyond the basic shelter, clothing and food you provide.

Desire is the greatest gift you could ever provide. And how can they desire something if they have everything?

You should be on the same page as a family unit. "I'd love for you to have a skateboard. Let's work together to learn how to acquire the resources and skills to make a skateboard show up for you." This means learning how to create a way for money to show up by either trading time for money or doing something entrepreneurial.

Let's talk about allowances.

Your child has chores, aka life skills. They can learn to *earn* an allowance. Don't just *give* them an allowance; that's nothing more than a welfare system. The worst thing you could ever do is give your child money without them earning it by doing *something*.

Instill in them the ability to earn privileges. Then, anything they want *above* the minimum requirements is worked for through effort and engagement as a family unit, as a team. This is not only a saving grace for your sanity as a parent, but taking this approach will help your child feel like a champion. They'll know that when they receive that money, THEY made it happen *on their own*. They will like themselves more because they expand their thinking and begin to see solutions.

"Mom, I want a bike!" "Mom, I want that nice jacket." "I want a cookie."

No matter how big or small the desire, it's the beginning place for transformation to be created.

Now you've got a *motivated* person. Use this as an opportunity to show your young person life skills by having them EARN privileges that are important to them.

That's the game.

My kids are older. Now what?

Maybe you've already fed your child plenty of fish and are now telling them, "You are going to have to learn how to fish yourself."

Okay, let's say you spent five, 10 or 15 years feeding them fish, just doing everything for them, and you haven't made the transition yet. Maybe you were behind the eight ball (you don't know what you don't know). Now you tell them, "You are going to have to start making your OWN bed every morning," or "You are going to have to start doing your OWN dishes," or, better yet, "You are going to have to start doing some chores."

Guaranteed, they will play three simple cards: *ridicule* and *violently oppose* you. However, once you stick with it, your kids will become your best friends and *accept you* beyond your wildest dreams with **self-evidence.** That's the third simple card.

Your kids may say things like: "I hate you!" "You're mean!" They may give you all kinds of eye rolls and attitude. They may have a complete meltdown or temper tantrum bigger than you could imagine them having. Similar to renovating a kitchen, things will get worse before they get better. They may even complain to family members. Well, guess what? Congratulations! You created all of that, too. Yes, I'm going to say it again. YOU created that. You can't blame them. Now, what are you going to do about it?

You will do one of two things:

1. You will take the easy road and continue to feed them fish. Guess what? Stop buying our material because we can't help you. Fair enough?
2. You will go through a transitional birthing process, which may be a little or a lot uncomfortable.

Remember that your children will *ridicule you*. "I hate you." "You're cruel." "I don't like you anymore." Especially if you are separated or divorced: "I'm going to go live with my *other parent* because they are nice and you are mean." YUP!

There will be days that tear your heart out. But, I know, and you know, it's time now to fix what we didn't know before. Yes? It's time to teach them the life skills they require to be successful. After all, you're not their friend. You are their parent.

Once again, the minimum requirements from you are:

1. Provide a place to sleep.
2. Provide them with something to wear.
3. Provide them with something to eat.

Everything else is a bonus, a privilege that must be earned. Know that they will fight you tooth and nail while you implement any new system in your best interest and theirs. They are children — they don't know any better.

The champion in your child is counting on YOU to do what is right by them, not just to make them happy in the moment.

When your child says, "I hate you!" or "I don't like you anymore," or "I'm never talking to you again," one of the best tips that you will learn to embrace is...

Here comes the secret, the magic...

Are you ready?

ACCEPTANCE!

When you truly make a shift and **accept** that your children may hate you for the rest of your life, you take away all their power. I will say this again: when you decide it's okay that your 10-year-old, 11-year-old, or 12-year-old hates you, you take away all of their negative power and make way for their champion self to come to life.

You may have never experienced this before. Do it once, and you will feel the freedom and blessing you will bestow on your children.

Simply say, *"That's okay. You can hate me for the rest of your life. You see, I have a job to do. I have skills to instill in you so you can be successful. Whether you choose to learn them or not, that's okay with me. I may not have known before that some of my behaviors as a parent were not correct. I didn't get a manual when you were born, but I know now. We've got another eight years to fix it and develop those skills in you."*

Your kids do love you. Deep down inside, they have been asking, pleading and wishing they could have a parent who would show them. As soon as you say this to them, you will likely not hear them say nasty things to you again. It will hold no power for them anymore.

Your kids will develop an internal desire to become *fishermen*. They will begin to understand that time is running out. They will begin to feel good about themselves internally and authentically because they are making things happen on their own. They will begin to realize that they will be on their own. In the end, it's going to be okay. Your family will be a beautiful portrait. In the beginning, it's going to be rough as hell. And guess what? If it takes six months and then all of a sudden, everything falls into place, you are perfect.

Let's talk about education.

What is your role when it comes to education? Your kids will learn to read, write, add, subtract and do basic things. The schooling system will prepare them to become really good employees — to follow orders.

Developing an EQ, an *"emotional quotient"* in your child is your job. You empower your child to truly understand that it is 100% their choice to be happy, angry, sad, or to feel joy or love. See, nine times out of 10, your role is to be the **"ER,"** not E.R., but **"ER"** as in happy or happy-**ER** to whatever the child is feeling. For example, anytime someone says, "So and so made me feel bad," it is your job to teach him or her another valuable life skill. You empower them and say, "No, you *chose to feel that way*."

Know Your Role as a Parent for your child and be the "ER" to what they choose. How empowering is it when you begin to understand how this works? Let's say they are angry. Well, guess what will happen? I'm going to be an "ER" because I'm going to be loving and happy. I am going to be an "ER" to whatever their choice is going to be.

"Well, you just make me angry. I hate you." "Okay, that's a choice you made. To be angry when you choose to interact with me isn't going to turn out well. I'm going to be an 'ER' I'm going to make you angry-**ER.** It's your choice. Do you want to be angry? I'll be the 'ER.' How about if you choose to be happy? Choose to be happy, and guess what? I will be the 'ER.' I will make you happy-'ER' when we engage and interact."
Parents often fall victim to the idea that it is their job to make their children happy.
Seriously?

If this is you, you are going to go broke and be totally exhausted trying to make your kids happy. The life skill here is for your child to be able to have and own both personal empowerment and the ability to choose what they want to be. Everybody around them is an "**ER**." So, if they choose to have a happy day, all the people with whom they interact will make them happy—"**ER**."

Your children's specific age groups have different roles, but they all should have certain expectations. We'll get more in-depth into those details in later chapters. It takes time to master this and to make a lifelong change. Seriously, we are talking about generational cycles here.

Let's say it takes a little while before this makes complete sense for you. For now, when you show up at the breakfast table with everybody there, you can ask, "Good morning?"

Your kids can all answer, "Yes, it is!" "What type of day are you choosing to have today?" "I'm choosing to be happy today." "Awesome!" And then you give them each a hug. That simple fact of hugging them was the "**ER**." Do you follow me? They are happy, the hug is the "**ER**," and they just became happy-"**ER**." "I think today sucks, everything...." "You've got a poor attitude!" They just became angry-"**ER**." How awesome is it that this can happen right at the beginning of the day, regardless of their age group?

You are the "ER" in their life.

You can start this if you have kids who are five to eight years old or even 17. When would NOW be the best time to commit to it? You can begin at any particular stage of life. That's part of your role.

You can now ask yourself: "Did I put that on the list as part of my job description? Did I put the fact that *my kids get to choose what they are feeling* onto my list of things I will have them be empowered with? Or was it in my job description to not care and 'whatever happens, happens'?" Or, better yet, "Did I make sure that I didn't teach them to be like a ping-pong ball in the surf bouncing around, where some days end up good and some days end up bad?" Whatever you choose, you will be 100% successful in creating the corresponding results.

Every.

Single.

Time.

Think about this again. Look at your children and ask yourself on a scale of one to 10: "How happy am I with their progress?" "How happy am I with what they're doing?" "Do I feel I'm going to create the most successful person I can?"

The person I'm talking to right now does care. It's YOU. The parents who don't care say, "Ah, I don't care. They're just kids. Whatever they are is fine." That parent is not reading this book, but YOU are. This means you sincerely care and want to become a proactive parent who understands their role.

There is a spark of hope inside you to create the necessary shift to produce new, exciting, positive results with your children. By understanding your job description and crafting it, then listing everything you would like them to have as life skills, know that you are making it happen. How good does it feel?

Take the time to go to the park. Go to the mall. Go to a childcare center. Go somewhere to watch other kids. Be observant of "What do I like best about all these kids?" If there are 50 of them, you can observe Timmy over there who listens and puts things away. "Wow! I will ensure that my child has the life skill of responsibility."

Do you follow what I'm saying?

The list that you made is right for you. It could contain two items or it could be 200. The point is when your child reaches the age of 18, your list of life skills should be complete. That's your job, **Your Role as a Parent**. Take on that concept. Accept your role. Everything else will fall right into place with your children.

You won't be sitting there wondering, "Why don't my kids listen to me?" Well, I don't know. Maybe you've been a great mommy but a really weak leader. If that's so, I wouldn't listen to you either. You haven't even known what you've been doing. Why would they listen to you? You will go swimming, and this guy who doesn't even know how to swim says he wants you to pay him to teach you how to swim. You wouldn't do that, would you?

Your children are extremely smart when it comes to intuition and intelligence on whom to follow. They know this instinctively. Perhaps you are smoking, and you are swearing, and you dictate, "Quit smoking." "Stop swearing." They will look at you and say, "I don't get this, and you are a hypocrite."

The more you execute simply by having them observe you and your actions, the more they will instill these essential life skills on their own. This is better than "Don't do as I do; do as I say!" That is a concept that rarely works.

They can model a clean office. Right? Focusing on leading by example will give your child a better understanding of what a clean room is. These are the true building blocks to creating success with your children. You have a list of things to teach them at every age group. You **Know Your Role as a Parent.** Always remember that when you stop feeding your child fish and begin the process of teaching them to be a fisherman, it will be a journey.

As I said earlier, first, you will be **ridiculed**. Next, you will be **violently opposed.** Finally, you will be **accepted by self-evidence** with your children when you commit to learning these 12 principles of proactive parenting. They will appreciate you and authentically love you more than ever.

You will have so much fun as you guide your children with love. Help them understand that you have a job to do. Because of past mistakes, your child may feel like they hate you during the initial stages of the transition. Know that your kids will get angry going into this new lifestyle. When they tell you they hate you, you can say, "Woo-hoo! I'm right on track!" You're going along right as scheduled. How long can somebody hate you when you do something good for them?

Here's an example you may understand. Let's say I am attempting to make you another 20 dollars an hour at your job. I'm doing things FOR you. You hate me because I am getting in your way and causing a little chaos in your life. You keep thinking, "Gosh, what are you doing? Stop moving my stuff around. You're irritating me." Then, when you get it, you exclaim, "Oh, my gosh, this guy's actually looking to get me more money at my job." "This guy is helping me have a better relationship, have more clarity in my thoughts, become more physically fit, or eat better food, for example.

"It doesn't take long (once you get past the ridiculing and violently opposing) for them to go, "Oh, you were on my side the whole time. You chose for me to be the best I could be."

That's the part that clicks for your kids.

"I wish for you to have a successful life. I wish for you to have a house, a family, a job, a career, or whatever you choose to do."

They'll know that you're on their side, and that's when they will begin to accept you. They will finally understand that you are there to teach them to become independent fishermen rather than feed them the fish.

They will be very grateful!

So what if you goofed up from the beginning? Guess what? You are in the same club with everybody because everybody goofs up. If not everybody, 99.999999989% of the population has goofed! None of us came with an instruction manual. Some of us had better parents to teach and train us, but until now, you have been searching. There's been something missing, and you have felt it inside your heart. That is why you purchased this book. Yes?

Don't think you must do this all perfectly before engaging. Decide to begin the transition now and "fail forward fast." Act, analyze, adjust and just do *something.*

Wherever you started with your game plan, you might have been completely off the mark. You may have ended up with spoiled brats. Great! What's the opposite of a spoiled brat? The answer is healthy, happy and productive family members. You can make the shift.

There is a step-by-step process for you to follow. As long as you engage in doing something, you have already improved your family and your relationship. Does it have to be an A+ right away? I don't know where you learned that. Maybe that isn't serving you now. No one ever has to be the perfect perfectionist out there.

I want you to understand that it will be rough initially, but it will all be well worth it. Your kids will eventually shift in their mindset and decide to grow with you as they become more prepared for life out of the "nest." They'll begin to think for themselves. "I've got five more years to learn all the other skills." They might even ask, "Mom, Dad, could you teach me how to do this? You are good at it. I know you won't be available to do it for me when I'm on my own. I want to be able to do it then." And that's what's so important.

Final thoughts by Bonnie:

Wow! What a powerful lesson. Can you see why I had to share this with you when Thomas shared this with me? I can tell you that I know and understand, as a mother who has gone through and is continuing to go through this process, how hard it can be. It can be heartbreaking as you watch your child scream things at you that I had no idea even existed! I love to spoil them. I love to spend money on them, and I love to be the one responsible for making them happy. In the end, they are children for 18 years. They are adults for the next 70 to 80 plus years!

Thomas' advice on accepting that they may hate me for the rest of my life was my best parenting decision. It has freed me spiritually when it comes to parenting my children. As soon as I said, "I am not your friend. I am your parent. I have a job to do. I can handle it if you don't like me for a while. I can live with myself because I know I'm helping you learn how the world works. I'm teaching you life skills. What I can't live with is being a contributing factor to you living a mediocre life through your entire adulthood.

I am choosing to follow the methods presented in this book and stick to my guns when adversity comes."

The short-term violent opposition was all worth it. The hugs I am getting now from all four of my children are tighter, bigger and more genuine than ever. We work together as a team. My kids love me now more than ever because I don't control every move they make. They choose!

1. What is your role or job description as a parent?

_____

_____

_____

_____

_____

2. How is this different from what you thought before?

_____

_____

_____

_____

_____

3. What are you taking ownership of as a parent?

_____

_____

_____

_____

_____

4. If you cease to exist when your child reaches the age of 18, and they are on their own, how successful will he or she be?

_____

_____

_____

_____

_____

5. What are five things that you are asking your child to do and are now going to take the time to teach him or her?

_____

_____

_____

_____

_____

Desire is the greatest gift you could ever provide. And how can they desire something if they have everything?

Chapter 2

Parent's Brain vs. Kid's Brain

~ What you say and what your child hears
ARE NOT the same thing. ~

Thomas C. Liotta

Bonnie: Watching a child's face open up like a flower in the morning sun because something new or colorful has come into their view makes the world a happy place. Am I right? It could be a shiny red balloon or an adorable little puppy that captures the attention of your bright-eyed, beautiful child. You know what I am talking about.

You keep a close eye on your child at a summer fair or any event like that. You want to protect him or her from getting lost, taken or hurt. Your child has no idea that danger could be creeping around the corner. He or she doesn't know they could get lost as they get mesmerized by pretty things and stop paying attention to where they are going. Can you see that your child sees the world differently than you do?

They see the world from a child's perspective, with a child's brain.

Do you even remember what it was like to think like a child? Do you remember the first time you saw a free-flying, colorful, beautiful butterfly? Or the first time you laid eyes on a bumblebee? You didn't know what any of those things were. You were excited, scared and thrilled all at once. Do you remember the feeling?

Children have the ability to believe in miracles. They have the ability to see good things happen. It is inherent in human nature to desire to advance, achieve more and be productive.

It's the same for children. Your child deeply desires to learn, grow and be an important producer, even if it is just tying up their own shoes. Your child would love to please you, make you proud, and accomplish good things now and in the future. They want attention and will find the easiest, simplest and fastest way to get it!

With all this being said, how often do we see a toddler screaming in the grocery store? How about a preadolescent child yelling at her mother or her mother yelling at them? How often is it that we find ourselves saying, "I can't get my kids to do anything around here. All they do is complain."

How does this breakdown in family communication begin? I know you love your children even more than you love yourself; at least, that's been my experience as a mother. I didn't even know what it meant to feel love until I gave birth to my first baby.

So, how do we get so off track with our children that we end up saying things like "Shut up!" "Stop it!" or "Leave me alone"? I know this probably doesn't happen in your home. If it does, it doesn't happen often, but you and I know this does happen. How is it that you could be offering your child a compliment about something, and they hear something that offends them? This can be heartbreaking in the moment, but in the end, how you handle these situations as a parent makes a difference in your relationship. You can either *guide* your children gently and elegantly into adulthood or *punish* them right into rebellious behavior.

As a parent, you will either learn this now through studying or later on in your child's life through teenage pregnancy, partying, teenage depression, or other similar experiences. So, yes, you will learn or pay the price for ignorance. Read on to find out what Thomas says here about the *Parent's Brain vs. Kid's Brain.*

Thomas: We will answer the question: "Is the parent's brain the same as the kid's brain, or are they completely different?"

As you explore this, you'll have many "Ah-Ha" moments. You're going to find out they work completely differently than each other. They are on two totally different frequencies.

The next time you are in a grocery store, walk to the fruit aisle. Choose one orange and one banana. They are both fruits, but they peel differently, taste differently and each makes a different mess, too. Similarly, these two brains have very different ways of computing the world around them.

We're looking to raise awareness and share ways to communicate better. To do this best, you must start with the problem. If there were no problems or issues, you would not need to find a solution.

So, here we start with a problem: "Well, the kid doesn't listen. I told him how to do this. It seems like I always tell him, and he doesn't listen." You already know what the issues or problems are for you. You're experiencing them.

As you begin to see the functional differences between the adult and adolescent or children's brains, you will be able to engage in a way that will create more success for you and your child. After reading this, you will have an amazing paradigm shift when communicating with your child, children or teen.

Many parents will begin to ask you: "How did you get your child to do that?" "Why is it your child does that and mine doesn't?" "I think the same thing, and you just make it seem so easy!"

It really can be.

You begin to understand your role when you listen to the audio or read the opening chapter, **Know Your Role as a Parent**. You've made some important decisions about what life skills you will teach your child by the time they are 18. If you have not done so, I suggest you go back and do that now.

As you move forward, understand that two different languages are being spoken in a conversation between an adult and a child. One language is the words adults use or hear to communicate a message; the other is the words children will use or hear to communicate a message. Here is an example I will share that 99.9999989% of you will be able to relate to.

The parent walks into a room and observes that it is completely messy or there are some things the children were asked to do that they did not do. The parent in this scenario walks in and speaks sternly, "What's going on here? I told you to clean this up a half hour ago!" Or, better yet, "I just left the room for 10 minutes; why is there icing on that wall and crayon marks down this side? And I don't even know what that is on the floor. I'm afraid to ask! Argh!!!"

The way you phrase comments, suggestions and recommendations can mean a whole world of difference in communication when it comes to **Parent's Brain vs. Kid's Brain.**

Let's take a moment to think about at what age a child will begin to conceive abstract thinking. Abstract thinking is *thinking* and *explaining* how or why things work when putting together an idea without actually *seeing* it.

A child will only begin to understand abstract thinking in the later stages of childhood, between the ages of 13 and 18. When you communicate with 12-year-olds and younger, you will go blue in the face if you believe your children understand what you are saying or asking them to do. Most of the time, your children do not. They will not have a clue what you are talking about. It will sound just like the Peanuts cartoon. Do you remember the teacher in the front of the room mumbling, "Ma wamp pa wa wam wam"? The words do not make any sense to them. They do not know enough to say, "Please help, Mom. I don't understand what you are saying."

What you say and what your children hear are not the same thing.

Let's go back to that messy room. So, what should you say? How do you ask your child questions about it? What's the best way to communicate?

Let's say you go in annoyed, yelling at them, "What the hell is going on!?!" Maybe you go in inquisitive. "Um, what are you doing?" Which one of those two is correct? I know that around your friends, you would probably answer, "Be inquisitive. Don't lose your temper. Count to 10." Okay, well, get past that part. You are going to show up as you show up. No one is here to judge you.

So, go in annoyed or go in inquisitive. Either is how the mom and dad's brains work because they assume so much on the child's side. They assume that the child understands the language. Whether you agree with this or not so far, it doesn't matter. You are just humoring me right now. You will be able to agree once you've spent enough time considering it and once you understand it yourself. I know that we will come to the same conclusion. The child has no idea why they did it, no clue and no iota of anything. They did not do it to be vindictive. They did not do it deliberately: "Oh, let's tick off Mom."

The truth is that the kids have no idea and no clue what you are asking them when you ask, "What the hell is going on in here?"

I can recall being around age five to six. A freshly completed paint job was on both walls on either side of the hall. I was running with the crayons, marking them along both walls! I was running full bore as I waved my arms. At the time, it made total sense of what to do. If you asked me why I did it, I couldn't tell you. I didn't have a clue.

I remember throwing rocks at cars as a kid, too. My parents would yell at me, "What the hell are you doing that for?" or "Why are you doing that!?!" I remember just going completely blank for an answer. Reflecting on those moments when I was probably around eight or 10 years old, I still have no idea why I was throwing rocks at cars. I knew it was completely wrong. I just did it.

When you begin to walk in and understand that they really don't know...WOW! That will be a step of empowerment for you, my friend. You will walk in and be aware that your children either know or don't know how to perform a given action or don't want to do it. You won't take it personally. You can always step back and know you have a life skill to teach them. That's it. How can you get mad at a four-year-old for coloring on the walls when they don't understand the consequences and haven't been shown *where* they can color?

Our parents raised us a certain way, and we pass those parenting skills on to our kids out of sheer and complete ignorance. When anyone offers another opinion, it's usually accompanied by "That's how my mom did it."

Whatever results you are experiencing with your child, you created that. Look at the creativity that the child came up with. How exciting to run up and down the hall with two fistfuls of crayons.

You must take full responsibility for your child's actions.

My parents said, "Here are the crayons. Draw." Okay, so I did. How could they reprimand me for doing exactly what they told me to do? They can't! I hope you are laughing because I am laughing inside as well. There is definitely something funny about that.

Go back to those life skills you should teach your children. It would be different if my mom or dad sat me down and said, "Look, here are some crayons. Hold them like this. Sharpen them like this. Then, you color inside the lines," showing me how it worked. "The crayon will be used only on these square pieces of paper." "Okay, I can do that."

Children understand simplicity. It's how their brains work. See how much attention your child is now getting? Isn't that awesome?

You might want to read that again.

Children are so literal. Their naivety can cause them to be unwittingly funny. I once watched a hilarious home video about a little boy named Timmy who was about three years old. He was standing holding his little baseball bat. Dad said, "Come on, son, hit the ball," as he tossed him the little wiffle ball. Timmy swung the bat and missed. What did Dad then say? "Son, keep your *eye on the ball*." So, there's little Timmy, just bright-eyed and doing his thing. He looked at Dad, then at the ball, and thought, "Dad just told me, 'Son, keep your eye on the ball.' Okay." So, he leaned down and *put his eye on the ball*. It made a pretty funny home video!

Keep your eye on the ball which means watch it hit the bat. Did Dad say that? No. He didn't. How did his son interpret it? He took what his dad said literally. Right? So, you have the fact that you are learning that children do not understand the abstract idea of keeping your eye on the ball.

Why did Dad not say that? He obviously has not heard of the **Creating Champions For Life** principles and does not understand *proactive parenting*.

A smart dad understands that he can speak the language his child comprehends and understands. How easy is it to become frustrated when you say something and your child doesn't get it? It's YOUR responsibility to understand how your child will learn best.

It's not THEIR responsibility to understand how YOU learn or teach best.

What I'm talking about here should be added to the *Universal Laws of Nature.* Like gravity, this works whether you know it or not, understand it or not, or believe it or not.

Here is a common outcome as we return to the messy room and the crayons. Let's say that you walked in annoyed. "What the hell is going on?" Maybe you could be inquisitive because you are so cool and collected. "What is going on here?" Either way, the child will almost always respond, "Um…I don't know." And that's when the parent usually begins to yell louder. The child will become flustered because they have no idea why you are yelling at them.

The next time there is a circumstance that is not to your liking, walk in and know that your child's intelligence is huge. Give him credit for its phenomenal potential. Your child will know the right answer. They will give it to you every time when you are *proactive in asking the correct questions.*

If Mom would have asked me, "Tommy, where is the best place for the crayons to be used?" I would have automatically answered, "On the paper, Mom." Then, I would take the crayons, sit at the table and go right to the paper. Mission accomplished!

Then Mom would have praised me and said, "I love how attentive you are. That is what I like best about you, Tommy. You are so smart because you know how to make beautiful pictures and only use the crayons on the paper."

But, if I'm like you and you're like me, you got smacked, you got ridiculed, you got punished, you got yelled at, and you sat there in a world of "I don't even know what's going on."

You may have a negative memory of something you experienced as a child which has become part of your creativity and strength today. It was and is a part of you. It was your imagination, dreams and exploring when you were adventurous. You were a free spirit, often ridiculed, condemned and not taken seriously. I encourage you now to embrace your free spirit. We will go more in-depth on this subject in Chapter 5, *Guiding Behavior vs. Punishment.* You will see how this works from another perspective.

You are now beginning to *Learn to Speak Kid.*

Ask your children key questions.

Rather than "What the hell is going on here?" you can ask, "What should you be doing?" Yes, you ask the question even though you know they are goofing off. That is their job as children. They will do this until you properly train them.

Here is another fabulous strategy. "Where should those crayons be best used to make Mom or Dad happy?" The child will answer, "On the paper?" See, they already know the answer, and when you approach it with the right question, you will bridge the gap between **Parent's Brain vs. Kid's Brain.**

Let's say they show up late when they are in their teens. You asked them to be home at eight o'clock, and they showed up at 11:30 at night. Awesome! You say, "I am happy you are home safe. When *should* you be home?" "Eight o'clock." See, they already know the right answer. Encourage that. "What would be the best way to be able to go out again? Make sure you are home when?" "Eight o'clock." "Excellent!"

Did you have to get into a fighting match with them? No. Did you have to get angry? No. Do they get a chance to go out again? No. Because they knew what the right answer was. They knew the plan in advance.

Isn't it intriguing how a police officer asks, "Hi, can I have your license and registration? Do you know why I pulled you over today?" When they pull you over, you respond, "Ah, yes."

You and I know right from wrong, right? From the native Hawaiians, you have it in your core; it is called your "Na'au." (Pronounced Nah—ah-oo.) It might be known as your gut or your intuition. You are spiritually connected to the correct answer. So are your kids. They are even more in tune with it than you are. Embrace that power and guide it correctly as we explore this further.

Let's shift to an idea where you have asked them to clean their room. Now you ask them, "Is your bedroom done?" They respond, saying, "Yep, I cleaned my room." Or, better yet, they say, "Um...." Or "Did you clean up after yourself in the kitchen?" (Right after they are all done eating, do they know what they're supposed to do?) "Yep, it's all clean."

Now, here's the fun part. Taking the time to properly train them on what to do in advance will eliminate any idea that something would be off the mark. When they say they cleaned their room and you say, "Okay," you are visualizing all the toys are off the floor, all the laundry is in the hamper and the bed is nicely made. However, when you go see the bedroom, stuff is stuffed over here, the bed is halfway made, and, nope, all the clothes are still there on the floor.

Now, it's time to *go back and teach them the skills*. What are your responsibilities as a parent to teach and to show your children systematically? (Chapter 1 *Know Your Role as a Parent.)*

See, their idea is correct. You cannot chastise them for that. They are correct. You say, "Well, that's not good enough."

There is a critical moment right there!

Did you sincerely take the time to teach them your definition of good enough rather than your abstract thoughts of putting things away?

"That book should be on the shelf. The blankets should be flat." They are over here thinking, "I do not know what you just said. I couldn't tell you. I do not know what you mean or want from me." In their minds, they cleaned up a few things, so it's done.

How do we do this in a more positive and productive way?

1. You take the time to pick up all the toys and have them *watch* you first. You put them on the shelves where you would like them to be or where they should be.
2. You put them back on the floor again.
3. Have them *mirror* exactly what you just did.

When they execute the task exactly how you like, the bridge between the two minds has manifested! Trust that your child can do a good job. Your confidence in them will be contagious. Make it fun!

Now you can say, "Yes, you can go out and play as soon as your bedroom is clean," or "What do you need to do before you go out and play?" "Clean my room?" "Good, clean your room and let me know when you are done."

That *life skill* will now be there. Now, when they say, "Mom, my room is clean," they understand what you truly mean by "clean."

What if it took you a week to go through those steps completely? Would it be worth it? How cool is it that you are going to have bragging rights with the other parents that your child already has their room clean? "I wish my child would clean their room that well."

You took the time to understand this conceptual aspect between the two brains. You avoid any struggle of "I did do it!" "No, you didn't!" "Yes, I did!" What is that going to do for you and your child?

Here's another point to consider.

I recommend that you get a good grasp on this. When it comes to things they are asking about or choosing to explore, you must ensure you *understand what they are saying or asking*. Always remember that children's and adult's brains are completely different.

Furthermore, advertisements stimulate children's brains. Advertisers know how to market to children using colors and other triggers. Therefore, they ask for this and they ask for that.

Another chapter explores this concept more in-depth, so we will touch on it here lightly. *You will decide and your child can make choices*; they cannot make decisions in their lives yet.

Here's an example. You may decide that the child is going to eat something nutritious. You have made this decision. It may be something in the vegetable category, meat category, organic peanut butter, organic jam, or, better yet, bread with no sugar. This is very important as sugar has been proven to affect your child's behavior at home and school.

So, you've decided: "I'm going to have my child pick a vegetable for dinner tonight." Do not ask them if they would like a vegetable because your kids cannot make that decision yet; that's your job. The kid's brain says, "I'm going to eat 'yummy' things." It's up to you to come up with three choices.

"For your dinner tonight, little Timmy, would you like peas, corn or carrots?" They will reply, "Hmm, peas, corn or carrots, hmm...I like corn." They have an illusion that they have made a decision, but it is just a choice because you, as the parent, made it for them. This is a crucial part to understand.

Let's say your kids would like to go out and play. You **make the decision** of **where** they play, not them. They have a **choice**. You have a half hour window to do playtime. Therefore, you can say, "Timmy, would you prefer to go to the park, play at home, or go over to your friend Bobby's house next door?"

Disguise dictation with questions.

YOU decide where they play, giving them **three** choices of what you have already approved. Now, you're being *proactive*. You can always say yes to them once you've established the *correct environment.*

"I want to go over to Derek's house." Let's say the scenario is that you don't like Derek's house for whatever valid reasons you hold. You are saying no to it. Now you get into that: "No, you can't." "Why?" "Because I don't want you to go there." "Why?" Whatever you say, they are going to keep asking *why*. There will be a 30-minute "why" session, and then most of the time, the parent will get angry and say, "Because I said so!" This is not conducive to sanity!

Are you with me?

You will always have the **Parent's Brain vs. Kid's Brain**, but be *proactive*. You know they will be engaging in certain activities you do not like. Maybe it's a sport they wish to play, like football. You would prefer for them to remain safe. They may get to engage in basketball, baseball or soccer because football is a sport you don't wish for them to play. It may be the contact and impact issue you are freaked out about.

The first thing is to wipe this sentence from your vocabulary. "What would you like to play?" Remember, children *cannot make the decisions yet*. You select the three from which *they will choose*. "Out of these three sports, baseball, soccer or swimming, which would you like to do first?"

Do you see how that is orchestrated? The child goes, "Oh, I get to make a decision!" Really, it is just a choice. Whichever one they choose, you can always operate in *"Yes Mode"* with them. Do you see how much nicer, more elegantly and correctly things flow when bridging parent-child communication?

You can use this for everything! Yes? Another example:

Let's say it's movie night for the family. You have already done your proactive parenting duties. You've looked at the movies available right now in the movie theater. You've picked three that you'll be happy with. "Which one of these three would you like to see tonight with the family?" "Well, I want to see the second one." You have already said yes. When they make their choice, everyone suddenly goes, "That is a great choice! Let's go see that." And then everything is smooth as silk.

When you find yourself experiencing a magnitude of frustration when communicating with your child, know that the frustration has to do with miscommunication. They are not being defiant on purpose. You should have the "Ah-Ha" moment of "Oh, let me speak THEIR language." "Let me craft an environment that is always a **"Yes Mode"** for them. A place where everything works elegantly because I screen everything first.

Consequently, you will see wonderful things happen in your life again and again. All these problems, these things that do not work, and all these power struggles will vanish.

What do you do when you have a screaming match with your child? Guess what? I do not have an answer for you because you know what? You are rowing upstream, my friend. Turn the boat around; go with the flow.

Teach and show rather than punish.

All of a sudden, your parenting life will become peaceful. "Oh, wow, rowing *with* the river is fun." "Parenting is fun." All children are a joy to be around when the environment is correct!

In the **Learn to Speak Kid Self-Study Course,** you will find a *Quick Study Guide*. You can see a systematical step-by-step approach to help you create a communication bridge between your brain and your child's brain. You will be able to reference this writing again and again.

It will require much repetition for you to really hit this home. Each time things fall into frustration, you are communicating in a different language than what your child hears. It takes time to perfect a new language and a new way of parenting!

Let's put this in perspective.

Let's say your child is 14. You have been misusing communication until now by saying things like "What the hell have you been doing?" and "What in the world is that for?" You are going to see an instant shift as you begin to craft things in a positive manner. However, when you begin to craft things, you must stay consistent with them because you will get ridiculed initially. Remember? But, as you undo some of that unnecessary programming, it will shift in a more positive direction.

No magical wand or pill can "poof" and make things click right into place overnight. However, you will see things click overnight in terms of: "This new way feels so good."

You will waffle back and forth from those old habits you brought to the table. You might ask, "What the hell's going on, or what did you do that for?"

And then respond, "I apologize. Hang on a second. Counting to 10 — okay. Where should the orange juice go, or where is the best place for it?" The child will answer, "In the refrigerator, Dad." "Excellent!" you say, "I love that you are so smart. You know where to put all of the things because you are responsible. Thank you!"

You are the one who is going to waffle. As you transition from the old dysfunctional way of thinking, acting and speaking to the new more productive way of thinking, acting and speaking, you will bounce back and forth. You are making a transition. As you study and become more effective, your child will naturally fall right into place and be able to be guided perfectly.

It is not their job to compensate for you. When you set the correct environment, they will follow and do exactly what it is that you are choosing to create. Yes, it happens.

Every.

Single.

Time.

One of the best things to truly understand about *attention* is that we all crave it. We all desire it, want it and yearn for it. We will do anything we can to get attention. Look at Evil Knievel. He would jump over *80 million* trucks so he could get applause. People strive to be on stage singing, acting and looking for recognition. Kids are exactly the same.

When observing the child's brain, they are looking for a stimulus-response. I drew a pretty picture. I showed it to Mom. Mom didn't notice. I knock a plate off the table and it smashes. Mom notices. "What are you doing?" Yelling, yelling and more yelling; it's attention. Whether right or wrong, we have that craving to have some attention come to us. Your child will do whatever it takes to fill that quotient. If you do not like what they are doing, it is because you are feeding them the attention that only responds to what they are choosing to be fed.

Can you blame somebody for stealing something if they are starving? No, you cannot. Your children are starving for your attention. They are going to do whatever it takes to get you to respond.

What if you focused all your attention on the things you would love for them to do and only praised them for those things? Let's say the child drew 10 paintings; only one was on paper, not the countertop. Praise them for that one and ignore all the rest. Yes, I know that can be tough.

What happens when you walk into their bedroom? Remember when we were talking about cleaning everything up? And, let's see, the laundry was wrong and the bed was messy, but somehow, all the toys on the shelves were perfect. "Wow! Look what you did here! The toys are perfect. Everything is in place on all the shelves!" They are getting wonderful attention.

"I would love to give you some more attention. When the laundry and bed look as good as the toy shelves, I've got more attention for you." "Okay." "How much more attention would you like? Would you like *some* more or would you like a *lot* more?" "I'd like a lot more." "Okay, so what do we choose to do to get more attention?" "Put the laundry away and make my bed." "See! That's what I love about you. You are so smart. You know all the right answers." That is how you approach it.

This will seem like a completely foreign language to you at first if you have always yelled at them, told them how stupid they are and pointed out what they can't do correctly. Yes, we do these things as parents, some more than others, but every parent falls into this trap at some point. This will be a 180 degree switch for most of humanity.

As you embrace these concepts more fully, momentum will build in the correct direction. Your child will clean the room of their own accord, and when they do, you praise them. This has to be big! This is huge!

How often do we get praised for the good things we do? Do you get praise for showing up on time for your job? No, they always emphasize the opposite when it comes time for review: "You were late three times this quarter. You were absent twice." "Well, you turned in the 10 reports, but that one was not handed in until Friday?" "Yes, you did that one late."

I get that they treat you that way — with negativity. It's easy to act like them and pass it on to your child. Maybe you did luck out and your boss always gives you positive recognition. However it is for you, good or bad, you have the power right now to break the negative cycle and shift it to create what YOU choose.

It is essential for you to actively find the things you will give hugs for. "Here is a list for extra spontaneous hugs posted on the refrigerator. Timmy, you earn hugs and special privileges when you do any of these things." Anything outside of the list will be completely ignored.

Yes, it really is that simple. Surrender to the idea that this is true and that this way of thinking with kids works! I already know it works and the more time you spend with us, the more you will come to the same conclusion.

Emphasize and focus on what it is that your kids did today that you absolutely loved. The house was a total mess when you came home. Yes, you address that. However, you pointed out that you saw all of the dishes in the dishwasher had been put away. "I appreciate you doing that!" You hug and praise and smother them with love. With all the other things, you say, "You know I have got more happiness to give to you when you make these other things look as good as the dishes look."

Tie it into things they like and want to do, such as going to their friend's house. That is where the upcoming *Star Chart* concept comes in. That's another piece of brilliance you'll get involved with as you continue to read this book.

Perhaps three or five stars are required to earn to go do a desired event. "I would love for you to go to your friend's house. What has to happen for you to earn that?" "Hmm, clean my room and put my toys away." They will always know all the right answers. "Excellent! You are on your way as soon as you get all those done."

Once again, you, as a **Big Kid Trusted Advisor**:

1. *Invest time* in your genius offspring.
2. *Show them* how it can be done.
3. Demonstrate *integrity*, better known as *standards.*

So, there isn't any "I did clean my room," to which you respond, "No, you didn't!" That only happened in the *past* because you hadn't taken the time to show them the correct standard. That is how it always progresses and moves forward positively and optimistically.

Stay in the negative mode if you like, but nothing ever works long-term there.

You will soon find that you have children who come up to you and right off the bat say, "Mom, I cleaned the kitchen and I completely straightened up the living room." You didn't even ask. It's not even on the *Star Chart*. "Wow! Thank you for doing that."

You'll hear things like "I did it because I'd like to earn a way to go to the movies with my friends this weekend," or "I'd like to be able to go to a friend's house on Friday night." Maybe there's a play they were hoping to go to, or they would really like to earn that specific jacket they had their eye on at the mall. Every single parent would love to get their children anything they choose to earn, provided they did it in this fashion. See what I'm saying?

How awesome is it that your children can come up to you and say, "Mom, what can I do to go over to Timmy's house tomorrow after school?" It's much better than "Can I go to Timmy's house?" "No. Your room's a mess!" "Oh, come on, can I clean it later? I promise to do it later. Come on, Mom. Why can't I go? Why?" You have been there. Do you see the shift? Can you see the value in this?

The farmer plants his seeds and waters the ground, cultivating it again and again. Carrots take seven days to pop out of the ground. Working through this transition may take seven and a half weeks before it engages your child because you have so many things you are re-creating.

Take the emphasis off the child; they are not doing anything wrong. They are actually rising up to the environment YOU have created. You are creating the environment for them to excel or fail in. Your child's intelligence is so strong that they can master whatever environment they find themselves in. If that environment is one of punishment and dysfunction, you bet they have mastered *that* environment.

What is the *opposite*? That is the other thing you can create. We are here to support you in every shape, form and fashion.

You will be able to use the information I'm sharing here elegantly. Now, you can say, "Oh, my gosh! I enjoyed communicating with my child!" Everything is in a "**Yes Mode**." You will be so happy next year that you made this decision and acted upon it properly right now.

You will think to yourself, "I had no idea what I was going to do when I had one teenager who was really giving me hassles and a nine-year-old who, oh, my gosh, was going to follow the same pattern as the older one. But, I found this information, this knowledge. I'm implementing it. I'm doing something!"

There you have it: *Parent's Brain vs. Kid's Brain.* The communication bridge is between the two, and when you understand the right language and linguistics, you will have phenomenal success!

Read each chapter as many times as you can. Take notes, highlight and practice the exact dialogue used here. Understand that you are working on yourself to make the paradigm shift. The more you make the shift, the better the results you will see in your child; that is how you **Create a Champion For Life**.

Final thoughts by Bonnie:

What an inspiring and insightful chapter. I remember when Thomas first met my two younger children, Jennie, age nine, and Zachary, age six. He would use this special language with them and it worked. It seemed like when I would ask them to do something or help me, they would complain or complete a half-assed job and call it a day. They knew I would take over and do it for them, didn't they?

I did not realize that I was creating a low self-image for my children by doing this. I was. Children do believe that you do not think they are good enough or smart enough to figure things out on their own. But, they are!

It was frustrating to accomplish tasks, keep a house clean, or take them on any outing. One day, Zachary, Jennie, Thomas and I were out running errands. When we got home, I pulled the car into the driveway and turned off the ignition. I turned to look at the children in the back seat and asked if they were ready to get out. They said they would be right in after they were done cleaning up. There's something funny about that. Thomas never asked them to clean anything. His conversation with my children inspired them to do something to earn time on his cell phone and they did.

He often encouraged them to do things that would put a smile on Mom's face and they did that, too.

Because of improved communication, it is fun to have cooperation from children who help around the house while running errands and when taking family vacations. Know that there are many more benefits to the strategies and lessons in this chapter that will represent your child's lifelong character traits.

It is the absolute most upsetting thing ever when I try to teach my children a life lesson only to have it become a fight. I see now that the language I was unwittingly speaking to my children for the first 13 years of my motherhood life was actually programming them to have a low self-image and become unproductive and lazy teenagers with deserving attitudes.

However, with the knowledge I have learned and applied from this lesson, I now understand how to communicate with children to achieve the desired result. My children respect me a lot more than they used to. The end results of family unit experiences are phenomenal. We all understand what the other person is saying. I also notice that they are authentically happy-ER, which makes me happy-ER too.

I now have the understanding, strategies and words to help my children learn the life skills they need not only to survive but to thrive in this world and now so do you.

1. Describe the essence of the Learn to Speak Kid program.

_____

_____

_____

_____

_____

2. What types of behavior will your child display when most of the attention he or she receives is from their wrong behavior?

_____

_____

_____

_____

_____

3. Clearly identify the responsibility of a parent.

_____

_____

_____

_____

_____

4. What does it mean when you feel frustrated when communicating with your child?

_____

_____

_____

_____

_____

5. What is abstract thinking? At what age can children begin to develop it and understand it?

_____

_____

_____

_____

_____

Chapter 3

Creating the Right Environment

~ Every child is a joy to be around when the correct environment is created. ~

Thomas C. Liotta

Bonnie: Whose job is it to create a winning **environment** for your child, children or teenager? That's right. It's your job. Whether you are a parent, a teacher or a coach, if you are an adult experiencing interactions with children or teenagers, then it is definitely your job to *Create the Right Environment. Creating the Right Environment* will allow you to raise, develop and produce a *Champion For Life*. And yes, it is just that simple.

I know, as a parent, you have a heart that hurts every time your child yells, "I hate you!" or when the school calls and says that your child has been bullied again, or when your teenage daughter gets pregnant. Other scenarios may include stressful mornings, sibling rivalry and children lying around the house while you do everything. How does this happen? I know you are a great parent, a wonderful parent and an outstanding parent. So, how do our children end up acting out, talking back and sometimes even becoming depressed?

When you complete this chapter, you can create a mindset and an environment at home that will produce beautiful results daily with your child or teenager. By making a few simple adjustments in the present environment, you will also create more peace in your life, witness improved self-image and behavior, and see an overall positive shift in your child's attitude.

In the beginning, they will fear and oppose any changes. When you stick with it and maintain **Your Role as a Parent**, they will develop much respect, admiration and love for you. In an environment where water consistently, continually and harshly splashes against a rock, the water will eventually turn the rock into sand, erode it and split it into two halves. It's just a matter of time.

The **Environment** always wins. Enjoy this chapter as Thomas takes you through it simply and elegantly.

Thomas: In this particular chapter, you will put Chapter 1 to work for you. What are the key things that you are looking to instill in your children? What are the skill sets? What is it that you truly want or expect from them? Here's an even more empowering way to look at it. Ask yourself how you choose to have your children behave. Would you like them to behave in ways that are honorable for you, prideful for you, or in a way that is your definition of what a good model citizen would be? When **Creating the Right Environment** at home, you will produce the results you choose every single day!

A *Star Chart* is a really cool tool for kids.

It's NOT a chore chart. It's a *Star Chart*. This will help you fuse the things you choose to create together with all the things your children naturally would like to have. It is possible that you are just giving all of your power away. You're not seeing that you have a gamut of arsenal right now at your disposal to win each battle and ultimately win the war on *Creating a Champion For Life.*

So, you might have spoiled brats, right? Possibly, they don't listen. Maybe you have teenagers and they are telling you to "EFF-OFF." You may be right there in a neutral zone. Maybe you are having great success with your children. Whatever stage you are in with your children, there is always more to learn. You can *Learn to*

Speak Kid quickly, but for most, it will take a lifetime of practice and coaching to master.

Let's say you are studying, working and implementing the new language with your three to five-year-old. Excellent! Let me tell you, every parent who engages with this philosophy wishes that they could go back 10 years and begin right there. You may already be on the path where you have been doing these things on an intellectual level, but it's more on the instinctive level. You just saw that it felt right, and you crafted it.

Yes, most parents use the please and thank you phrases. As you know, and I know, no matter what number you pick in life, you can always add one more number. Allow me to add a *"Plus 1"* to the great skills you are already doing by doing something more.

So, let's begin at the ages of two to four and go up to the spectrum of 18 plus. This works for *every* age group. You will see that your overall results will roll out slowly over several weeks. Then, it will seem like all of a sudden, everything falls right into place.

What do you crave, desire or choose for your household and your children? What are you wishing for and are now creating for and with your children to do, be and have? These might be questions like "Oh, my gosh, I must think about that one for a while. I never really thought I had a choice. Hmm, okay. Well, let me get out my pen and paper and get started on this exercise. Let me write down the top 100 things, or the top 50, maybe even just the top 10 of what I would like my children to be able to do, be, have or demonstrate."

Let's begin to write down some lists.

For example, some of the most common items on a Mom and Dad list would be:

- Clean up after themselves.
- Earn their own car insurance.
- Be productive so they can pay for their gas.
- Use manners like please and thank you.

You can help them create a habit of asking, "Hey, what could I do to earn this thing?" Before now, they might ask or, rather, whine, "How come I can't do it?" or "Why can't I have that?" or "If you loved me, you would pay for...."

You may spend the first week or two simply manifesting your lists. What if it took you 30 days to explore childcare centers, malls or parks to observe other parents with their kids?

Now, I'm not asking you to set your mindset on what you *don't* like.

For example, "Well, I don't want them to be bratty." "I don't want them to curse." "I don't want them to steal." "I don't want them to lie, and I don't want them to be messy." None of that works, ever! That's NOT what we're looking for here.

I am asking you to set your mindset to what you *choose* to create. What would you like them to have or be? Use your observations from the care centers, malls and parks to discover the great characteristics of other kids. "Hmm, I like that one. That one has really good table manners." Yes, table manners, eating properly and using a napkin." Did you see ones who would help with household chores, who would be respectful to their parents, or who always seemed to have good relationships with their brothers and sisters? Ones who were cooperating? As you observe the world around you, you can manifest what you choose.

You must have your list created before you go forward to have any success with this.

Period!

You may read the entire book in one sitting and state, "Okay, I get it. I'm on track. I know now." But, if you're like me and I'm like you, *writing something down* is a hundred to a thousand times stronger than anything you could merely stick into your memory. The faintest of ink is stronger than the best of memories.

Write down your lists and post them for your kids to see.

Think of it as cooking with a recipe; your ingredients are listed. Are you going to memorize those ingredients and go to the grocery store? You would get to the store and forget a few items because you didn't have your list. I know there is a rare exception to the human race. Some of you are thinking, "I would remember." I am speaking generally. Yes, I know it sounds simple and might sound odd, but I am telling you it is worth it. Do it for your children's sake.

Now, you have created your first list; these are important things to whom? To YOU! Break the list into appropriate age groups:

0-2 years old
2-4 years old
5-8 years old
9-12 years old
13-17 years old
18 years and older.

Let's say you've got a five to eight-year-old. You are beginning to manifest a list of what you will be working on now. Ask yourself, "What would I like them to be, do and have when they're teenagers?" You can observe teenagers; that's the 13 to 17-year-old category. Make different lists. One is for wherever you are currently, and then you have other lists manifesting to work on later.

Repeat to yourself, "I am a co-creator in life. I know that as I **Create the Right Environment**, all the things I have on my list will manifest."

The Environment always wins.

Now, let's look at some things that your kids like. You are going to be putting together this **Star Chart**. You will be asking your kids to do certain things they haven't done before. They probably don't want to do them either. "Oh, my gosh, Mom, you've been doing all the dishes for me. Why the heck would I even remotely choose to wash dishes?" "Dad would always clean my room or clean up after me; He always gave me five dollars every Friday. Why would I start working now when I can get it all for free?"

So, there is a **transition period**.

On a new sheet of paper, create another list of the things that are important to YOUR children. What things are your children asking to be, do or have every single day? For example, "I wanna cookie." "Can I watch TV?" "Can I play on my iPad?"

We are talking about things such as what they like to eat. There's breakfast, lunch and dinner. Do your kids like entertainment? Do you have games they play on PlayStation, for example? Do they have some sport or activity they enjoy doing? You are getting the idea.

These are things your child or teenager asks for. "Mom, can I have five bucks to go to the mall?" "Can I have twenty dollars to go see this?" "Can I have...?" Whatever it is. You know what they come up and ask for in YOUR home.

You've written down all of your little golden eggs which happen to be their GOALS. This list is your arsenal to motivate them to engage in things that are important to YOU which is where we are going next.

Now, what life skills do you choose for them to have and develop? What other things are important to you? Are there any character building skills you would like them to learn? Is it being self-disciplined? Is it being responsible? Is it having self-control? Is it having focus in life? You've got all these on your list, right?

There are many things to think about. They come up to you on a regular basis and ask, "Mom, Dad, can I...?" "Mom, Dad, can I go...?" Do you see what I am saying? Excellent! I'm going to repeat myself often because, as you know and I know, repetition is the second law of learning —

repetition is the second law of learning — repetition is the second law of learning.

You will write these lists and have them posted all of the time. A list of your child's GOALS and a list of the LIFE SKILLS you would like them to have.

Your wants and your child's wants begin to merge. The transition evolves into a true manifestation of happiness, cooperation and productivity. It's like a zipper. The little teeth go click, click, click, click, click, click and all of a sudden, your plan is bulletproof.

You have now formed the foundation of the **Star Chart.** It is the beautiful tool we use to **Create the Right Environment** by merging these two worlds.

Visit our website for *FREE* access to the **Star Chart PDF,** where you can also download an in-depth training video.

CreatingChampionsForLife.com

Do you remember from Chapter 2 how adults and children understand the same words differently? The *Star Chart* creates a bridge between the parent's brain and the kid's brain. This is just an introduction. You will learn more over the next three chapters. Trust the process as you start on the most empowering and imperative journey of your parenting life.

Furthermore, the *Star Chart* coincides with what YOU would like to begin developing and what THEY like to do.

With a desire for something, aka "**Goal Power**," THEY will be motivated to learn the life skills that are important to YOU. Trust me, they will pay the piper. When they get hungry enough, they'll ask, "What would you like me to do so I can earn this?"

And what a perfect place to be.

Take a typical day. You have a huge window of opportunity every morning. Let's say YOU expect your child to make their bed, put all their clothes away, have breakfast and clean up when they are done. They should wake up and be on time for school. Whether getting on the bus or waiting in the car, they're ready.

My advice is to pick *three key things*. Even if there are more life skills you wish for them to learn in the morning, *begin* with only three things. What if the expectation was that they would make their bed, clean up after themselves, and then be ready to go to school on time? When they do this, *all without being asked*, will that make a difference in your life?

Keeping your expectations extremely simple in the beginning will help smooth the transition. It takes time to **Create Champions**, so be patient. Once you and your child or teenager master this simple list of things to do, you may add on up to three more expectations.

Then, when they do all three, they have the three checkpoints to earn a star in the *morning* (or a signature for older children and teenagers) on the **Star Chart**.

1. Did they make their bed? ★ 7̶I̶
2. Did they go ahead and do the dishes after they had their bowl of cereal and cleaned up? ★ 7̶I̶
3. Were they right on time to go to school? ★ 7̶I̶

All three of them, boom! They earned a star with a happy face, a little watermelon, or whatever you have as a sticker. It's cool to see your child choose what to use as a marker on the **Star Chart**. You may just put your signature in that space when they are teenagers.

You have the things you want them to do displayed on a list. You'll see what actually gets done on the **Star Chart**. At the end of the week, the child will get to cash these stars in for things that are important to them.

I will assume that it's important to you that your kids *participate in school*. How would you like them to participate in school? Maybe you would choose to work with their teacher? Would you like to get weekly or maybe even daily progress reports? Make it happen. So, there's another star. They went to school. They go to school every day and earn a star just by *doing something.*

Are you with me?

Then, they make it home on time, get a snack and do their homework right away, which is important to YOU (input what is important to you here).

So, you've taught them the life skills you need them to know. What do you want them to do *after school until dinner*? You have that window of time to fill. They get their homework done first. They get their 20 minutes of reading in. Maybe they have one or two chores to do, like feeding the bird or cat. You're beginning to take these things off YOUR life skills training list. Are you beginning to get excited? I know you are because you're getting this concept.

When your kids complete what they are expected to do, they get a star and you have dinner ready for them. Make sure also to have their list broken down for the window of *evening time* expectations. After dinner, it's reading time, bath time, getting ready for bed and being in bed on time.

So, you have three, four or five different stars (as many segments as you choose to create) throughout the day.

Begin to execute your ideas. Again, start small. You can always build more as the concept generates new habits and a new lifestyle for you and your child or téen.

There are the things that you would like them to do and some skills that you would like to begin to manifest. Now, what's important to them? For example, let's tie it into *Friday Fun Day* or *Friday Pay Day*. Maybe there's something they always love to do on the weekends. Do they like to go outside and play all Saturday or Sunday? What fun things do they have access to that are important to THEM?

Let's say you have a weekly allowance you give your children. It could be a *playtime allowance* for the little ones. Saturday is about 10 hours worth of playtime; they've got all day since they can start at nine o'clock in the morning and be home at six at night. They have a whole day of a potential window to do something important to them.

Or let's pick a $20 window. When you tie the *Star Chart* into $20 worth of money at the end of the week, they have learned that ***everything in life is earned.***

An allowance is a learning-to-earn opportunity. Rather than just giving them fish, we teach them to become fishermen. See how this is all working together? When Friday comes, you can add up all their stars.

IMPORTANT:

Now, do they *have* to earn these stars? NO. Do they *have* to do any of these things at first? NO!

If your kids are used to always taking the shortest path to their desires, the **Star Chart** won't mean much to them in the first week or two. They haven't gone through the first cycle of stars. This is still the old environment, which was, "Oh, well, what's the minimum I can get away with without having to do much?"

The more you study and apply these strategies, the more you will see the results you want to create. So, here comes Friday. Say there are 20 stars to be earned during the week, five each day for four days; that's 20. Or better yet, there are four on all five days. Either way, you're going to harmonize it and you'll be able to make this work well for YOU.

Remember, Saturday has the potential to be 10 hours of whatever is important to your child or teen. "I always love to go to the skate park. I get to play with my friends and that's my day to do whatever I choose to do."

What if each of those stars represented 30 minutes? Are you beginning to see what I'm saying? You have 20 stars, 30 minutes each, and 10 hours total. The child we are using, for example, already has an established routine of

"I like to go ahead and play all day Saturday." This is where you add something like "Perfect! I'd love for you to go play all day on Saturday. These are the things you'll do to earn it." If they did 10 stars, you guessed it, they have actually earned five hours on Saturday to go play.

In the monetary example, if it's 20 stars, it's $20 if each star is worth one dollar or $10 if each star is worth 50 cents. At the end of Friday, you say, "I would love to give you the $20. You earned 15 of those $20 by earning or achieving 15 stars.

"Here's the kicker. You will love this window when they first respond, "Well, I want the $20." They will always whine, ridicule and tell you, "It's not fair," or something like that. The **Environment** you are beginning to create is that *they learn how to earn things rather than just begging for that fish.*

"I would love for you to have those $20." Here is an example of how important the linguistics part of the philosophy is. "What must you do to earn the full $20?" "I don't know." "I know you don't know, but if you had to guess?" Hint, hint: *Star Chart,* right? "Well, I have got to do the bathroom thing in the morning. I have to clean out my hamster's cage and ensure my..." as they list what they know they needed to do on the *Star Chart* to earn the dollars!"

See? Children's intelligence is superior. They are so smart. They know the right answers every time when you ask the right questions.

The key here is that they only "have to" if they wish to earn privileges, which changes it from "have to" to "choose to."

"What must you do to earn all $20, all 20 stars, or all 10 hours?" They will know what the answer is. You will guide them through the process and say, "Well, excellent. You earned 15 now. See here, when you missed this one and this one? Next week, you have a choice. You can go ahead and make sure you get those done and then you'll have a full $20 on *Friday Pay Day*."

To explain in real life terms, if you were a farmer out there, you and I both know what would happen if you only collected *half* the hay. Can you really demand the full $200 for a $100 job? No one is going to pay that. If you did half, you might get half or fired and lose the contract.

When you **Learn to Speak Kid,** you are **Creating the Right Environment** that will put your children or teenagers in the best position to be successful now and later in life.

It really is that simple.

You will understand the *Star Chart* more in Chapter 6, *Know the Reward*, where we'll explore this further.

With each star, you have the opportunity to check and balance. It's easy when you tie it in with each window of time:

• before school or morning
• school time
• after school until dinner
• after dinner until bedtime
• bedtime

These "windows of time" are when you naturally get their highest level of attention.

Will this develop when the *parent wants something* or when the *child wants something*?

Yes, you guessed it; it's when the **child wants something**!

"Mom, I'm hungry."

Here we go. It's breakfast time. Now, before breakfast, you have something on the schedule. Here's an opportunity to have your child complete these other two things before breakfast. So, when you're sitting down, they have completed what you choose to have accomplished.

It works like this. "I'm hungry, Mom." "Perfect, I'd love to have breakfast with you. Let's check and make sure that the two things on the *Star Chart* are done." Say it was to have your child make their bed and put their laundry away in the hamper; you know what's on your list. It's easy to see what comes next.

There are only two reasons things don't get done on these *Star Charts*.

1. They don't know how.

You haven't taken the time yet to teach them how to make the bed. You've got to physically *show* them *your standard*, mess it up and then have them do it correctly in front of you so they demonstrate the level that you choose to have done. You must have them demonstrate that they know how to accomplish the task to your chosen standard.

It is important to demonstrate it first and then have them do it second because the worst thing you can do is tell them, "Well, go make your bed," when they throw the covers over it, you say, "It's not good enough. Do it again." They will not be able to comprehend, abstract-wise, what the heck you are even talking about. They start protesting, "I did make my bed." "No, you didn't!" "Yes, I did!" "No, you didn't!" "Yes, I did!"

You must digress and back down here, understanding there are two reasons things aren't getting done the way you want them done and with this first one that we just talked about: *they don't know how*; it is up to you to take the time that you must spend to truly SHOW them how. Make the effort to demonstrate it to them repeatedly as often as necessary. Once it's done correctly, they will always be able to make the bed exactly the way you want it. They can't play the ignorance card anymore; they only get one chance at that.

2. They don't want to.

The other reason is that they plainly don't want to do it.

You don't have to say anything negative like "Well, if you don't do that, then you aren't getting this."

Don't even go there; reframe that old bad habit of punishment. It will never work long-term. It works short-term at best. Even then, it's not very successful.

Go through this with them and ask, "Did you get your bed made? Ah, look at that, beautiful. Okay, well, there are still clothes on the floor. So, did you already teach them how to pick them up and put them in the hamper? Did you demonstrate and SHOW them exactly how to do it? Yes? Would they earn a star for the laundry part of their day? Or no, because they made a choice not to do it. The more you hold your ground on this, the more successful of an outcome you will see.

Your job is simply saying, "You either don't know how, or you don't want to." So what? It's perfectly fine. Tell your child, "Excellent, Timmy or Susie, you earned ONE of your stars this morning, excellent. What does a good student or a self-disciplined child do to earn *both* stars?"

And your child will respond, "Put ALL the clothes in the hamper?" "That's what I love best about you, Timmy. You are so smart. You already know what the right thing is to do. It's up to you when you choose to earn that."

And then, boom! They do it because they are beginning to tie everything together. Again, this will take a little time. The more consistent you are here, the sooner it will manifest. Remember what happens when water washes up on a rock? It doesn't just turn into sand overnight or cut in half in a day; it keeps moving and eventually erodes away.

Your children will eventually fall right into place with your plan now that you have one. At the end of the week, all you have to do is *praise* them.

Let's say they only earned five of the stars. You give them all your love and say, "Wow, look at this. You earned one dollar for this one, one here, one there and five big dollars. Look at that! Man, that's awesome. You are a champion!" Little Timmy might say, "But, I want $10." Excellent!

You want to hear these words because those are little windows of opportunity where you get to answer, "Great. I would love for you to have two of these five dollar bills. What do you have to do, or what has to happen for $10 to show up?" "Earn five more stars?" "Aw, that's what I love best about you; you're so smart. Which one of these are you going to do next time?" And Timmy might say, "I can do that one and that one." "Awesome, let's do that!"

Then, you will be empowering yourself with highly productive children.

Or perhaps it goes like this: "Let's see, I didn't fully teach you how to do that skill yet. Maybe that's why it didn't get done. Now, we can fix it."

Your child will still get a paycheck between one and $20. Your child's total empowerment is knowing how much of that $20 they truly choose to EARN.

Again, you would never say, "Well, you didn't do this; you aren't getting that amount of dollars."

Get rid of that; remove it from your vocabulary quickly. That talking will never work magic with children.

As you begin to shape and craft what you want them to do, they will build with that "**Plus 1**" every time. You saw the five; well, I want 10. They'll move up, with a little rise in the level of the Environment. You empower them and they step up.

Every.

Single.

Time.

Do you understand the *Star Chart* concept?

Are you beginning to understand that the *Star Chart* molds and bonds both worlds? The parents or the teacher would like the child or teen to *learn life skills* and the child or teen would like to *earn a privilege*.

Remember, what is your number one job? Is it to make them happy? No! Is it to give them everything they want? No! Your job is to help them *learn life skills* so that they are *Champions For Life* when they transition away from you.

That's what we are creating! What's the opposite of *Creating a Champion For Life*? You might as well get a big barn and keep all the family members there. Never let them leave. I've never seen a momma bird have eggs and get a bigger nest, so they never fly away. No, she gets to the point where it's "Look, I'm done throwing worms down your throat. I fed you 'fish.' Now you've got to be a 'fisherman.' It's time to get out."

That's the job. It's a transition. We can make this as much fun as we like, or we can be in denial and kind of figure it's just supposed to work out on its own. Know right now; it won't.

This book empowers parents who think, "My kid didn't come with an instruction manual. I want to do some right things but, need some help here."

When you focus, work together and blend your desires, you'll work this *Star Chart.* Only then do you manifest whatever you want to create as a team.

There will be some transitions at the very beginning when you, as the adult we like to call "***Big Kid Trusted Advisor***," may be off the mark for a while. Perhaps you have some teenagers who never performed any of these concepts while young. It's okay. You didn't know any better. It might start with something as simple as a cell phone. It might start with dinner or some electronic device they expect to have shown up.

Let's pick dinner. They usually get a big plate of whatever they want, but they have been a little resistant to doing some things you have asked them to do. So, does dessert normally come with dinner? Ah, you see the correlation? They love the dessert, so you tie it in with the stars. Maybe you have two or three stars of things you'd like them to begin to complete *before* dinner. As long as those things are done, dessert shows up.

"But, I want dessert." "Excellent. What has to happen for dessert to show up?" "I don't know." "I know you don't know, but if you had to guess?" "Well, I've got to do that stupid stuff...!" "See, that's what I love about you. You are so smart. You know exactly what to do and it's your choice to make the dessert show up."

Or, even better yet,

"If you know how to do this but don't want to, you are telling me that you are choosing not to have dessert." "But, I want dessert." "Okay, what do you have to do?" "I've got to do those things." "Great!"

Do you see where it will be a rub at first when you've got a lot of reprogramming to do? I get that. I've been there. It doesn't happen overnight.

When you are *Creating the Right Environment* in your home, remember that it always wins.

Stick with it. Stay on track.

Be like the water that comes up on the rock again and again and again and again. You'll probably be all over the spectrum with this in the beginning. We will be behind the eight ball, right on track, or somewhere right in the middle. What matters is that you start by *doing something* and follow the guidelines.

Let's recap what we've discussed in the **Creating the Right Environment** chapter as we move forward, keeping you on track and supporting you in your journey of doing the right thing as an awesome parent.

You have a list of things that are important to YOU, which contains skills and ways that you would like them to behave, be, do or have.

Then, you create a list of all of the arsenals of the things that are important to YOUR KIDS — cell phone, skateboarding, talking on the phone, watching movies, hanging out with their friends, eating dessert, having a pizza party, whatever it is — you've got all of those things written out.

Yes?

You're beginning the process of merging the lists of desires with the *Star Chart*. Training, teaching and helping them learn life skills is your job. **Know the reward** of things that are important to them and they will always rise to the occasion.

Knowing that you are doing something in the right direction with your child or teen is a wonderful feeling.

Creating the Right Environment will have an amazing positive effect on your entire household. You will love this concept. The longer you stick with this, the better the results you will always have. The more you do it and use it, the more you will like that you decided to do something.

Final thoughts by Bonnie:

I am extremely grateful for this lesson. When I began to associate with Thomas, my four children were, unbeknownst to me, walking all over me. There were constant power struggles between my children and me. We were all trying to accomplish things that were important to each of us.

All four of my children would go in my room and play in my office on my 27" Mac computer whenever they wanted. They seemed to push me enough to wear me down until I just said, "Okay, fine!" And then I was forced to nag them to get things done. I had definitely created an **Environment** of chaos. The harder I tried to create peace, the more I would flounder!

I have implemented many reward charts over the years, but none worked because I never took the time to find out what was important to my children. I was focused on how to have peace in my life and make them happy. I always planned trips, bought them things and did things for them. Then, I would be upset because they were never grateful. I seriously wanted to run away from home sometimes. I did not realize the power I had with everyday desires that were important to them, like freshly baked homemade cookies. I could have used the power correctly if I had just stuck to my guns and let them earn things!

In trying to keep peace in my family and wanting more than anything for my children to be happy, I was actually stealing their opportunities to feel good about themselves by stepping in and doing everything for them. This program is the best thing that ever happened for my children and me. I have seen depressed children become happy, the *victim* becomes a *victor,* and anxiety turns into enthusiasm.

The way Thomas lays out the *Star Chart* and reward system really puts everything the child or teenager chooses to buy or create on THEM. With the added responsibility, they have to step up and become Champions. They will step up every time, but only if you *Create the Right Environment.*

They are begging you to set up the structure and care enough about them to stick to your guns. They would love for you to follow through with teaching them life skills and then believe in them enough to allow them the opportunity to create greatness for themselves. They are very intelligent and want to do it, but the want is deep inside. They don't know they want to because they are used to having everything given to them.

It is scary at first with and for your children. The older they are, the scarier it is. They will not want to give up the lifestyle they are used to, not right away, because they have never built the concept of solutions in their minds. Chances are, because of this, they have no belief in themselves. They never had to believe before.

When you stick to your guns and follow through with the lessons and agreements you make with your children or your teenager, such as signing 28 "*signatures*" to EARN a paid vacation, they will step up and begin to find solutions.

You will always say, "Yes, I would love for you to have or do that." This will make both you and them feel so good.

It will set you free as a parent and set your child up for successful relationships, careers and families for the rest of their lives.

1. What key skill sets are you looking to instill in your child or teenager?

_____

_____

_____

_____

_____

2. What is it that you expect from your child or teenager?

_____

_____

_____

_____

_____

3. How do you choose to have your child or teenager behave?

_____

_____

_____

_____

_____

4. What is your definition of a good model citizen?

_____

_____

_____

_____

_____

5. What are you creating for your child or teenager to be, do and have with this new philosophy?

_____

_____

_____

_____

_____

When you Learn to Speak Kid, you are Creating the Right Environment that will put your children or teenagers in the best position to be successful now and later in life.

Chapter 4

Making the Transition

*~ Your role as a parent is to teach them to be fishermen,
not just feed them fish. ~*

Thomas C. Liotta

Bonnie: The initial stages of implementing this parenting philosophy will seem like a ton of work for you. There is much to put in place. We must teach them step-by-step how to do chores, make lists and create the *Star Chart*, for starters. Then, you must be present to give them their stars, stamps or signatures. If your children are anything like mine, they will fight you tooth and nail to return to what they know and are used to. You will also experience times when you want to give up. Don't.

Your children are begging you to follow through with this.

Believe me.

It will feel like work and it should. You are a parent. You have a job to do, and trust me, it is worth it. When you begin seeing authentic positive shifts in your child, you will love yourself for being strong. You will have peace in your life and have so much respect from your child or teenager that life will seem very different to all of you.

You will have good days and bad days. The more you stick to what you said you would do, which is teach your children the life skill of earning anything above and beyond food, clothes and shelter, the more success you will have in guiding your children to become *Champions For Life*.

I will hand this lesson over to Thomas now. He will brilliantly guide you through the psychology of **Making the Transition** from feeding your kids fish to creating fishermen.

Thomas: Imagine you have been working at a job for 15 years. You can come and go as you please, use the phone whenever you want and take days off if you finish your work early. One day, you arrive at work and someone new has taken over. All of your privileges come to an end. You actually have a pay reduction. You now have to pay to use the phone. You experience the loss of your freedom. How do you feel? I know! Horrified! You would either throw your weight around to see if you could get away with the old behavior, or you would find a new job. Am I right? In this chapter, we will dive into the psychology of **Making the Transition.**

You and your children will go through a journey as you go from feeding your children fish to turning them into fishermen.

This is where you may get **ridiculed, violently opposed,** and then **accepted by self-evidence** with your children.

You will be going through what I call "waffling." You will think to yourself, "We were good for a week, but then what happened?" You may ask yourself, "What am I going to go through psychologically, from my own doubts, fears and anxieties because I thought this was working? But, I don't know if it really is. Can I do it? I don't know if I'm able to do it."

It is important to be aware of all the emotions you and your child might experience so you can feel empowered when they show up and know that you are on track.

In the beginning, you have your *baby*. Oh, you love your baby so much. Everything your baby needs, you provide, of course, they are babies! You have to do everything.

You feed them, prepare their meals and bathe them. You provide for them, pick out their clothes and decide everything they will do with their time. Now, you have this six-year-old, or 10-year-old, maybe even a 15-year-old, and you are still providing for them. You're cooking for them and picking out all of their clothes.

You may find yourself begging them to keep their room tidy daily, but to no avail. It can become so frustrating that it seems easier to do everything yourself. Okay, fine. Let's say you do everything, pay for everything and drive them anywhere they choose to keep them happy.

This is Making the Transition from feeding them fish to teaching them to become fishermen.

You have kids. You give them the tools they need and desire. You make choices for them. When they are 18, they are on their own. They're working on their career, living in their home and building their family with kids. Even though they will fight you on this **Transition**, you love them enough to realize that you only have a certain window of time to teach them the necessary life skills so they may have successful experiences, careers and relationships throughout the rest of their lives. Now, you might cuddle with them, love them and wish they would never leave. Eventually, there will come a time when they must go.

Do you really want a 40-year-old man living in your basement? With all that being said, **Creating a Champion For Life** does not remove anything from the "I love to give them things and do things for them! Can't I spoil them? Can't I give them everything that they like?" You are supposed to give them everything they like as they *Learn to EARN* it.

Where does it start?

Making the transition begins as they become individuals around one or two years old. It is at this time you begin to show them how the world works, giving them more and more responsibilities. The process is like peeling back an onion, beginning with holding their own bottle, and feeding themselves until they are two, and putting their toys away. It's like layer after layer after...does this thing ever end? No, it's perpetual and it continues to expand and grow year after year.

Consistency is the seed that grows the greatest fruit.

If you have a two-year-old or older child, your persistence in doing it through each age group will continue to **Create the Right Environment** for an easy-**ER Transition**. When you implement change or add responsibility as they hit the next level in **Making the Transition**, the ridicule and violent opposition are minimal. However, it's not minimal when you raise them to their teen years, having pampered them for 10 or 12 years and then suddenly implement some new behaviors.

There's a process like a Fibonacci sequence.

Start small with 0, 1, 1, 2, 3, 5, 8, 13 and let it build in nature's natural growth cycle. If you're looking to gain a little more information on what I mean by Fibonacci, he was from the 1200s and was an Italian mathematician who found the natural growth sequence in nature. The numbers go 0, 1, 1, 2, 3, 5, 8, 13, 21, 34, 55, 89, 144 and it keeps growing perpetually. Everything starts small and builds. That's what you are going to be experiencing.

Think of this: how long does it take a person to become 500 pounds? If it took five years to get there, would this person release the weight back to normal in a week or two? This process takes at least half the time it took to get there in order to return to normal.

This means I will lose all that weight, or release it, in about two and a half years if it took me five years to get there. Okay? Are you with me on this? Give yourself some time. Permit yourself to be patient. Give it the persistence it truly deserves and your kids truly do deserve it.

Wouldn't it sound funny if a farmer took a seed, dug it out of the packet, stuck it in the ground, watered it and then showed up tomorrow expecting to see apples? Okay, let's chuckle a bit on it to keep it in perspective. Many people think, "I said that. I did that. It worked once," but know that it is extremely easy to fall back into old habits that don't serve you.

Be consistent and persistent. Your children will love and appreciate you so much for this someday — and sooner than you think.

"Why do I have to start making my bed?" "Why do I have to do the dishes?" "I don't want to vacuum." "Why do I have to empty the cat litter box?" Do any of these statements ring a bell?

You will receive *opposition*.

The opposition is exactly what you would do at work. "What do you mean I've got to start doing all the janitorial jobs? And even clean the toilets? But, I'm the secretary." Right? You would give them opposition. Think of it in exactly the same way. Ease into this if the **Making the Transition** strategy is new to your family.

I'd also like you to understand that when you encounter some opposition, that's your opportunity to implement more of what you're learning here.

Implement even more of the *Star Chart*. They are going to test your will. Especially if you've pampered them for 10-plus years. The older your children are, the more violent the opposition you will generally experience. They are going to say hurtful things. They will play every card they can to tug on your heartstrings. "I hate you! I don't like anything about you." They might even start threatening to break this or do that. Or even worse, they might break this and go do that, not just threaten.

It is intriguing that once you persevere, they will love you for it. They will have high levels of integrity and respect for you. Most importantly, they will thank you because THEY have learned missing life skills and YOU will be *accepted by self-evidence.*

If history is any pattern that shows how powerful and important it is to understand the process of change, you can read about it in history books. At one time, everybody believed that the earth was flat. The first person said, "Hey, I think it's round. Let's keep going." Everybody in power or an area of authority said, "No. The ship will go right off the edge. You're crazy. You're stupid. Who are you to talk like that?"

Ridicule.

Are you seeing the analogy here? "No! I know it will work. It will go around. I can sail the whole thing." Okay, they would jail that person and label him a kook, a quack, a witch or a weirdo. They would also whip him. They would hit him. Stone him to death.

Go back to any time in history. You will see the pattern: *ridicule*, then ***violent opposition.*** It could have been anybody, but history always tells us Christopher Columbus sailed around the world. He didn't fall off the edge. I guess it is round.

Let that be your inspiration. We used to believe the earth was flat and was the center of the universe with the sun going around us. Anyone who opposed that was ridiculed and violently burned at the stake before being accepted. "Oh, ha, ha. I guess they were right the whole time."

Accepted by self-evidence.

Obviously, you are not going to be burned at the stake. That's not what I'm saying. I'm stressing the point to let you know that those three steps happen every time a new change is implemented.

This could include new business management, a restaurant menu change, or your kids *Making the Transition* from feeding them fish to teaching them to be fishermen. They're supposed to show a little opposition. It is a normal part of the process. Accept it.

Get excited when they oppose it rather strongly because, "boom," right after that, everything clicks into place for them and you've got yourself a *Champion For Life*.

The psychology here is that you will be able to create an intention instead of just going through your days, weeks and years with no direction. Most people end up just existing with each other, hoping everything will eventually work out. It won't.

This is part of YOU *Making the Transition* from feeding them fish to becoming that fisherman. You have a mindset and a way of running things that is comfortable for you. This philosophy will initially push you out of your comfort zone and it will be as uncomfortable for you as it is for the children.

As soon as you get out of that comfort zone a little bit, you might relapse and say, "Let's go back. I don't know if I'm really going to implement all this stuff."

My advice here is to *keep the intention*. Ultimately, your child can hate you if they choose, but your job is to teach them missing life skills! Love them enough to stick to this.

When you *Make the Transition,* you will experience three main emotions, better known as going through a **F.A.D.** – **Fear, Anxiety** and **Doubt.** When these overwhelm you, you may end up going right back into your comfort zone. Be aware of this. You intend to do good things in your life and that's what this is all about. When in **DOUBT**, stop doing what brought it out. You are very close to having a breakthrough of truer **UNDERSTANDING**.

When facing your **F.E.A.R.**, just choose **P.O.W.E.R.** to persevere.

False
Evidence
Appearing
Real

Positively
Outstanding
With
Every
Result

When you feel **ANXIETY**, just ask yourself "where's the 3?" Can – Can't – Don't Care. Who else is there?

The opposite of it is **ENTHUSIASM**. I love en-thus-**I.A.S.M.**

I
Am
Sold
Myself

When you know, with the utmost confidence, that whatever you are doing is right, who can stop you? Be that modern day Christopher Columbus. Be that Modern day Moses who parted the Red Sea with absolute power and conviction. Be like Galileo, who knew that the sun was at the center of the universe and that the earth went around it.

Your kids will love you and will develop the utmost respect for you.

Making the Transition is one of my favorite things to witness when I work with kids and hear feedback from parents on the same path as you. When the kids ridicule you, they're going to play a *victim.* "Poor me. Oh, my gosh, why ...." You name it. You will see it.

The Power of Opposites:

What's fun about the awareness of opposites is when you realize that, at times, you have a child playing the *victim.* We talked about fear and power, right? Doubt and understanding are also opposites. Anxiety and enthusiasm. Well, what's the opposite of *victim*? Well, the first thing that comes to mind could be a *victor*. Up and down, wrong and right, not working and working, and *VICTIM* and *VICTOR*.

When they subconsciously play the role of the *victim* within their personality, they are looking for attention. Usually, the attention that is easiest to get is *negative*. When your child plays victim, they are going to say things like "I hate you." "Why are you being mean to me?" "I can't believe you're doing this." "Other kids don't have to do this." On and on and on, they're going to play the victim role.

When you talk to a *victim*, you know and I know that no matter what you do, what's a nice guess as to what they'll do? They find some way that they are a what? They are a *victim*. You got it.

Embrace the victim. Tell them, "Yes, I love you as the victim." Your child will probably tell you how awful and mean you are. They won't believe you're making this transformation. It's been the old way for 10 years. You used to do everything and now they've got to do the work. The beauty about that is that's how the *victim* talks. Once you become aware and make them aware that they are choosing to be a *victim*, they usually change quickly.

No one wants to be a victim.

The other important part is creating awareness of the *victor* who also exists within your child. Let them know that is how the *victim* talks. Now, the *victim* will always say negative things. If you stop the process, then the victim wins. He doesn't have to do any chores or *Make the Transition* to learn any of these skills and the *victor* will never get a chance to step into his or her true power, now and forever.

You give them the choice to wake up as *victims* or *victors* in the morning. Find the opposite of whatever they are being negative about. They both coexist. You're saying, "You know what I love best is that I love you as a *victim*, but you know who I love to spend the most time with? *Victor*."

The *victor* will find a way to learn all of these really cool life skills. They will find a way to EARN their stars. They'll begin earning $20 at the end of the week or be able to spend all day Saturday playing outside. That's what a *victim* doesn't see...yet. The *victor* does.

The *victor* says, "Oh, yeah. Let me learn more. What can I do to earn more?" "Hey, Dad, what can I do to earn enough so we can go play ball?" "I can earn some money so I can buy some tickets to go to the movies with my two friends." You give them examples of what a *victor* is. Show them what they talk like and what they sound like. When you do this, you allow them to step up to their potential. They feel like Champions.

Conversely, the *victim* is the one who will come up with every story in the book of why he *can't* do it. Here is another life skill that can be added to your list now.

You can empower them with a choice. You get to be the "ER" to whomever they decide to be that day or at any other time. Do they wish to be the *victim*? By engaging with them, you are just the "ER" to their chosen emotion. You are going to make them more "**victim-ER**." Everything they hear is "Poor me. I can't believe you're doing this, " and everything else is *victim*.

When they choose to be a *victor*, you get to be the **victor-ER** when engaging with them. That is so powerful!

I love this story that was shared with me. Grandma was watching the grandkids. There were three of them. She went upstairs and said, "Okay, time for breakfast. Let's rise and shine." The two granddaughters got up while little Timmy whined, "I'm not having a good day. I'm having a bad day." Wise Grandma said, "Okay. You're right. You should stay in bed and not go to school if you are having a bad day today. I get that."

So, he bought right into it. He went back to sleep for a little bit and pretended to do his whole cough routine. You likely know all of the games that kids play. They are going to attempt to dupe you as much as they can.

Sometimes, I think they should go to Hollywood and win an Oscar for some of their performances.

She sent the girls off to school. Little Timmy showed up downstairs two hours later. The *victim's* performance began at eight o'clock in the morning. It was now 10 or 10:30. He shuffled his feet into the kitchen and Grandma asked, "Can I help you? What are you doing?" "Well, I was going to get something to eat." Grandma says, "Ah, breakfast was actually about an hour ago." Timmy says, "Oh, but I'm hungry." Grandma says, "Okay...and?"

See, he had already shifted from not going to school to what was convenient at the time. "Cough, cough, I'm sick. I'm having a bad day. I can't go." An hour or two later, when it's no longer convenient, he's ready to have a good day, eat breakfast, watch TV and play.

Grandma took him by the hand and put him right back into bed. She said, "Remember that you told me you were having a bad day." Timmy said, "Why are you being mean? I want to have breakfast. I'm hungry." Grandma said, "I know. You told me you were having a bad day. So, no TV." He complained about that. He couldn't do any of the things he thought he would do. He couldn't play with his toys. He couldn't talk his way out of this. Now, he was having a really bad day.

What a genius Grandma. When his bad day was over, she gave him one of life's best gifts: the *power to choose* what HE decided to create that day and each day for the rest of his life.

When little Timmy was over at Grandma's house the next time, Grandma said, "Rise and shine! What kind of day are you going to have?" Timmy said, "Oh, I'm going to have a good day!" He knew that if he didn't get up, go out and eat breakfast and go to school, then he wasn't going to be able to have any fun. He couldn't claim, "Ha, ha, ha, I'm sick and I can dodge school to watch TV all day." The tough love that Grandma showed and the consistency of sticking to her guns is what children need to complete *Making the Transition* successfully.

When they choose to be *victims*, write down the words they use so they can see for themselves what they are saying. For example, let's call him Todd. Todd says, "I hate you. Everybody's mean to me." You think, "Excellent! That is a great *victim*." Acknowledge it. Give him praise. "Well, what else is bad? What else bad happened today? I mean, you're the *victim*. Everybody must have taken advantage of you. What else?" Get serious about it.

See, the *victim* was looking for a hug. They were looking for attention like anybody else would. I'm like you and you're like me. We all will do things to get attention. Why would you punish that? How could you correct that?

GUIDE their behavior.

"You know what, Mr. *Victim*, I'll spend five minutes with you here. Do you know who I'd really like to work with? I'd really like to work with the *victor* who knows how to be that *Champion*. I want to spend time with the one who is so smart and knows how to figure things out, who is a genius and who loves to have great days every day."

That's part of the **Making the Transition**. You are going to have resistance. Embrace it. Don't suppress it. When you begin to suppress something, it will come back up more fiercely and in a more negative fashion than you could ever imagine.

Let's talk a little about EMOTIONS.

Just a side note: I go more in-depth with this when I do one-on-one and group coaching with people I select to work with. However, I'll tell you this here. Each one of our emotions is just like a little child. It starts as *immature* and evolves into *mature*. What are some of your emotions? Anger, jealousy, love, happiness, sadness, name them all. Each one must be *praised*. When you deny any of the emotions, force those down and select the few you like, the ones you suppressed will catch up with you later.

For example, it would make no sense for a mom of 10 kids to pick three of her favorites, shove all the rest of them down in the cellar, tell them to shut up and expect them to be happy and open. You see, that's what we do. I am lightly touching on this here, but it is a choice YOU get to make.

When you get opposition from your kids, let them know that you will say thank you whenever you are ridiculed and violently opposed. One of the neatest things that represents a sincere compliment is when people who are *victims* ridicule you and *violently oppose* you. You can choose to say thank you to them. When they say ugly hurtful things, it is their gesture of love. It's in the language that they speak. It can be misinterpreted. Okay?

So, are you with me on that?

Let's jump back into the *Star Chart* to understand how this process of **Making the Transition** from feeding them fish to helping them become fishermen really works.

You've got to understand that it's not just a "Hey, I put the *Star Chart* up and all of a sudden everything is as smooth as silk." No, there will be a *waffling* effect. There will be layers to work through as if you were peeling layers off an onion.

Now, Friday Pay Day is the fun part. Let's take an extreme case here. There are 20 stars available to earn throughout the week or $20. At first, they know they have to clean up their room, do some homework, read, and clean up their dishes. Then, there are new things that you implement. They go, "Yeah, right, Mom. Whatever."

Right?

In the past, you've asked and they just blew it off. You asked again and again. You may have started feeling like you got into this nag mode and pretty soon, you said, "Fine. You know what? I'll take the garbage out myself. It'll be faster and easier." "I've asked him to pick up the clothes again and again. I've got company coming over. I'll pick up their stuff."

Long ago, they learned that there isn't always a consistent follow through when Mom asks or Dad says something. This became a neurological pathway in their brain.

Now, they know they can nag Mom eight, nine or 10 times and she'll finally give in. Better yet, Dad only told them what to do once or twice and the kids know he really doesn't mean it. It ends up not getting done. Then, they ask, with full expectations, "Hey, can I do something I want to do?" And the answer is usually "yes." That's how the pattern typically goes. Am I right here?

Now you've got your *Star Chart*. It's all right there and you started exchanging some of their things. For example, they are used to getting $20 every week, or they have a cell phone for which YOU pay the bill. They are used to having things paid for them.

Now, when they complete the full 20 stars, they can keep their cell phone or receive $20 each week. That's some of their *learning to earn.* That's peeling back the layers of the onion. This is called little growing pains. You are helping them build new neurological pathways in their brain, with "Hey, I've got easy street," developing into "Oh, now I've got to be productive and put some effort out."

What do you prefer?

Here's an example:

Let's say they earned one star as they went through the week. You caught them off guard and they happened to have one day when they said, "Well, Mom, I'll do one thing. Whatever. Yeah, my clothes. This is stupid." They made fun of you the whole time they did it, right? They ridiculed you and violently opposed you. They mocked you. "Okay, doing the dishes. Duh."

You will experience this. It's funny at first, but it can be serious. It is time for *Friday Pay Day*: "Mom, where's my $20? Dad, where's my cell phone?"
You could easily fall into punishment mode, as I was raised in: "If you don't do this, you can't have that."

You could use corporal punishment, which was used in the school system when I was a child. I can tell you countless times that there was always a dad amongst all my friends, mine included, who would smack the taste right out of your mouth when you back talked or you got out of line. There is a place for that and that is something YOU decide on.

That's not what I'm talking about here. I'm talking about *Guiding Behavior vs. Using Punishment* to get them to comply. Punishment only works short-term. Nobody goes through a prison system and comes out saying, "Okay, I'm a golden boy now." **Punishment** does not work. **Guiding Behavior** does.

Every.

Single.

Time.

Now, when it comes time for "Where's my damn phone?" "Where's the $20?" or "Hey, I got my $20 coming!" they're demanding. You know what I'm talking about? "Well, let's look at the *Star Chart*. How did you do? Well, I can see you earned one. So, here's one of the $20. Congratulations. You did a great job!"

That might seem a little funny at first, like you're being a smart mouth, but you teach them the life skill of *cause and effect*, or you reap what you sow. You are teaching them to work, just as you do, to earn things. You know, the way it works in the real world. You may get, "What the hell is this?" But, whatever you get back, remember that it is part of the process.

As they realize you are sticking to your guns, they say, "Huh. Wow, I've given them a whole arsenal. I've threatened this. I've yelled here. I've called them this name. Huh." Heck, I've even had parents experience their children swearing at them for the first time when they implemented this program for many months. It's a building process that will let your children know that you are serious and that taking the easy route is no longer cutting it.

Ultimately, what was the goal when you had kids? Would you like to be nice so you can get them up to 18, pretend they're ready, and send them off? Suddenly, they show up and say, "I'm 20 now, Mom. Can I move back in? I knocked up a girl and have two kids already." I'm telling you the facts. You can deal with it now even though this is tough, or, guess what, you just adopted a grandson. You've got someone who can't help himself. Will you do things for them for the rest of their lives? I'm not here to place any blame or judge. I'm telling you what the statistics are.

How much wiring is there to unravel? It's almost like a tangled ball of yarn. Will it take three months or a year to unravel the wires? Is the mind nice and clean right out of the package, like in an infant or toddler? It hasn't even been tangled up. You can pull the string right out and it's as smooth as silk. I'm giving you some worst case scenarios so you'll know you're right on track when you come up against it and see it.

Stay plugged in.

Remember the Fibonacci sequence? They did one star. Next week, they might do one more or two this time. Then, they start to get the pattern and you hear, "Wow, Mom, Dad, Grandpa, Grandma, Aunt, Uncle, I got all 20 stars this week. I am outstanding. Look at me!" Yes, they're really serious. And you ask them, "Who did that?" and they proudly answer, "I did!"

They finally get it.

Let's use the cell phone as an example. "You've earned five stars out of the 20. Okay, you get your cell phone one day out of this next week." "But, I want it the whole time!" "Excellent! What has to happen for you to have it all week long?" "Do 20 stars." They already know the answer but have been sitting in the welfare lane for so long, begging, "Well, I can't do anything about this."

The worst thing you could do is keep them in that same state of disempowerment. I know this was not and is not your intention, but if you continue to GIVE them things, that is exactly what you are creating. Begin to embrace the *victim* to become the *victor*. Believe in them.

Stop feeding them fish! Turn them into fishermen.

Let's say they have got all the basic things down pat. Take it simply and go easily. The momentum will continue to grow; keep the momentum going. As momentum builds and they begin to buy in more, you can "*Plus 1*" it and add more. Consider different age groups, five to eight, nine to 12, 13 to 17, and 18 plus; see what skills and learning moments to add to each age group. It is beautiful to see once the momentum is headed in the right direction.

Their minds begin to think solution-based on all levels. When the *victim* shows up, they realize, "Oh, my gosh! I don't choose to be a *victim* here. I choose to be a *victor*." That empowerment follows them everywhere throughout their entire life. It follows them while they are at school.
They begin to have the ability to choose this or that. They will waffle, too, switching back to a *victim* mentality when they hit an obstacle that may seem difficult. Then, they shift right back out of it when you give them a choice — you give them *personal empowerment.* You will be so proud as you experience how amazing it is to witness

them grow and build and become all they are meant to become.

When you go through this process, your children will play all kinds of games with you. They will be on board one day and then the next day, they will revert to "I don't want to do anything." "Awesome!" Do you have to nag them? Nope. Do you have to convince them this is good for them? Nope. Sit patiently and wait until they have a **burning desire** to do something.

"Oh, man, I want to go to the movies with everybody. Mom, can I go?" "I would love for you to go. Remember we talked about how it takes at least 10 stars to earn going to the movies on Saturday?" "Yeah, but I'll do it later." "I understand and you will have a chance next week."

Do you see the windows that you have to work with to help you create success? Stick to your guns. Decide. Be patient and persistent. Until they want something, their tank will have no fuel for them to learn.

They will always want something. Right?

As they transition into becoming fishermen and when *ridicule* and *violent opposition* become accepted by *self-evidence*, your children will fall right into place. They love this. They think it's one of the coolest things in the world. They begin to manifest a new approach. They become resourceful and begin thinking things through in their minds as victors.

They immediately ask, "Mom, Dad, what can I do to earn going to my friend's house this weekend?" Or "Tomorrow night, my friend is having a sleepover. I want to go. What can I do to earn that?" "I have something over here at the mall that I'd like to buy. It's a beautiful dress (or a new pair of sneakers). What could I do to earn this?"

How awesome! How many parents would pay millions of dollars to have their kids be able to be proactive like that? It happens! When you master **Learn to Speak Kid**, YOU will make this happen.

Deep down in your heart, your kids will know you gave them the best you could. When they are ready to make their way, you'd like them to come back for a visit rather than hear, "Okay, I'm $20,000 in debt. Dad, could you bail me out?" Statistics are statistics. You've heard the stories. You know they're out there; yes, they are very true.

Now, I talked about this in the beginning. **What is Your Role as a Parent**? We'll talk about it a little bit more here, too. It is so important to understand that as a parent, you have a job to do. It is not your job to make your kids happy. It is not your job to do great things for them. Your job is to instill great gifts and skills in them. They will play every card they have to make you feel bad, to have things go back to the way they used to be, and to get a free meal ticket. Back when they didn't have to do squat—nothing.

So, they make you feel bad. They hate you. They're going to play all of the tricks in the book. You can respond with "That's okay if you hate me. I don't like it. But, I accept that you hate me. It's alright to hate me because I have a job to do. It's to equip you with life skills and to prepare you to live a successful life on your own. Whether you like me or not, hey, that's okay. I'm still going to do my job."

That is one of the most freeing parts of the bondage. Kids are very smart. They've been able to manipulate you to keep you at bay. Almost like a servant because they know you love them so much. They've been mentally whipping you. Not physically with a whip, but *mentally* whipping you so they don't have to do anything more than they must to survive. Until now.

Now, let it go.

They don't hate you. They might say it. They might play the game. When you let that go, it is freeing. It is empowering to know you have a job to do and when you follow through with it, they will thank you forever and appreciate you later.

Ridiculed, violently opposed, and then *accepted by self-evidence.* It's 0, 1, 1, 2, 3, 5, 8, 13, 21, 34, 55, 89, 144, etc. That's the pattern of how this will grow for you. Stick to your guns! When your kids pull out the punches, don't take it personally. No matter how bad you feel.

"Oh, my gosh! Am I doing this wrong? I don't want them to hate me. I feel like I'm being a meany here, a monster." Yes. This will come up immediately and the children will win for anybody who doesn't understand this quickly.

When you stand strong and reply, "That's okay. That's just the way a *victim* tells me he loves me." The *victor* deals with situations using hugs. The *victim* says, "Get away from me. I hate you. I don't want you to touch me. You're evil." That's just how the *victim* says, "You're the best in the world. Love you, *Mwah*."

F.E.A.R. is **F**alse **E**vidence **A**ppearing **R**eal. That's all it is when your kids are crying and saying, "My life sucks!" We all did our best because we didn't know better for the first five, 10 or 15 years. Don't beat yourself up or place judgment. We're not placing any judgment. It's all about making better decisions now that we DO know. Move forward and learn a new approach.

We're emphasizing the worst case scenarios they will come up with. These can come up. They can manifest. Make a decision now to move forward and make this work. It really is that simple. Get the momentum moving in a positive direction. Different successes can happen quickly, within one or two weeks. Then, there will be some waffling and some protesting as you go from a couple of weeks into a month. Maybe again after a month to two months and so on.

Eventually, there will be a tipping point when they suddenly say, "You know what? This is pretty cool. I love being able to choose *victim* or *victor*. Wow! Oh, my gosh! Is it my choice? I don't have to be a *victim* the whole time, where everybody's out to get me and the world's evil. The world is fun. I can find everything I choose to find."

Setting the right mindset with your kids is imperative.

Whatever you set your *reticular activation system* (R.A.S.) to, you will always find it. Let's play with this, maybe for the first time, so you can see how true this is. Think of a color. I'm going to think of green. Now that you have chosen your color, close your eyes for five seconds and think about that color. Then, open your eyes and give yourself five seconds to scan the room and count how many items you can find that are your color.

Ready? Go! Okay. Time's up. I saw different green things because I set my reticular activation system on what I chose to see or find. All the things in this room that I'm seeing, things of all different colors, I didn't count, did I? See what a victim does with their reticular activation system? You can give them 1,000 great things: hugs, kisses, gifts, loves, toys, trinkets, you name it. What are they going to find? They will scan over all of that and find the ones that support them as a what? Yes! A *victim*.

The opposite of the *victim* is the *victor*. You will examine all the negative circumstances and conclude, "You know what? All of these bad things happen to me. Do you know what the best part of today is? Coming home and having a hug, getting a ride, seeing I could get a text from a friend, or seeing I got a letter." They will begin to find those few things that always support the *victor*!

Maybe this is an "Ah-Ha, wow" moment for you. Now, you can play with this and begin to engage. That's why reading the book repeatedly to build that repetition, which is the second law of learning, is so important. You, too, are forming new neurological pathways of understanding that are no longer limited to "I just want to love them and make them happy and...."

It's almost like being on a political campaign. You can be the best candidate or their favorite person, or you can choose to have them become productive citizens and ensure you get them the skills to succeed.

Whether you agree with or like me or not is irrelevant because you know what I'm telling you is true. I'm all right if you don't like me because I know what I stand for is TRUTH. As you engage with the ideas illustrated here, I know you will see success and thank me later.

Sound familiar yet?

Every parent who sticks with this program loves me and they will for the rest of their lives. They think this is the coolest thing that ever happened. I have seen so many **Learn to Speak Kid** recommendations and I've seen them accompanied by much enthusiasm. There's no way anybody could tell me that this doesn't work.

Take these gifts. Allow yourself to know and understand that the process will take a little while. What if it took you a year on just this one chapter, but you stayed consistently with it? Your **Star Chart** would grow tremendously. It could be a matter of just a few weeks or even a month. It takes 21 days to create a habit and 90 days to anchor it in. That habit is part of a neurological pathway, as a habit that genuinely produces results.

Permit yourself to have fun. Enjoy the journey. You can set your reticular activation system on "What was my mini victory for the day?" What was the best part of the **Star Chart** for you? You can focus on growing it. Turn your doubts, fears and anxieties into understanding, empowerment and enthusiasm.

You, too, my friend, are on the same path to greatness. Be a *victor* rather than a *victim*. The program will work exactly how you, yes, I'm talking to you here, exactly how YOU choose to see it work. The *victim* does not work. *Victor* works every time.

Once again, I appreciate all you're doing and love hearing the success stories that consistently keep coming in.

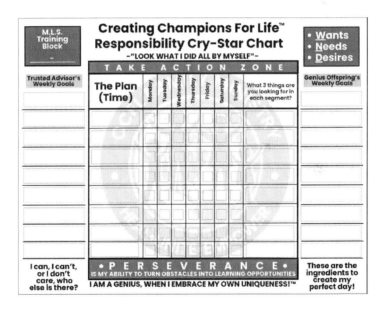

Final Thoughts by Bonnie:

When I first began to *Learn to Speak Kid* with Thomas, I didn't have this book or the 12 modules and videos with the self-study course. I had Thomas seeing my kids and their behavior with me. He was implementing the only way he knew how to deal with kids, with loving guidance.

The results I saw were amazing. I was embarrassed because my youngest, who was seven then, came to me and asked me to make him juice. Thomas asked me to go get something. While I was gone, Zachary made the juice all by himself. Thomas taught him what to look for and asked him questions. Zachary was so excited that he figured it out all by himself! He literally beamed with joy and confidence. He has never asked me to make juice for him again.

I began to copy Thomas' methods. When he did it, it seemed effective. When I did it, they thought I was stupid! All four of my children did exactly what Thomas says children will do in this chapter. I have shed a few tears because of how hurtful they have been in some cases, especially the older two. I know that if I am going to live with myself, I have to do what is in the best interest of my children. Not what is in MY best interest. It is in the best interest of my children to let them go, let them make mistakes, and allow them the opportunity to struggle with the juice can. When they work on something and succeed, they feel awesome about themselves.

This may be the most difficult thing you ever go through in your life as a parent. Remember, your children know how much you love them and sometimes use that against you.

They are extremely intelligent and will push their limits to the edge. Your children must learn to live alone in the world at some point. Buying things for them, making them happy and stepping in to save them is NOT setting them up for success later in life. This type of parenting sets them up to never understand why they can't provide for their family, maintain solid relationships and develop successful careers as they move out and into adulthood.

If you are not going to go through the process now, when is a good time to do so?

I know you can do it. You will succeed. The authentic love and gratitude that your children will give you later will bring peace, harmony and happiness to your family and future generations.

1. What is the most common reaction from children and teenagers as you begin to go through the Transition from Feeding them Fish to Creating a Fisherman?

_____

_____

_____

_____

_____

2. What psychological emotions will you go through during the transition process?

_____

_____

_____

_____

_____

3. What are three great reasons for making the Transition to a Fisherman?

_____

_____

_____

_____

_____

4. What are the different age groups for a natural Transition?

_____

_____

_____

_____

_____

5. Describe the Fibonacci sequence.

_____

_____

_____

_____

_____

Stop feeding them fish! Turn them into fishermen.

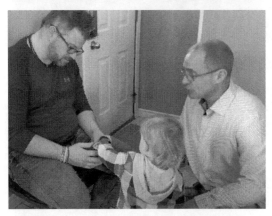

148

Chapter 5

Guiding Behavior vs. Punishment

~ Give your child the opportunity to grow, learn and think lovingly on their own. ~

Thomas C. Liotta

Bonnie: The word *punishment* brings to mind spankings, groundings and the removal of privileges. *Punishment* has been used to mold and control behavior in children and adults since the beginning of time. Spankings have been outlawed in many parts of the world, such as Sweden and other European countries. It's controversial everywhere else. Combined with the fast pace of today's society, *punishment* has taken on a whole new form. The term *Guiding Behavior* is a new one.

I was, and still am, a good parent. So are you. I know you are because you are taking the time to **Learn to Speak Kid**. It's time to become a GREAT parent. I know that the main way people know how to parent is by how they were raised by their parents. Yes? The only way I knew how to parent was to use discipline and *punishment* techniques. Those worked when my children were little, sort of. As they grew older, I just saw unproductive, depressed kids who were ungrateful and were diagnosed with disruptive behavior disorders like ADHD and ODD (oppositional defiant disorder).

When Thomas began introducing me to the idea of *guiding* my children's behavior, I thought, "Yeah, right. I've read books. My kids are pretty good. I don't know what else there is I can learn." But, I have always kept my options open to possibilities.

When I witnessed my seven-year-old and nine-year-old children clean the Lexus without being asked, I knew something was up. I gave Thomas a funny look out of the corner of my eye and asked him, "What did you say to my kids? They have never done that before!" From that moment forward, I began to become even more open. They weren't just cleaning it without being asked; they were happy doing it.

I know you are excited to learn about the principle of *Guiding Behavior vs. Punishment,* so here we go. Get a notepad and a pen ready for use as Thomas explains another amazing power principle.

Thomas: Ah, how awesome is it that you and I, who are just alike, would love to be able to have our children and teenagers learn the lessons of the life skills you choose for them? But, in the vibrations of love rather than the opposite of love. That could be hate, anger or distrust. How awesome will it feel when you can operate with your kids in a "yes and yes" mode rather than a "yes or no" mode when they talk about things that are important to them?

These concepts will make plenty of sense as we move forward.

Your child's attitude will dictate how things work. When you went through the earlier chapters — **Know Your Role as a Parent** and **Parent's Brain vs. Kid's Brain** — you engaged fully in those. Right? If you have not, NOW would be a good time to go back and practice the contents of those chapters. Go through them again and again. Knowing that your child's brain thinks and sees the world differently than your adult brain does can help a lot in aiding and **Guiding Behavior**. It also might bring awareness to those "Ah-Ha" moments of "Why do I always feel like I have to *punish* to make anything work?"

When you engage in *punishment*, you're, in a sense, forcing the other person to do something against their will. It's usually something parents will desperately grasp when nothing else works. It's a default technique taught to us by some older generations. When you really and truly engage with the exercises outlined in this book and more thoroughly with the actual *Self-Study Course of Learn to Speak Kid,* you are learning how to empower your child to make better decisions for themselves. See, if I'm like you and you're like me, we'll always ensure we can acquire exactly what we want...whether others agree or disagree, including your parents. Yes?

Do you remember your "*sales training*" when you were perhaps only two years old? You asked Mom "Why," and then you asked Mom "Why" again. Then..."Why" again...see? You have the ability to keep going after what it is that you'd like to acquire. So do *your* children.

You and I can engage in this process of **Guiding Behavior vs. Punishment.** Your child will be able to make things become his or her decision as you, unbeknownst to them, guide them. This is part of the empowering process rather than saying, "You are going to do this," and then they feel they have no choice. They have to do what you tell them to do. No person I have ever met loves to do things because they *HAVE to.*

The ideas presented in **Guiding Behavior vs. Punishment** will shift the words your children use from "I have to..." to "I choose to...." Let's take a moment and reflect on that. Think about the last time you said, "Well, I *have to* get this done. I *have to* do that." When you look at it, you're thinking to yourself, "I'm not even happy doing this and if I had a choice, I'd rather be doing something else." When you feel inspired and ready to do something, you say, "I choose to do this," and a smile begins to form on your face rather than the frown that comes with the "have to" thought.

Congratulations on making it through the other chapters and progressing this far. Sticking with this process will pay you back huge dividends. I encourage you to go through and answer the questions from the previous chapters to ensure you have all of your expectations, life skills and your child's goals and rewards written and posted.

One of my favorite places to post these lists is on the refrigerator. Every time someone is in the kitchen, and the entire family cycles through there, it will be a mind trigger. The concept begins to sink in and engage with your children.

There is a foundation of four building blocks:

1. **Goal**
2. **Plan**
3. **Take Action**
4. **Perseverance.**

Many of these building blocks go hand in hand with **self-control.** We **Guide their Behavior** by teaching them:

"I am in control of my body and actions."

They go from *renting* their body to becoming an *owner* of their body, from borrowing something to "I actually OWN it." When you were younger and rented your apartment, you didn't paint the walls or take great care of everything, did you? It was up to the landlord to take care of his property. It's different when you buy your OWN home. In fact, I know some people who paint their fence EVERY summer!

When your children begin the first building block of self-control, *"I am in control of my body and my actions,"* you will teach them what is known as an "attention stance." They do this in sports, school, and now at home. This is also common practice in a customer service line or as you get ready to check a book out at the library. So, don't tell me your teenager doesn't need to know attention stance. We ALL do. Yes?

When you want them to hear what you are saying, instruct your child, "Show me your best attention stance." Teach them to stand with their feet together, hands at their sides, body straight up, and eyes straight forward, making eye contact. That's establishing an attention stance. This saves you from continually barking orders of "Hey, pay attention!" Teaching them how to get your attention with an attention stance is *Guiding Behavior.*

Create a simple game that can teach the technique; we used to call it playing "statue." If your children are older, eye contact and focused attention are the best ways for them to hear and understand with clear comprehension. "Show me your best statue. See if you can overcome everything inside your head that asks you to move, scratch, twitch and look around. Those are distractions that take away from your self-control."

Just like math always has a formula that will get you the correct measurements, what we're teaching you here is so sound that there is an exact formula for anything you choose to create with and for your child. This is how you guide them.

Let's say they ask you for a candy bar at the store. A common starting point is when they start saying, "Hey, Mom, can I get this? Hey, Mom, can I have that? Mom, can I go do that? Dad, what about this?" Any time they begin asking for something they like, you should first say, "Wow.

It sounds like you have a **Goal.** You've found something important for you."

As your children begin to desire to acquire things and you identify what they are, you recognize them as opportunities to teach. Your child or teenager will want something soon. You'll hear, "Mom, Dad, I want a new bicycle. Mine is the oldest one of anyone in the entire school! It's embarrassing!" "Wow," you respond, "you would like a bicycle? Great goal. Well, tell me about the bicycle you want!" "It's got these handlebars with oversized pedals. It's got a really cool seat and I can put...!"

Your kids will share all the things that they love with you. Get more details about what they like. Get as many details as you can. Once you *acknowledge* something important to them, which we'll go into more in-depth in the next chapter, ***Knowing the Reward***, you can execute the second part of the ***Guiding Behavior*** formula.

Part two of this formula is to have a Plan.

In ***Knowing the Reward***, when they ask for something, "Can I have this? Can I have that?" we start to create a subtle shift where your kids begin to ask, "What can I do to earn a bike? What can I do to earn some outside time? What can I do to earn something else I desire?"

"I would love for you to have the bike. What has to happen for you to earn it?" "Well, I don't know." "Excellent." See, there's another *life skill.* You can slide this in there and say, "Well, let's figure out the plan. How much does it cost?" "It's only $200." "Excellent! Do you have $200?" "No, but you do, Mom. So, buy it for me."

The **Guiding** part is **Knowing Your Role as a Parent.**

Just buying them a $200 bike does not count as teaching them life skills. Does it?

Does it fall under the formula of *Making the Transition* to being a fisherman rather than giving them fish? It's YOUR job to help empower them to create a **Plan**.

"Well, I can earn some money doing this. I can earn some money doing that." Then, suddenly, they start building on it until they figure out how to buy the bike on their own. Once you help them with a **Plan**, they can **Take Action**, which is part three, and *do something*.

Two things will happen through the process of that formula: **Goal — Plan — Take Action — Perseverance.**

1. You just saved yourself $200 for a bike that'll be left outside in the rain, stolen or abused and not taken care of very well.

2. During the process, they can say, "Gosh, you know, I've been earning some money and I don't know if I really want that bike now."

You'll probably come to the same conclusion as any parent who has bought their kid toy after toy after toy and *punished* them for not taking care of them later: "You can't take care of what you've got now. Why the heck would I get you something new?" Now, you're back in *Punishment* mode.

As you're learning the process, you may *waffle*. As soon as you catch yourself, forgive it and return to **Guiding Behavior**: "I'd love for you to have a bike. That is called a **Goal.** What do we have to do?" "Come up with a **Plan.**" PRAISE the correct answer. Now that you are working together with your life skills lined out and have a **Plan,** let's **Take Action**. "Excellent. Let's go ahead and do that. Now that you have all these chores over here on a list, let's do them step-by-step and figure out what you CAN do so that you can EARN that money."

This takes you into the *fourth step,* which is **Perseverance**. Here's where you can turn obstacles into opportunities. Any time your child has opposition, that's a good sign. Now, you get to return to the life skills list and use this as a teaching and learning opportunity. Teach them the game of opposites.

The conversation might go something like this with your child saying: "Well, I can't do this because I don't have that." "Excellent. Now you told me what you can't do. What's the opposite of can't?" "Can." "So, tell me what you CAN do." "Well, I can do this." "Excellent. That's going to help you move towards your goal. Very good. Look at that. You're very smart. I like how you can see what you're supposed to do."

You may also find them doing something they aren't supposed to do sometimes, right? You ask them, "What are you doing?" And they answer, "I don't know." You remember this from **Parent's Brain vs. Kid's Brain**. Instead of asking, "What are you doing?" ask them, "What *should* you be doing?" "Well, I should be finishing up my chores." Or ask, "Where's the best place for that?" "In my bedroom."

Every time you ask these questions, you will instill in them the opportunity to feel the *positive* vibration of "I know what the answer is" rather than "I don't know why this place is a mess." Walking into a room with "Why is this place such a mess?" immediately falls into a *punishment* mode. Your kids have to defend it. Instead, "Hey, where 's the best place to put everything in here?" Get a positive answer before you move on to the next one. They will always know the correct answer.

Follow this simple process: **Goal — Plan — Take Action — Perseverance** every time they ask you for something.

We were in the store at the beginning of Bonnie's kids' journey and were looking to get some organic raw honey. The kids immediately went into "I want" mode. "I want some honey, too. I like this jar. That looks like a teddy bear." It would be so easy to go into **Punishment** mode here and answer, "No! Stop asking for things!"

With **Guiding Behavior**, you use the formula: "Excellent. That's called a what?" "A **Goal**." "Excellent. What's your **Plan** to make it work?" See, now you're **Guiding** them to put their thinking cap on. They begin planning things to find a solution. They were waiting to be fed. Now, they are thinking.

Once your kids have a *parent-approved* **plan**, they should take action. In the beginning, nine times out of 10, you will make the plan for them. They now have direction. Every time the kids run into something, encourage them through. Do not take over. Obstacles are expected.

Perseverance is the key. Help them turn all their obstacles into opportunities. Get excited when they find reasons they can't do something. "Oh, my gosh! That is so great. I'm glad you found that!" Remember, the opposite is always there. Right? Left hand, right hand. Top, bottom.

Front, back. Opposites always exist. There's the law of polarity. Positive, negative. They go hand in hand.

Get excited if your kids show their intelligence on why something *can't* work. Guide your child to the opposite. "What is the opposite? Tell me the way it can work."

There's a great affirmation that works with them. It's personally one of my favorites to perform before having them engage in any activity. Have them go through the affirmation of:

"I am a genius. I figure things out easily and elegantly. The answers immediately come to me because I know I am a genius."

With that mindset, all obstacles automatically shift into opportunities. When you choose to play the game of opposites and **persevere** at turning obstacles into opportunities, you'll always be in the right environment to reach your, you guessed it, goal. G-O-A-L (Goal). What are the first two letters in the word goal? G-O. Where are we going to GO in life without a goal? You got it. Nowhere.

In your child, the **victor**, or **Champion**, begins to formulate a *plan* by searching for a solution. "Well, I don't know." Opposite. "What's the opposite of I don't know?" "I do know." "So, what would that sound like?"

Ask questions.

Give your child the opportunity to grow, learn and think independently. They will be so proud of themselves when they come up with the correct answers — they will every time.

Children are extremely intelligent. You'll be surprised to discover their capabilities when you **Create the Right Environment** for them to step up. Now that they have a **plan**, you are here to support them in that plan. "Let's **take action** on it. It's up to you." "If it's meant to be, it's up to me." They start to take *OWNERSHIP* of their lives. That's a great place to be!

Every study shows that from when a baby is walking around until they're three, the brain literally hears the word "No" massive amounts more often than it hears the word "Yes." "No, don't do this. No, get down from that. No, don't touch that. No, no, no...." A UCLA study from a few years ago reported that a baby will hear the word no on average 400 times daily! Have you ever visited the swimming pool and seen that big rule list? They say *no* running, *no* spinning, *no* jumping, *no* diving... You're a kid asking, "Can I go in the water?" They are always reading and hearing no, no, no, no, no...

Here are some other things you can do to **Guide Behavior** when you see signs posted that say no, no, no.

Play the awesome *game of opposites* with them again. What's the game of opposites? No running. Walking only, please. Same message. Higher vibration. No diving. Right? No diving? Please walk into the water.

As you **guide behavior**, these steps will make the whole thing work smoothly for you. As you begin to **guide behavior,** you will be able to operate in a more loving, caring manner.

Let's return to that "yes, yes" and "yes, no" concept. When operating in *Punishment* mode, you will either say yes or no. Sometimes, it's a 50-50 split. When you operate with a **Guided Behavior**, you're always in the operation of YES.

"I want this." "I want you to have it, too. What has to happen for it to work?" "Well, I've got to do this and this." "Awesome! So, let's go do it." When you hear yourself starting to go into the "yes, yes," this might sound a little odd.

Here's an example. "How was your day today?" Most people ask, "Did you have a good day?" To which your child or teen will answer a yes or a no. They had a good day or a bad day. What if you always had a good day and some days were even greater? That's a kind of "yes, yes" mode. It keeps you on a higher scale of vibration.

Let's say you have some kids with a behavior that is natural for them to do but irks you. For example, you're happy when they are in the park running, but if they're in the house running...not so much.

Guiding Behavior is *Creating the Right Environment* for them to run in and be able to *guide* them there.

Punishment is they are running, which is great physical exercise, and you're telling them that they're doing something WRONG. They think, "Oh, running is NOT a good thing." They don't hear there's no running *IN THE HOUSE*. You went right back to that big list at the swimming pool of no, no, no. Really, they're asking you, "Okay, what *CAN* I do? All I get from you is that you yell at me about what I *CAN'T* do."

Guiding Behavior vs. Punishment is "yes, yes" versus "yes, no."

See, "yes, no" is when I told them, "No, you can't run," but in the "yes, yes" mode, it would be: "I'd love for you to run. Where's the best place for you to be safe and run?" "Outside." See? They are already going to know the answer. If they don't, then there is a life skill for you to show them. Once it's already been learned one time, they know they can run *outside*. We use walking feet inside.

Guiding behavior guides them in what they choose to do in their life.

Here is the other part. Let's say they're fighting with brothers and sisters. Guess what? They are normal. They are not expected to always get along. If they get along and don't get along, they are perfect. You have cooperation and non-cooperation. You encourage both of them. "Hey, I noticed you guys are doing a really good job of not getting along. That is awesome. You guys are doing so well." Here, we have two areas where these opposite behaviors can operate. "Cooperation is an indoor and outdoor activity. Non-cooperation is an outdoor activity only. Indoors, you guys are expected to play well together. Outdoors, you can yell at each other all you like."

You never have to say NO to them for arguing or fighting.

Now they're arguing, so you say, "Hey, I think you guys are doing great here. It sounds like you are really into arguing. Where's the best place to argue?" "Outside." "Excellent. Let's go." You move them outside. Put them in the backyard. "Now, you guys can just yell, argue and do all the things you want to do that involve arguing. Get it out of your system. Make it work."

"Well, we want to be back inside." "Excellent. I would love for you to be back inside. That is a **Goal**. How does it work for you to be inside?" Now, you have defined expectations for them of what they *CAN* do inside. They are expected to have walking feet and cooperation indoors. Running feet and non-cooperation are outside-only activities, whereas walking feet and cooperation have the choice to be inside and outside.

You could use this analogy: "Well, little Timmy, you have a stick you're swinging around. Would that be a good activity *inside* or *outside* the house?" "Outside." "You've got it."

Let's say they love to do those things inside, the running and the screaming. "Excellent. Can you share with me a restaurant where we could go and you could run around and scream?" Obviously, we mean besides Chuck E. Cheese'. We're talking about a Denny's or some family related restaurant. What would the owners of a house or restaurant do if you were to yell, scream and run around? Yes! They are going to ask you to leave.

Punishment mode usually kicks in here because no one has ever taught you about *Creating the Right Environment.* They say, "Oh, inside is for good behavior. Outside is for not-good behavior. Once again, the principle from *Guiding Behavior vs. Punishment* is praising them "yes, yes " on both sides of the coin. Either way, you are there to support them on how they can make a choice.

Things will click for them and they will exclaim, "Wow, I'm beginning to have really good power here. If I'm outside not cooperating and choose to be inside, I know exactly how to make it happen." They feel more empowered. You guide them on what behavior you'd like to see more of. YOU set the stage. YOU are the parent. It is YOUR home. What are the life skills you wish for them to learn? Hmm, etiquette. "Walking inside the house. Excellent, that's an inside behavior." "You'd like to run? I'd love for you to run. Where's the best place?" "Outside." "You got it — outside." Then, they do that; they go outside.

Now, they always hear yes from you versus yes and then maybe a no, or from many of us, no, no, no and then maybe a yes. There's going to be a difference in communication. Understand that you are choosing either hate, anger or distrust — the low vibrations or joy, happiness and love — the very high vibrations, based upon the method you vocalize with your child. You may share the exact same message, but what method are you choosing, *high or low vibration*?

Once again, will this be simple the first time if you have already done years of negative training? Probably not. Remember the chapter on *Making the Transition.*

You must have certain things in place for your children to know. They love structure. Kids love to know what has to happen or what has to be done. Let's say you would like their room to be cleaned. That is a basic life skill. Maybe you would like them to be responsible for cleaning the bathroom they're using.

Always break down everything that's expected to be done into **threes**. When a bathroom job is complete:
1.   All countertops and sinks are completely clean and the floor is swept and mopped.
2.   All robes and towels are hung up on the back of the door.
3.   The mirrors and the bathroom accessories are all wiped and clean.

Three simple steps will be easy for them to understand. Now, when you hear them say, "I want something (a **Goal**)," choose to **guide** them. "Excellent. Well, what do we need to do?"

1.   Room Clean
2.   Bathroom Clean
3.   Everything Put Away

They have a **Plan** broken down into **three** parts. It's up to them to **Take Action**. "I'd love for you to do whatever it is that you'd like." They know what has to be done and **Take Action**. It's up to THEM to get it done now.

You go right back through that same one, two, three, four-cycle: **Goal — Plan — Take Action — Perseverance**. You can answer YES to them every single step of the way.

Guiding Behavior keeps you in "yes, yes" mode. You NEVER have to take anything away and are always building towards what is important for them.

It works when they have a want, a need, a desire, or something to choose that is important to them. They have a little *fuel tank*. When there is something important to them, it *fuels* them up to make these things happen. They may want something. They may know exactly how to do it. If they're unwilling to **Take Action** because they don't want it that badly, you will save much time and money. *Doing things for them* to make things happen is NOT *Guiding Behavior*.

It must be up to THEM to follow the steps.

"Well, I'd like to have some breakfast with everybody." "Excellent. We'd love for you to join us for breakfast. What has to happen?" "Well, I've got to get the bathroom done." "Excellent. Do you know how to do it?" "Yes, I do." "Great."

OR

"Well, I don't know how." There's an opportunity to teach them a life skill. SHOW them. Remember the three steps?

You demonstrate how to do the life skill, mess it back up and have them show you how to do it correctly. That's how it works. There's a great chapter you will come to called **Complaining** which talks in-depth about "either they *don't know how* to do these things, or they *just don't want to.*"

Another example in **Guiding Their Behavior** is called *pre-framing*.

Pre-framing allows you to be a proactive parent.

Have you ever been in a car with a friend and the kids are in the back seat? As you drive around, every three to five minutes, you hear, "Mom, Mom, Mom. Dad, Dad, Dad." This is where *pre-framing* comes into play. The life skill is called *self-control*; I am in control of my body and my actions. Their mouth is part of their body and their actions. The car ride is a perfect time for them to practice and demonstrate good self-control.

During the ride from here to the store or Grandma's house, you always tell them their expected behavior through *pre-framing*. You would say, "Between here and Grandma 's house, I will answer one 'Mom,' so pick your 'Mom' carefully. How often will I answer you when you say 'Mom'? I am going to answer you only one time."

Here's a *punishment* scenario. You're in the car. They keep asking, "Mom, Mom, Mom." Five, 10, 20 times on a 15-minute drive. "Can't you see I'm busy here? I'm driving here. Shut up. Knock it off. What do you want?" It comes across as *punishment.* When you do that, you operate in a "yes, no" mode.

What if you got in the car and *pre-framed* this: "Excellent, we've got a 15-minute ride. You're more than welcome to use one of your 'Moms' to get my attention. Unless it's an absolute emergency, all you get is ONE time." That creates the value for them to think, "Hmm, I've got to make this valuable." When they use the "Mom" right away, you can always say, "Yes, now you've used up your 'Mom' already. When's the best time you can use up another one?" "When we get there." "See, that's what I love about you. You're so smart. You know exactly what to do." It's called *pre-framing* and it works. It allows you to *guide their behavior instead of punishing* them.

Guiding behavior also goes hand in hand with praise.

Praise is so important. What is it that you would like to manifest? What would you like to see? First off, parents will say, "I don't want them to be disruptive." Okay, that's what you *don't* want them to be. What would you like them to be? "I'd like them to be cooperative and quiet." Excellent. So, the only time they could get your attention is when they are being cooperative and quiet. So, you ask them, "What's the best way to earn my attention?" "I'll be cooperative and quiet in the car." "Excellent." See. Look how awesome it is.

1. The **Goal** is "I would like your attention, Mom or Dad."
2. What's the **Plan** to get it? To be cooperative and quiet.
3. What is up to them to take? You guessed it again. **Take Action**. They might not get it right away.
4. That's called **Perseverance**. They're turning obstacles into opportunities so that, eventually, they will reach their goal.

You can always operate in YES mode with them.
"Mom, Mom, Mom." "When is the best time we can talk? What kind of behavior is Mommy looking for?" "Quiet and cooperative." "Awesome. Once you've demonstrated that, I'll be able to go ahead and talk with you."

That's **Guiding their Behavior** with *praise*. You're giving them votes. You're giving them energy on that which you would like to see grow. That's *praise*.

Always give energy to the things you choose to see versus the things you don't want because whatever you give energy to will grow. If they keep yelling and then they get attention, guess what they will do? They're going to keep yelling to get your attention. That's how kids operate.

Let's talk a little bit more about *praise*. A neurological pathway forms when a child has heard the words "no" and "you can't do this" many times. As I have mentioned, they hear it an average of 400 times daily as babies. We say things like "No, don't do that!" "Go to your room!" "Go outside and don't do that in here!" "If you guys are going to yell and scream, go outside and do that!"

They develop associations about some of these places, with feelings like "Gosh, I am in trouble" or "I'm being ridiculed for I'm not sure what." Part of the process here is that the kids are operating in either "I'm being *praised*" or "I'm being *punished*." How do you want your child to develop their brains?

Your child WILL develop *self-discipline* as you progress through the principles. They will tell themselves, "Whenever I choose to run, I'm finding the *correct environment*." It's just like finding the correct behavior in an environment such as a restaurant, library or airplane. That usually represents quiet and good self-control. Right? It's not swinging around sticks and running around yelling. That would be appropriate in a playground area.

Every time they are in a grocery store or where they use that extra energy, you ask, "Where's the best place to use that great activity or great energy of running?" "Outside." "Excellent. Is a loud voice welcome inside?" "No." "Excellent. So, if you use the loud voice, let's be sure to go outside." Put the child outside. "Well, I don't want to be outside." "Well, yes, you do. You just told me the loud voice place was outside. A loud voice was not inside. Where would you like to be if you're using a loud voice? You'd like to be outside. It's just like they'd do at a restaurant. They'd ask you to leave and go outside. We are helping you to be in the right place."

Now, somewhere along the line, *punishment* was introduced as a way to CONTROL a child. *Punishment* is a perfect short-term tactic. It doesn't build any good, long lasting relationships, not by any means. It's just a quick fix for the situation without being able to *praise* or *guide* them.

Repetition is a key to learning; again, you are *pre-framing* and interacting: "Where's the best place for your shoes?" "I don't know." "Well, shoes are worn outside or inside?" "Outside." "Excellent. So, if your shoes are on, you should choose to be where?" "Outside." "Excellent. Oh, but you're telling me you'd like to be inside. So, where would be the best place for the shoes?" "Over here, in the closet, in my bedroom, or over by the front door." "Excellent. That's what I like best about you. You're so smart. You know exactly what to do."

This is going to take a little bit of time and practice. How often did we get communicated to by our parents and told that what we did was wrong? "Yeah, everything looks good. Damn, the bathroom's a mess." "The rest of the house is clean, but the bathroom didn't quite make it."

Now, *Guiding Behavior* here is to say, "Hey, your reward for the end of the week would be 90 minutes of swim time. With two rooms not quite up to par, you have earned 30 to 60 minutes of swim time. Congratulations." "Oh, but I wanted to do the whole 90!" "Awesome, what has to happen to earn all 90?" "Well, the whole house has to be clean." "Now, see, that's what I love best about you. You already know exactly what to do. Now, you've got to do what?" "**Take Action**." "Can you show me what it looks like?"

Remember in the above example where they only cleaned one room? Either they *don't know how* to clean the bathroom or they *don't want to*. If they DON'T know how, that's a life skill and it's your job to show them. If they DO know how: "Well, then, if you'd like to have 90 minutes of swim time, you know exactly what to do."

Like you and me, if we were ever at a job where you make $20 an hour, you do this and then you'll get that. "Do you want money?" "Yeah." "Well, do this." "Okay." It's a simple thing. Just forget the statement: "You don't do this, then you don't get that."

That's really how simple this technique can be.

Almost every kid who is born in today's society comes with a cell phone. Buy diapers, get cell phones. I'm saying that whatever their item is, it's very important to them. "I would love for you to have a cell phone. That's called a **Goal**. Exactly what has to happen?" "Well, it's $50 a month, $100 a month, 'X' dollars a month." "Okay, who's going to pay for that?" "Ah, well. I just thought you would. Tommy's mom bought him a phone." Okay, remember what your role was in Chapter 1? Remember your role was to teach your child life skills? Remember the other chapter where we talked about going from feeding the child fish to them becoming a fisherman?

And the conversation continues: "Let me understand this. If I just paid all your bills, then pretty soon there's going to be a point where you won't be able to pay them, so I'm always going to have to. Understand my role? Would it make sense for me to keep buying your cell phone for you right now?" "No." "Okay. What is going to be more important for you to do?" "Set a **Goal**." "Exactly. Let's come up with a **Plan**. How's that going to work?"

Then, the child **Takes Action**; you go right into number three again. If they really want the cell phone, kids will find a way to make it work. Their intelligence is always there to rescue them.

When they are setting **Goals**, creating a **Plan** and **Taking Action**, you've got someone to work with; when they say they can't work, you've got someone to *guide*. If they don't have anything going on, which is very, very rare, then they don't have any goals. They have nothing that's *filling their tank* to move forward. They're not even asking for a cell phone. When they're asking for a cell phone, their tank is full. You help them come up with a **Plan**. That tank becomes such a *driving force* that it makes them eager to do the activities and learn those life skills. Then, eventually, they'll reach their **Goal**.

Let's approach this from a different angle:

"I want a cell phone." "I'd love for you to have a cell phone." You're operating in the "yes, yes" mode again versus the "yes, no" mode because then it would just become an argument. "If you loved me, you'd get it for me." "I do love you which is why I'm NOT getting it for you."

Any parent who buys their kids stuff doesn't truly authentically love them. They have the idea that they love them, but don't have the right intuition to love their children. If they did, Mom or Dad would know there's going to be a point when they're not going to be there paying their child's bills anymore. It makes as much sense as teaching them to be on a welfare system.

Always remember the transitional part of the process. Your kids are going to test your *perseverance.* See, if I'm like you and you're like me, they will engage in the same behavior as electricity or water. They will take the path of least resistance. If we've already trained them to be dependent, it means we did a lot of stuff for them. They've never known how to do their own dishes, laundry, or whatever it may be.

For example, they will say, "I want something and that's called a **Goal**, yeah. I need to work toward the **Plan**. Got it. Yep. **Take Action**." Once they come across an obstacle, old habits may kick in. "Well, I started and it was just kind of hard." They will go through whining episodes to see if you will do it for them again. You might say this: "Oh, okay. Well, let me help you and do it for you." Do you see what is missing in our 4-step cycle?

That's NOT *guiding* and it is not forming the right behavior. You've got to stick to your guns and say, "I would love for you to have it. What do you have to do?" "Well, I've got to put all the things away." "Awesome. Let me know when you have it done and then we can take the next step." Then you walk away. This is YOUR part in teaching THEM to **persevere** and YOURSELF to **persevere** through the obstacles.

What ends up happening is they start to build the part in their brain of "Oh, if it is to be, it's up to me." It used to be that Mom never did say no. She said yes. Dad said yes. All they had to do was ask. Now, instead, you're testing it. You're measuring. How much do they really, really choose that, or how much do they really want it? You could easily save $200, as discussed earlier in the bike gift experience.

If you just bought them the bike, they'll be happy for a day, maybe even a week. Then you will find the bike outside in the rain, not neatly put back in the garage. "Wow, if you can't take care of this, I'm just going to have to take it away from you." How's that *punishment* thing working?

I know it doesn't work. You've been doing it for too long. If that child went through and did all of the steps to earn it, oh boy, that bike would be respected. You wouldn't even have to ask your child to put it away. They know where it goes.

They might say, "I got distracted." "Okay, that's good. It's easy to get distracted. How does that help you with your goal?" "Oh, it doesn't." "Excellent. That's what I love about you. You know where to refocus your attention. When your attention gets stronger, then you'll reach your **Goal**. So, let me know when you want to get that done."

Once again, operate in **YES** mode. You don't have to ever tell your child no. Tell them how it is. Give them the structure to let the environment empower them. Their intelligence will master any environment they're in. If they know they can whine a little bit, and you'll do it for them, well, congratulations, you might as well move out of your house and go to college with them, too, and do their laundry and all the other stuff. They'll milk you right along the whole way.

You will fall short many times as you engage more in this **Guiding Behavior**. You'll default back to *Punishment* mode. You have some good strong neurological pathways that must be readjusted.

When you engage in it and it's your **Goal** to make it work, it will. You've got the **Plan.** All the materials are right here. It's up to you to **Take Action**. Turn obstacles into opportunities. You might tell me, "It's not working with them." "Well, what part's not working?" "He's not listening." "Great. So, what's the opposite of not listening?" "Paying attention."

Remember that **attention stance** we talked about? Self-control. *"I am in control of my body and my actions."* How often did you do that training with them? "Stand at attention stance. Let's see if we can do it for 10 seconds together. Let's do it for 20 seconds, 30 seconds, 40 seconds, up to a minute." See if they can stand in an attention stance and not let that little voice in their head go, "Oh, I've got an itch. What was that noise?" You don't have a snowball's chance in hell of doing anything else unless you get these important building blocks put into place. At best, you've got a three-second attention span to work with.

When they develop the ability to focus, pay attention and exercise self-control, they will stay focused on the task at hand and become more efficient.

This is when ADHD is reversed.

They will not be diagnosed if you teach your child *focus* and *self-control*. When things get done correctly, wow, privileges are achieved as their reward. Let's say you're going to go swimming. You've got a task to do before you go swimming. The sooner they get it done, the sooner they can get there on time. If they want to take 20 or 30 minutes to do something because their focus is really short, they spend their swimming time.

You never have to say no to them. "Okay, when you're all done, we're going swimming." They took a half hour longer than expected. Now, you go swimming, but there are only 15 minutes left. Oh, well.

"I'm so happy, grateful and excited you got to go swimming today." "Well, I wanted more." "That sounds like a **Goal**. What would be the **Plan** to go longer next time?" "Well, get my stuff done sooner." "Look how smart you are. Oh, my gosh, what would happen if you got it done sooner? What would that be? Would that be *self-control*? Would that be *focus*? How about *self-discipline*? Or maybe *responsibility*?"
"Oh, I'm responsible for my actions and my belongings."

When they have self-control and you ask them, "Come over here and show me your best attention stance. I have something to share with you," they stand perfectly still and look you right in the eye. They begin to become more *responsible* for their actions and their belongings. The whole story of why things don't work begins to disappear because you put it into *praise* and you are **Guiding Behavior.**

Self-discipline: *"I do what I am supposed to do by being asked only once."*

So, what if we wish to go swimming? "Kids who have *self-control, responsibility and self-discipline*, with good *focus*, always earn 90 minutes of swim time. The other ones earn 60 or 30. Maybe 15. Which one would you like to have?" "I'd like to have all 90 minutes of swimming." "Well, what are some good characteristics you always show?" "Good self-control, good responsibility, good self-discipline and *focus*." "Excellent. It sounds like you have a plan. It's up to whom to take action on it?" "Me." "Great. Now, remember that sometimes you're going to have some obstacles. You've got to turn them into what?" "Opportunities." "That's what I love about you. You're so smart."

Now, let's say they only had one of these characteristics. They had good *self-control,* but you had to keep asking them for *self-discipline*. You go swimming and they earn

30 minutes, not the full 90. Always "yes, yes." "Well, I only got to go 30 minutes." "Yes, you did. Congratulations! I am so happy, grateful and excited that we got to go swimming today for 30 minutes." "Well, I wanted to go longer." "What's that called?"

Goal — Plan — Take Action — Persevere.

Guided Behavior always says, "Yes, yes." Eventually, they'll start saying, "Wow, Mom and Dad are pretty cool. They're my best friends. They're always on my team. I feel that if there is anything I'm looking to acquire, they always say yes to me because they love me. And they're teaching me life skills so I can be self-sufficient."

Right at the very beginning, this will be so weird and awkward for THEM and YOU that you may experience more opposition than productivity. When you push through that initial bubble, they'll realize, "Oh, my gosh, they love me more and more." They'll be so thankful, especially when you interact with the other parenting styles. "Yeah, Jimmy's mom just buys him stuff. He doesn't take good care of his stuff. He doesn't have any responsibility. He whines a lot and his mom does stuff for him. I'm so happy that I'm learning these life skills."

They begin to see the two opposite sides. It is a fun journey to be on.

Begin parenting with love rather than anger. "I'd love for you to earn that. What would be a good way for us to work as a team and make that happen?" That's more positive than: "Well, we can't afford that. If you act better, I might get you something." There is a lot of hate and anger verbalized as *punishment*.

The *environment* you create is so important for them. They love to run and yell. *Guide* them in understanding the best place for them to do that. Never tell them no for yelling. *Praise* them. "You've got some great lungs there. I'll bet you could be a great opera singer or rock star. Where's the best place to practice that? Inside or outside?"

"Outside." "Awesome. Let's go." "Well, I don't want to be outside." "Oh, well, if you don't want to be outside, where would you like to be?" "Inside." "What's the best voice to use inside?" "A quiet voice." "See, just let me know where you want to be and I'll help you get there. Loud is out. Quiet is in and out."

Always *praise* what you want more of. Once again, know what's important to your child. What's their **Goal**? They'll always tell you. "Mom, can I have that?" "Mom, can I do this?" "How can I earn a new bike?" "How can I earn a new movie?" "How can I earn a new book?" "How can I earn a bedroom set?" Or whatever it might be.

Enjoy **Guiding Behavior vs. Punishment.** It keeps you on a higher vibration of love. As you *guide* your children, you'll always be able to say yes to everything in your children 's lives.

Final Thoughts by Bonnie:

Once I learned how to *guide* my children's behavior by asking them questions and always saying yes, I began to experience more and more success with them. Especially after I stuck to it for some time. At first, they tested me, and once in a while, they still work on getting me to go back to feeding them fish, to doing everything for them for free. I know better!

Amazingly, putting the *responsibility* on your child inspires them to do their work, while *punishing* or telling them they have to does not make them want to. Does this make sense?

I love to watch my children come alive, take action and persevere in what is important to them! Using this philosophy is the key to learning how to guide them in that direction.

It warms my heart when I see them turn obstacles into opportunities because I know these life skills will set them up for future success in all areas of their lives. I feel so good now in everything I do with them because I know everything I do is lovingly guiding their behavior.

All four of my kids like themselves better. They now know how smart they are. They choose their own lives (with parent-approved decisions) and are extremely grateful for learning life skills.

1. Describe punishment.

_____

_____

_____

_____

_____

2. Describe *Guiding Behavior.*

_____

_____

_____

_____

_____

3. What does it mean to raise your child or teenager in the mode of "yes, yes" vs. "yes, no"?

_____

_____

_____

_____

_____

4. How can I learn to use this philosophy better and more consistently?

_____

_____

_____

_____

_____

5. What does it mean when you see opposition from your child or teenager?

_____

_____

_____

_____

_____

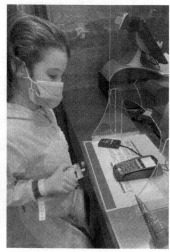

Chapter 6

Knowing the Reward

~ Find out what is important to your child or teenager; you will always have cooperation, love and peace in your home. ~
Thomas C. Liotta

Bonnie: I love being a mother. My greatest joy is watching my children grow, learn and advance. I also love rewarding my children with new clothes, family vacations and special treats they don't know about. It is fun to watch their faces light up! Can you relate with me on this? The words "Mom, you're the best! I love you!" are heartwarming. I am sure that you love this feeling, also.

This being said, I have made a terrible mistake! I have unknowingly spoiled my children. Let me describe what I mean by that. I have always thought I could spoil my children with material things but still teach them manners, morals and respect through my parenting style. I thought that using discipline techniques and sticking to them was the right thing to do. Isn't that what we have all been taught?

I would plan a camping trip or an outing at the water park for the day. You know what I mean, something fun. Then, I would tell my kids that I wanted them to clean their room or do their chores. Honestly, when the work did get done, it was half-assed at best. We would get into the car and they would fight with each other, driving me crazy. Even still, I would stop at the store and make sure they had juice boxes and something to eat so they would be happy. And quiet.

You see, I never found out what THEY wanted to do. I did not take the time to determine what was important to them. I always chose what I thought they would like. I bought them cell phones, let them play on my computer and allowed them to run the show of what would be seen on the TV. I have found through studying this chapter that kids love to EARN things. My children are happier when I find out what is important to them as a reward and then help them earn it through the work they produce. Read on to learn what Thomas says about the importance of **Knowing the Reward** for your child or teenager.

Thomas: When was the last time you found yourself procrastinating? It's easy to procrastinate when you either don't know how to do something or don't want to. Right? Like when it comes to tax season or when a job has become overwhelming. Usually, it comes down to action at the last minute when it has to get done because there will be a consequence if it doesn't get done. How do you feel when you are working under those conditions?

As adults, we know what has to get done. We know why it has to get done. We know that if we do not go the extra mile at our job, we will be the first ones to go when it comes to layoff time; we know that if we do not get up and work our job or our business, then we won't be able to provide for our families or survive in this world. We have a "why!" And the better the lifestyle you choose for yourself, the more disciplined you need to be. ***Knowing the Reward*** is a great principle. It is the key element to any motivation. Truly learn your child's "why."

What motivates us as parents, adults, teachers or anyone reading this book? What wakes you up in the morning? What gets you to move to act? What pushes you through? What makes you give that extra effort? Sometimes, you will have those days when you feel like you have tons of energy. You're motivated! What does it come down to? It is all about knowing your "why."

It's a reward. Why am I doing this? Parents and teachers will study this program because they have a clear vision of their reward. They understand that their reward is more time, building a deeper bond with their children, or seeing the reward of self-confidence in their children.

Maybe you will return to Chapter 1, **Know Your Role as a Parent,** and make a definite decision. "My gosh, my ultimate job is to instill *life skills*. So, with what I know, in a very short window of a couple of years, I can instill all of these life skills in my children." What will be the reward for doing an outstanding job with the **Learn to Speak Kid** program? Pat yourself on the back as a parent or a teacher, an uncle or an aunt, or another family member because you'll pass on what you've learned to the next generation.

That is the "why" that is extremely important. It will push you through the obstacles and opposition that are bound to arise.

Now, when it comes to the kids, what are you going to do to *motivate* them? What is their *reward* for helping around the house or being outstanding at school? It is easy to have consequences when things don't get done because it is important to you to keep a clean home. I get that. But, have you ever asked them repeatedly, "Hey, are you going to get that done soon?" "What was it that was supposed to be done?" And you felt like you had to *beg* them to do their chores when you knew they should do it of their own accord?

Knowing the Reward for your child is essential for getting them to **Take Action** and have a positive mental attitude while doing so.

You can begin a very simple technique of creating a *vision board* or a vision book with your children. What is a vision board? When did you last sit down and talk with your children about what's important to them? Have you ever?

"Hey, what's important to you?" "What are some things that interest you?" "What are some wishes you have?" These are wonderful words to use. "What are your wants and your choices?" "What are some desires you have?"

If this is new for them, they will be uncomfortable sharing with you — just like you are when doing something new — they will be completely out of their comfort zone. You may say, "If I could pay you a dollar for every item you put on a list that is important to you, would you be able to come up with 100 of them so that I could pay you $100?" "Oh yeah, I could do that. Oh, I want a bike, I want this and I want this." You let them go, go, go. And you get a big huge list. Do this! Then, go out and collect some magazines and other publications. Allow them to clip things out that they like. Have your children put them all together on a vision board. They can visually see exactly what is important to them every single day. Then, they can focus on the vision board when it comes time for chores. *Creating Champions For Life* parents know what the *reward* is for their child. That's their *motivation*. That's what gets them to move, to act.

Picture your lawn mower running on gas fumes. It is not going to do the greatest job on your lawn. It will probably give out on you before the job is done. Something must fill up your kid's gas tank. Their *desires* are their fuel. This gives them enough *motivation* to learn the life skills that it is your job to teach them. Be patient. Wait for that right window for them to feel motivated about something. It could be *"Friday Fun Day," "Friday Pay Day,"* or anything they are working towards on their list. As they use that fuel as motivation, they will be directed into building a life skill.

When their fuel tank is empty, their motivation is gone. Be patient. Wait again.

Here's a simple window of opportunity. "I'm hungry." There are at least three times this happens throughout every day: breakfast, lunch and dinner. Their fuel tank fills up so quickly when it's time to eat. "Oh, my gosh, I'm hungry, I want...." Excellent. **Know the Reward** is food! Yes, you have to feed them after they complete their tasks. Know that the reward could be an activity, a cell phone, a skateboard, tickets, or "X."

Know that "X" is vitally essential. That's their fuel to get them to motivate themselves. But, it has to be something THEY have asked for. Something that they really, really want. They will be internally motivated as you show them how to EARN their privileges.

You will motivate them without having to really motivate them as you teach them to EARN their privileges. Just knowing that is powerful. When you begin teaching them life skills so they can earn their OWN rewards, you'll have the right timing to execute your **Plan**.

Now, we begin adding the missing pieces to the *Star Chart*. The *Star Chart* goes hand in hand with the previous chapter, **Guiding Behavior vs. Punishment**. You are going to be in a stage right now where you're creating a list of the things your child desires.

The *Star Chart* is for your understanding of what your child is producing. *Praise* the specific behaviors you like as often as possible.

Here's an example of how a *Star Chart* is divided into segments throughout the day. Please note that you may choose some or all of the segments we provide below. Your *Star Chart* will be unique to you and your situation.

Each segment on the *Star Chart* could be as follows:

1. Before breakfast
2. Breakfast time
3. Before school
4. Morning time
5. Lunchtime
6. Afternoon time
7. After school to dinner
8. Dinnertime
9. Before bedtime
10. Bedtime

Maybe you'll have a special event time in there somewhere. Break your days down into different sections or segments. Depending on circumstances, you might have as many as 12 sections in a day! For example, if you are dealing with an ODD child, the more checkpoints you have throughout the day to show them their greatness, the better.

These are like *checkpoints* on a rally race. Realizing the whole race takes a long time and an entire day is a really long time for a child, we need to break it up into *bite-size chunks* to encourage your little genius to succeed.

These *checkpoints* will allow your child's fuel tank to fill up each time. Then, they will have enough juice to continue building on those life skills. After the tank fills up, you have a chance to deplete it with guidance and role-play. Their tank fills up when they have a desire (iPad, Video games, going to the park, for example) and as they EARN goals for each segment, it empties. You have to fill it back up and then get a chance to deplete it. You build momentum through repetition.

During the day, your child might have five, six, seven, or a dozen segments to EARN stars. Every segment is a potential opportunity. Whatever way it works for you, the philosophy is sound.

Base your Star Chart on life skills that are important to you as you fill in the blanks.

To support this part of your parenting journey, visit our website, *CreatingChampionsForLife.com* to download the *Star Chart PDF* and, if you desire, request the accompanying tutorial video to dive deep into setting up your own.

As you create your child's *Star Chart*, focus on the checks and balances. "Okay, breakfast time, awesome; what has to be done in order to EARN your breakfast (or be "qualified" to eat breakfast or *before* you eat breakfast)?" Let's say that you have picked out **three** things for your child to do.

Here's an example of what this looks like:

Segment: Before Breakfast (7:30 am)
Life skills to complete: *Before Eating Breakfast*

1. Organize room
2. Have a shower
3. Get dressed

Let's say these are all the things you want done every morning before breakfast. Excellent, you're ready to go, "Bada boom, bada bing."

Let's say they missed one, were running late, or slept in. Do we punish them? Well, you probably used to, to some degree. "You don't have that done, so you don't get a star." Okay, wow, that's **dysfunction** at its best. This behavior or parenting style stems from our grandpa's grandpa's grandpa, right? That's a thing of the past. You will not even talk like that anymore now that you're following and implementing this new philosophy.

What's their motivation? What is their fuel? It's the *reward* way over there; they have to EARN a *certain number of stars to get it.*

Do they HAVE TO earn stars?

NO!!!

They have to EARN stars to get their reward.

Here's the life skill: Do you have to work a job? No. You have to work a job to get money to pay your bills. When your focus is on **their** reward, their "**why**," they are **motivated** enough to do each task at hand. They'll do it.

Every.

Single.

Time.

Checks and balances are the life skills of responsibility. "I am responsible for my body and my actions."

Therefore, they did those three morning things. Excellent, they earned their pre-breakfast star. **They never have stars taken away.** They can ONLY **earn** them.

THIS IS IMPORTANT!

"Well, I want to earn a star." "Excellent, you've got a **Goal**. What has to happen?" "These three things. Make my bed, have a shower and get dressed." "Did you **Take Action** on them?" They tell you an excuse. You answer, "Excellent. You earn stars when you complete these three things. Do you know how you can earn all three?" And they'll get a chance again tomorrow to earn *pre-breakfast morning stars.*

Then, they go through segment #2, breakfast;

1. Eat everything on my plate.
2. Put everything away when I am finished.
3. Make sure my dishes are rinsed and in the dishwasher.

After they finish, have them come to show you their empty plate. This is giving them *positive attention.* They're learning the right life skills. They have to know how to eat what you choose for them to eat. Right? They might be taking too much and not eating it all. Did they learn a life skill or earn a star? No.

When they learn to take the amount they will eat and finish it all, they earn a star if that's the life skill you're teaching. *Praise* them only. Yes, that right there is *Creating Champions For Life*, my friend. Great job and they earn a star.

It's important to have these *checks and balances* throughout the day. They are lighthearted, so you can have fun with them. Take baby steps. As the *Star Chart* becomes easier, you can build on it.

When *Friday Fun Day* comes, there is the paycheck. Add up all of the stars that they could potentially earn. Let's say there are seven segments multiplied by five days in the week. Basic math: 35 potential stars. Let's say they earned 28 of them, or maybe only 15. Whatever the number, *congratulate them* on earning 10!

Then, that big reward at the end is proportionate to the number of stars they earned that week.

You'll *patiently* wait for them to decide. "Well, I want to go swimming more, just another 15 minutes." "Excellent, what has to happen?" "Earn more stars." "How do you do that?" "Well, I have to do this, this, this and this." "Excellent." Sometimes, they play the "I don't know" card. "Well, if you didn't know and had to guess, what would it be?" See? Your kids are really smart. The less they find that you will do everything for them, the more they will continue to step up. I'm going to say that again because it is so important.

The less they find that you will do everything for them, the more THEY will continue to step up.

They click. They begin to go, "Wow!" and then do even more. They see that they can earn more because their reward is proportionate to what they put into their learning. The *Star Chart* is an *"earn only"* type of process, just as the *Creating Champions For Life* philosophy is *always focused only on the positive.*

You **never** have to say, "Well, if you had done this, then you would have gotten a star." No. You don't have to put them down for doing nothing. Congratulate them, even if they only earn three stars out of all 35 possibilities. "I only got three stars." "Look at you! You got three stars this week. Look what you have earned."

When they say, "But, I want to go to my friend's place." This is their *"fuel"* or their *reward,* and it takes earning 14 stars to go. You can simply ask them, "That sounds like fun. What do you need to do to be able to go to your friend's place?"

If you have been working with them and staying in integrity with their *Star Chart,* they will know EXACTLY what they need to do to earn a chance to go to their friend's place. You can *"let go"* of the outcome. Let THEM "own" it. There is no need to say, "You can't go," only "Of course you can. What do you need to do?"

The news has conditioned us to focus on *negative* stories. There are 100,000 cars driving around, but what do they do? They focus on the five that got into accidents that day. It's not even 1% of the whole population. Thousands of planes fly, but they only talk about the one that crashed. Can you see how dysfunctional that is?

So, instead of focusing on the negative, *praise* them. "My gosh, look at that, you earned three stars. Man, that's three more than zero, congratulations! Here is your reward in proportion to your work." And then, as soon as they click and say, "I wanted more," you reply, "I would love for you to have more." And you go right back into the repetition of the magic formula.

Goal — Plan — Take Action — Perseverance.

And, voila, they get it! Remember, the *environment* always wins. You are creating a *winning environment* with the *Star Chart*. You can now operate in a "yes, yes" mode with your child for the rest of your life. You'll see more success with a "yes, yes" mode rather than a "yes, no" *punishment*, fear-based mode. *Punishment* is a thing of the past and is pure ignorance.

YOU are in the driver's seat, my friend. When you have the right tools, the parenting drive becomes simple. The only reason you haven't been able to create parenting success before now is that no one has shown you how to think in this new way before. Or maybe you sort of did, but then you didn't have anybody to agree with you or guide you along the way, so you found it difficult to remain consistent like you are required to do in order to create success. Staying in integrity is key to creating lifelong learning that will allow your child to become an independent thinker and cooperative family member.

Making sure that they can earn all of their privileges as rewards makes a lot of sense in the long run. In the short-term, if you buy things to give to them, you may think you're doing them a favor. However, when you do that, you're missing an important life skill teaching moment. You don't even know that you don't know that you're supposed to teach and show them. You NOW understand that you must show them what to do. From the first moment of birth, we should be teaching life skills.

Every newborn baby must be taught how to latch onto a nipple or breastfeeding will be unsuccessful.

Repetition is the *second law of learning*. Going through the chapters repeatedly and sticking with the program for at least a year can create authentic change that will flow through future generations.

Why do we teach the life skill of "*Earning the reward* or *privilege* instead of just giving our children everything?"

To help you understand, I recently heard that a lady won the lotto when there were 14 $1,000,000 winners. Two happened to be in the same state. She had had a conversation with her friends. "Oh, my gosh, how much fun would it be if we might be one of those winners!" So, they checked their tickets. She had one of the winning tickets for $1,000,000. She also had the second winning ticket for the $1,000,000! She actually won $2,000,000.

Now, everybody thought that she wouldn't have to work ever again. Temporarily, yes, that was true. But, if you look at the statistics of all the lotto winners, you'll see that most of the winners wish they had never won the money. It ruined their life. It didn't do them any benefit. Within six months to three years, they were worse off than they would have been if they had never won.

It might seem great while you're buying your kids things they like or YOU think they might like. They're always saying, "Who-Hoo!" so this seems magnificent on the surface. Look, everything is happy as long as you keep getting them stuff and doing things for them. However, in the long-term, they are going to be worse off.

Doing things, buying things and making life too easy for your children are NOT at all beneficial to them. They can and should EARN privileges. You'll see the characteristics of what I'm talking about come shining through in your child as soon as you *Create the Right Environment.* It will be the end of scenarios where you bought your kid a brand new bike, and within a week to three months or so, it's been stolen, left outside, rusted, or broken. You get them a nice cell phone or a computer and become frustrated when they get broken or lost. "Mom! My cell phone is lost. When can I get my new one?" They misuse, lose or drop it. *Does this make sense to you?*

In the beginning, when you do stop giving them things, my gosh, that's when the complaining really begins. "How come I don't get this anymore?" "How come so and so got one?" "How come they get to do that and I can't?"

Knowing the Reward is ESSENTIAL because they learn the LIFE SKILL of EARNING things rather than learning to be completely dependent on you, FOREVER!

Again, remember the image of the 40-year-old man living in your basement? That's YOUR motivation to teach your children life skills. Move beyond the welfare system. Go beyond thinking that the lotto is going to be the one fix-all for everything because, like *punishment*, it's a temporary fix.

You've been conditioned to buy their love, do everything for them and give them privileges first while expecting that they're going to earn it later — well, how's that been working for you so far? That's why you're here studying THIS information. It's because you KNOW that it's not working and you're looking for *long-term answers.* You ARE making the right choice.

Let's get back into **Knowing the Reward.** What is one of the simplest ways to remind yourself what the reward is? "Hey, Mom, can I have this?" "Mom, can I do that?" Ah, let's go back to the *Creating Champions For Life* basic formula:

1. **Goal.** "Hey, I would love for you to have that new bike (go to the park, go to the concert). That's called a **Goal**. What's the best way for you to EARN it?"

Remember the sequence? Ask what they can do to EARN the **Goal**.

2. Then, help them establish a **Plan**. "Well, it's $20 each to go to the concert. There is the *Star Chart* and the other things that I can do to earn money. If I do this, this and this, then I can earn this amount of money." "There you go. Then you'll have $20." You establish a **Plan** together.

3. Now, it's up to them to **Take Action. Knowing the Reward** is what YOU use to *fill up their fuel tank;* it's THEIR *motivation* to learn life skills and to **Take Action** on their **Plan**.

4. Help them overcome all obstacles by encouraging them. It takes **Perseverance** to turn obstacles into opportunities. Believe they can learn!

Continue to encourage them until they achieve their **Goal** or until they decide that they don't want it after all. "I don't really want to do it now." "Okay, let me know when going to that concert works for you." Sometimes, all they're doing is playing the role of "If I clean it a little bit, you'll do the rest."

Let me warn you: If you continue to overcompensate for them, they'll never have to work hard to EARN *privileges* on their own. Once again, are you going to spend the rest of your life with them? Are you going to go to college with them? When they get married, are you going to move in and still do their laundry? These are extremely important life skills and milestones of separation. Are you with me on this?

ALL children will eventually step up in this winning environment. At first, they will be a little bit or a lot reluctant, of course. When you stick with it, they'll say, "Wow, Mom and Dad would love to help me get whatever it is that I would like." We call that a **Goal.**

We discussed the **Plan** and how to make it work. "If it is to be, it's up to me." They start to reprogram themselves neurologically. "Wow, I can make anything happen in my Life. It's MY choice.

I have to **Take Action**. Do this, this and this, then that shows up." It's as simple as taking water, putting it in the container, lowering the temperature and seeing that it'll freeze. It's basic simple logic.

Perseverance is the act of finding a way over and through the obstacles that will always come up, especially when learning new life skills.

They will go through the cycle of "Well, I kind of did it." "Okay. Would you say that you earned *some* of the movie, *all* of the movie, or *none* of the movie?" **Know the Reward.** Operate in a "yes, yes" mode.

Say *Friday Fun Day* comes around. That's when your children look at all the stars they earned during the week. You and they **Know the Reward**. It might happen to be swimming at a public pool for up to 90 minutes. That's their **reward**.

What motivates them to continue to do the dishes, their homework, their laundry, use manners, show cooperation, and all of these things? You always say "yes" to the swimming activity on *Friday Fun Day.*

The amount of time they get to swim directly reflects what they have EARNED.

They know swimming will be available for 90 minutes. As they go through the week, they're going to be working towards EARNING their reward. That's "yes, yes" mode. So,

"Yes, we are going swimming. How much time did you earn?" If they did half of the model, worked half of the steps and earned half of the stars, that's what they EARN when it's time to go swimming on *Friday Fun Day.*

They earned 30 minutes, 60 minutes, or 90 minutes of swimming. Keep it CLEAR and SIMPLE. Once they have identified their **Goal**, show them what this looks like before they start their week.

Let me repeat this: Show them the options of good (90 minutes), bad (60 minutes) and ugly (30 minutes). Let them CHOOSE their REWARD with their actions. The beauty of this is that you can "LET GO" of any CONTROL and give them the freedom to choose what they want. This is called FREE WILL.

The first time you execute this, chances are you're going to be dealing with the *victim*. Right? You're a *victor* and you don't communicate with a *victim*. You know what I'm talking about. Your child will whine, "I don't get to go the whole time?" Great, it's back to the game of opposites. Teach them to say, "I am so happy, excited and grateful that I got to go swimming and that I earned 30 minutes. Next time, I'm going to earn 60 minutes."

They are going to whine, "I want to swim the whole time." They might get into a crazy funk with an hour of screaming. Stick to your guns. "I will talk to you when you are calm." "I would love for you to earn the whole 90 minutes. What has to happen for you to earn 90 minutes of swimming?" "Well, I am going to earn all of my stuff!" "Okay, it's up to you, right? Let me know how you can do it."

You're breaking habits. It's not going to be easy every day. But it's not easy now, is it?

Once they have this *earning* life skill in place, it's a matter of overcoming obstacles, rising up to the occasion and putting in a little extra effort. So, if they put in a *little* effort, they only earn a *little* bit of the reward.

This life skill will benefit them throughout the duration of their life. After all, when you reward them everything for nothing, eventually they will get to the same place as everyone else who cuts corners.Think of those who work on commission. They will get paid directly proportionately to what they produce. Yes?

"Congratulations, you did something perfectly, so you get to go to the swimming pool." Their stars might even be so low on the totem pole that they just got a chance to go and *watch*. "Oh, I want to be in the pool." Ah, there's their **reward**. "That's called a **Goal**. What has to happen for you to be in the pool?" See, their tank is full RIGHT THEN. Negotiation begins, training kicks in, and then their fuel tank depletes.

Each time you stick with this formula and maintain your integrity, they will rise up more and more with their part of the formula: **Take Action** and **Perseverance.**

Up until now, they've learned to use non-helpful behavior to get what they want. They are very good at whining, screaming and arguing. You have given them things, done things for them, and been in control of what they can and cannot do with no clear plan on how to get what they want without you. For example, you GIVE them a cell phone, then TAKE IT AWAY when they do something you don't like.

This is the CAUSE of ALL defiant behavior and disruptive child behavior disorders, like ODD and conduct Disorder. There is ALWAYS a cause to the effect.

The reward is that they can earn 30, 60 or 90 minutes at the pool. Now you have a way to motivate them. "Let's hit some yard work, rake up the leaves and pull up the weeds." You know and I know, what an "A+" looks like, a "B" looks like, or what a "C" looks like, don't you? If not, make sure to *clearly* define what "A," "B," or "C" looks like to you because you need to SHOW your children crystal clear expectations, not just TELL them.

Their fuel tank reflects *how much* the chosen reward means to them: how much effort they'll put forth to accomplish the life skills you want them to learn.

For example, helping with the lawn is a life skill that teaches:

- Work ethic
- Responsibility
- Focus
- Money sense

There's a power struggle when parents think that their kids are going to do this great big job without the motivation to do it. You expect them to do the full job, but they don't really care that much about it. So, if you give them the full paycheck when they only put in a little bit of effort, you're reinforcing a behavior that is not good. So, pay them proportionately.

Winning with **Knowing the Reward** is a game of patience, waiting for the right time, like the punch line of a joke. Could you imagine if a comedian were to reveal the punch line first and then tell you the joke? The joke definitely wouldn't have the same impact, would it? If they don't know how to say the joke correctly, it will come out all jumbled up at the same time. Tell the joke, hit the punch line at the correct time and you'll receive maximum laughter.

The same thing applies here. **Know what their reward** is and execute what you want with perfect timing. Now, if you ask them to do something when they have zero reward for it, like when their tank is completely empty, guess how much motivation you're going to get out of them? VERY LITTLE TO NONE.

"Hey, would you like to carry the groceries in?" "Oh, no thank you." It's all about using the right timing. You're using the wrong window if sometimes you ask them to do a couple of things and they yawn and say, "I really don't want to." You know that whine because they're so good at it.

Whining will show up when you miss the teaching window. If this continues to happen, YOU need to make a DECISION. Be coachable and follow the principles outlined for you in this book. Be aware that this is a progressive development like anything worthwhile. Give yourself grace as you embrace this new empowering lifeSTYLE. It will take time, effort and energy, just like any new habit Does. Practice until you have *Learned to Speak Kid.*

My favorite checkpoints are breakfast, lunch and dinner. It's the perfect segway because you never have to ask them to show up or be hungry — their fuel tank is already full. It makes *logical* sense. This then that. An opportunity to go from disorder to order. Simple. Natural. God's way.

In the Universal law of cause and effect — the effect would be breakfast — aka **Goal**. What is the cause — aka **Plan?** What must happen first? *Self-Discipline.*

These are great windows for your daily non-negotiables. There are things that must be done throughout the day, every day, such as getting up and out the door on time. As your child engages in bare minimum, average or outstanding effort during these segments on the *Star Chart*, the points add up for longer-term goals, such as swimming on the weekend or a bicycle they are saving money for.

For daily non-negotiables, you execute the criteria for certain things that must be done before enjoying breakfast, lunch and dinner. Stick to your guns on this. "But, I'm hungry." Yes, you are going to feed them. Of course. Your child knows what needs to be done before each meal. Yes? Don't fall for emotional blackmail.

"I would love for you to eat. What did we agree upon that gets done before you eat breakfast?" "Well, let's see…making sure my bedroom is clean, I get dressed and I pack my bag for school." "Awesome. As soon as those things are done, breakfast will be ready." "But, I'm hungry now." "I'll bet you are. How do you make breakfast show up sooner?" Then, LET IT GO. They are counting on you to be a great leader.

It's now 7:30 am. You have to be out the door in 10 minutes and the room is still not clean. This is the part where you feed them *something*. They are dressed and the bag is packed, which is average on the *Star Chart* because they did two out of the three expectations!

You NEVER deny them food. However, if they have chosen to neglect their room, have they earned the three course outstanding breakfast with syrup, jam and orange juice? No. They get toast and water or oatmeal without sugar.

At the end of the day, we want them to have oatmeal with sugar and milk, toast with jam, or syrup on their pancakes, just like you do. However, this is the perfect opportunity for you to *Create a Champion* with *self-discipline.*

This window gives them something to work for. Their fuel tank is full and they may be motivated to do what is necessary to EARN an outstanding breakfast. This is an example. You create whatever is right for you. They choose the result by **Taking Action.**

They need YOU to fill their fuel tank, not just give them an outstanding breakfast because they are "cute" or you feel guilty.

Follow this same pattern with clothes and shelter. There has to be something for them to wear, so give them some clothes. They don't have to match. The third one is they have a right to shelter and a place to sleep. This doesn't mean a five-piece bedroom suite with all the bells and whistles.

Can you begin to see now why starting at a bare minimum is the best gift we can give our children?" Mom, I want that canopy bed my friend has!" "Can I get those cool shoes we saw in the mall the other day?" Only NOW do they have desire. They're not being denied anything to which they have a right.

So, when they play this game of "You're mean!" they'll use mudslinging worse than the politicians. They'll throw you under the bus. They'll make you feel like you are the worst parent in the world. And as soon as you break, they are the ones running the show again.

Provide your kids with their basic rights, food, clothes and shelter, and progressively allow them to EARN more.

Goal — Plan — Take Action — Perseverance.

Following this formula puts the responsibility squarely back in their lap.

Every.

Single.

Time.

You never have to deny them anything, but if you pay them *outstanding* for *bare minimum* action, they're going to get a reality check when they go out in the real world. The reward they get is directly proportional to what they put out. There is no free lunch.

Your kids will love you for this.

At first, they'll be quite ticked off because you've been training them for five or 10 years in the wrong direction. All of a sudden, it will shift, and you'll have a superstar child who is and will always be a **Champion**.

"Ah, I have to keep up with them now. They are so self-sufficient. They're able to create everything on their own. I support their actions and choices now; it feels much better."

It does work! Be consistent.

It's all about *patience* and waiting them out. Wait until their *tank is full* to get them to *engage*. "Well, I want this, I want that." Now they're getting ready for *Friday Pay Day.*

I'd like to congratulate you on beginning to implement the *Star Chart*. As a quick reminder, you will be dealing with *ridicule* and *violent opposition* from your kids or maybe even your friends and family. It's going to feel very mechanical, but through practice, perseverance and positive results, you'll be *accepted by self-evidence*.

You can save so much time by not arguing with your kids:

"Ah, I don't want to do it." "Cool, don't." Walk away. They're going to think, "Oh, that was easy." They're going to think they won. Here comes dinnertime. "I'm hungry." "Can I help you?" "Well, yeah. I thought I was going to eat." "Well, excellent. What are you going to do to have dinner?" "What do you mean?" "Well, it requires having the chores done and your homework completed." "Well, wait, what?"

There must be *checks and balances*. Could you imagine going into a movie and they say, "Where's your ticket?" "I didn't really do too much for it. I know it's a $10 ticket, but I did about $2.50 worth." They're not going to let you in. You can't go anywhere in life and slide through. So, when you think about it, you're doing right by your kids.

Now, they've got the *life skills.* They've got the **Plan**, the *Star Chart,* and the *ability to create anything and everything they choose.*

Parenting...the way God intended. Begin at zero and add.

Think about how much time and money you will save. Have you ever bought them a $500 bike that they rode twice and then left in the rain? If you had done it the *Creating Champions For Life* way, you never would have had to buy the bike if your child lost interest in it halfway through earning it. The same thing will happen with toys; it will happen with everything. When they've earned it, they take care of it.

When you execute these steps, your child or teen will take care of their bed, toys, clothes and all of the fancy stuff, not just exist with the bare minimums that they have a right to. I guarantee you right now that when it's done correctly, you will never have to go into their bedroom and tell them, "Clean up your room."

Self-discipline: "I do what I am supposed to do by being asked only once."

Do these things happen overnight? No. Think of how many years you trained your child prior to now. Was it two or five years of heading in the other direction? Give it six months, whatever it takes. Your job is to get it done; that's your **Role as a Parent**. How much you put in is how much you're going to receive. And that, my friend, feels really, really good.

Final Thoughts by Bonnie:

Wow! What an important lesson to grasp. I have heard mothers say, "He doesn't seem motivated by the reward."

Was it a reward YOU chose for your child or one THEY chose for themselves? It may have sounded like "If you do this, I will do this for you," or "If you do this, you can have that." The funny thing is that when your *child asks for it,* **THEY** chose it and *when you offer it*, **YOU** chose it. Even if it was something that they asked for yesterday, it may not be important to them today.

I have learned the lesson of offering my children anything. I discovered they would take what I offered them, but it wasn't important to them because it wasn't what THEY wanted.

For instance, I told my daughter that if she earned her signatures (from school) every week for three months, she would earn a trip to Mexico for 10 days. This set her up to fail. I know what a trip to Mexico is like and so does she. She was excited about the trip, but did not have the *fuel to motivate herself* to take action on her responsibilities enough to earn it. However, she was willing to take immediate action on her idea of a hair straightener that cost $40 and $150 cash for her 13th birthday.

When I came up with an idea that was important for me, taking her to Mexico, I had the false assumption that this was just as important for her.

I now know to **discover** what is important to them by listening to what they ask for and then asking them questions to get clear on the *fuel that will fill their tank.*

This becomes a winning combination when you *Know the Reward.*

1. What are the two reasons a job will be procrastinated?

_____

_____

_____

_____

_____

2. What is the key essential element to any kind of motivation?

_____

_____

_____

_____

_____

3. What two things are bound to occur while you or your child is striving to reach a goal?

_____

_____

_____

_____

_____

4. How can you keep your child or teenager in a positive mental attitude while doing their work?

_____

_____

_____

_____

_____

5. What is a vision board?

_____

_____

_____

_____

_____

Chapter 7

Parents Make Decisions; Children Make Choices

~ Children feel important and empowered when they get to choose something that is already parent-approved. ~
Thomas C. Liotta

Bonnie: In the great Star Wars series, Luke Skywalker began his journey as an apprentice or a baby Jedi. He was introduced to the Jedi by Obi-Wan Kenobi. Obi-Wan became Luke's teacher and mentor. Luke was trained on every principle, technique and belief of the Jedi before he was able to operate on his own. Throughout the entire series, there was one mentor and one apprentice. At the beginning of his training, Obi-Wan sent Luke to train with

Yoda, a master of the Force. As Luke approached Yoda's planet, he lost control of his jet and it crashed into the swamp. Yoda explained to Luke that he had the power, on his own, to lift the ship out of the swamp. Luke did not know what Yoda was talking about. He ended up failing to do so. Yoda showed Luke what he was talking about and only then did he begin to believe in the "Force" and his own power!

I love the movie, Star Wars. I can now see that we should be working with our kids right from the beginning when they are babies and continue to do so until age 18. I can also see that I have unwittingly trained my children in the wrong ways. I was begging and nagging my children.

Before learning the parenting principles from this chapter, I experienced many scenarios that all parents dread with their kids — for example, going to a fun center, out for dinner, or taking a basic car ride and getting a thousand Mom, Mom, Mom, Dad, Dad, Dads. I was definitely willing to take the time to work with my kids. I didn't know how. Let's see what Thomas has to share in this chapter.

Thomas: This chapter of **Parents Make Decisions, Children Make Choices** will bring you a whole new level of peace, time and a great-quality environment. You can get your work done and still be able to spend quality time with your children.

This chapter will help you refine the first skills and organize everything in a way that makes sense. You and I know that living in a "yes, yes" mode works and feels much better than punishment and "yes, no." It allows the children to build independence and self-esteem versus being caught in the punishment mode of fear.

Before we jump right into **Parents Make Decisions, Children Make Choices**, let's cover just a little bit of background on why it is that children can make choices and why they are not able to make decisions. Yet.

When you ask them, "What do you want for dinner?" you are really asking them an open-ended question requiring them to make a decision they are not ready to make. "I want macaroni and cheese."

If you buy anything off the shelf and start doing your homework, you'll see that there is no nutritional content in macaroni and cheese. You are feeding them *fun food,* but are you really teaching them anything? Remember, your **Role as a Parent** is to help them eat the right food.

When you have taught them nutritional life skills in Chapter 11, they will feel like they can make a decision. Very rarely would you ever have a five or 10 or even a 15-year-old girl decide what will be for supper. Can you imagine this: "You know, Mom, I think it will be important that you buy all organic foods because my body is an organic instrument. And the more organic the food is, the better I am going to be and feel. And I know I am only five years old now, so having more vegetables and fresh fruit and things without high fructose corn syrup as my food is really going to help me become a *Champion for Life*!"

Do you see why they can't even come close to making that decision? Remember Chapter 2, **Parent's Brain vs. Kid's Brain**? They are not able to think abstractly. Yet. This developmental phase for kids usually starts to kick in around age 13. That's when they can begin to think abstractly. So, the best approach is to use what is taught in this chapter: **Parents Make Decisions, Children Make Choices.**

Okay, so what about this scenario regarding dinner? Your **Role as the Parent** is to make sure that they eat properly. You are going to pick a vegetable for them.This is how YOU can *Make the Decision* and allow your CHILDREN to *Make the Choice.* When you plan your meal, expect that there will be a vegetable. Don't ask your child, "Do you want a vegetable?" That anticipates a yes or no answer. The result would be that you have to convince them to eat a vegetable.

You are making them pick something that they may or may not be interested in. More often than not, kids are not interested in vegetables. Decision making is the same for you and me. If we pick up the phone and we hear a telemarketer talking about anything we are not interested in, we hang up. We chuck it away. We are uninterested, even if they give everything for free. It is the same for children. So, moving forward, you are now going to give only what is called "**parent-approved decisions.**"

For this example, we will pick peas, corn and carrots. Those are three different vegetables the kids can choose from. A very efficient way of raising your kids is to offer a choice that makes sense for them. You must decide what is *parent-approved* BEFORE you make the offer. So, when you have them CHOOSE their dinner, you ask, "Great, Tommy, which one of the three vegetables is going to work the best for you tonight? Peas, corn or carrots? What's your choice?"

You structure the question so that it has an "alternate ending." Thus, they can answer, "Hmm, peas, corn or carrots. Peas, corn or carrots...." Let's go against the norm and say, "I don't want any of those."

From our previous chapter, **Know the Reward**, you are now aware of how important it is to focus on THEIR reward for internal motivation. Yes? Tonight, the reward happens to be that there is a plan to go over to their friend's house after dinner. That is the big reward. You know it *motivates them*. You remember that **desire** is filling up their fuel tank. It's full now. Part of being able to go out with their friends is eating and finishing everything on their plate, including the vegetable. So, their tank is full; they and you **Know the Reward.** They may say, "Well, I don't want a vegetable."

"Oh, okay. I thought you wanted to go to your friend's house, but maybe you decided not to go. That's okay. You don't have to eat your vegetable. It makes it a little tough not getting to go to your friend's house, but I understand "Oh, no, I do want to go." "Excellent. What has to happen for you to go?" "Oh, I must eat my whole dinner, including the vegetable." There you go. You're right back on track.

"Now, for your dinner, peas, corn, or carrots, which one is it going to be? " And they start to think, "Hmm, peas, corn or carrots. I like corn." So, now, in their mind, **Parent's Brain vs. Kid's Brain**, they believe that they made a decision.

But, you know and I know what happened here. They are not developed enough to make lifelong or important decisions. What's awesome about this is that ALL three of their choices are *parent-approved decisions*! The key here in this section is *pre-framing*. We have covered it many times before, especially in the last chapter.

Pre-framing means you take a few minutes prior to an event to think about your expectations of the event.

It's where you spend five or 10 minutes *sharpening the axe.* Then, you can just cut through the tree in a matter of minutes and have enough energy to go on to the next tree. Your *pre-framing* before dinner happens in the exact same way.

Otherwise, they are sitting down and eating. You put out some vegetables and they say, "I don't like that, Dad." Now, you find yourself in a power struggle and in battle mode. However, if it is already *parent-approved,* whatever choice they make out of the ones you have offered is acceptable because they are *pre-framed.* It's an instant yes because now you are operating in a "yes, yes mode."

Here's another scenario. Costco seems to be a pretty popular place. Kids love to go around and find all the little samples offered at the tables. A pre-framed scenario here, where **Parents Make Decisions, Children Make Choices**, is that we have a grocery list. The kids already know which type of organic items to find, that is if you have taken the time to show them this life skill. If not, when would NOW be a GOOD time to work on the life skill of grocery shopping?

The list says we need eggs, dairy and bread. First, you *pre-frame* by saying, "Okay, how many of these snack stands would you like to go to? Would you like to see how many you can find in three, five or seven minutes?" "Umm, seven minutes." They make their choice.

"Excellent. We have 20 minutes and you would like to have seven to run around. Basic math: how many minutes will it take for us to get everything done?" They will subtract seven from 20 and come up with 13. "Okay, excellent. What a great game plan we have. We can get all of our items on the list. We are sharply focused. Remember the focus life skill? You will keep your attention on the task at hand because this plays the key role here." "Okay," they respond, thinking about being able to work towards the seven minutes of finding the sample tables!

Now, the kids can go throughout the store with laser-like focus and get everything on the list in 13 minutes. When they do it in 13 minutes, they will earn the seven extra minutes. And, yes, you guessed it. They can go to as many sample tables as they can in that timeframe.

What if it takes 15 minutes? Then, they only have five minutes to visit sample tables. If they did it in 17, they would have three. You notice we're always operating in a "yes, yes" mode. Now, let's take the worst case scenario. They took a full 20 minutes.

"Congratulations, you were successful in getting everything on our list. If you would like to be able to have a snack or a sample from one of those sample tables, what has to happen next time?" "Oh, I have to have sharper focus." "Excellent!"

Yes, they can develop the ability to focus. Believe they can learn.

They know the right answers. Therefore, they know that in order to have time for snacks at Costco, they must pay attention to the task at hand. The sharper the laser-like focus is, the more time they can earn for snacks. Simple.

Can you remember being a child and asking, "Can I go to the movie?" "Can I go to the mall?" "Can I have this?" "Can I have that?" When you are a kid, money magically comes out of your parents' pockets and you just run and spend it. Right?

Let's say you are on a budget. Your kid asks for something and you tell them no. "But, why not?" All of a sudden, you have to admit the truth. "We can't afford it," "It's too expensive," or "It's not good enough." Whatever the truth might be, your child will start to feel that somehow they are not worth it.

It translates that way to little kids because they don't understand what else it could be. Talk with them from your heart so they understand it. Your primary directive is not to make them feel like they are not worth a $5 or $10 item. That's how powerful this is. You can shift that from a "yes, no" mode back into a "yes, yes" mode. EVERYTHING your child desires comes from their "paycheck," i.e., the *Star Chart.*

Your children will feel empowered when they see the stickers on the Star Chart because they can see and feel that they are worth something.

Let's use another example and go to the Fun Center. Oh, my gosh, it's New Year's Eve. A place with a big bowling alley, flash laser tags, a pizza parlor, and some games and toys they have *EARNED* to get to play. I have seen parents go there with one or two kids. Each kid is just running around and going all over the place, like letting the air out of a balloon. It flies everywhere with no direction. Every few moments, they're asking, "Mom, can I have money for this?" "Dad, can I have some for that?" "Dad, Dad, Dad?" The typical reactive way of "yes, no" is not the plan. Pretty soon, Dad sighs, "Wow, I think I just spent $100 and I haven't even done anything."

If your goal as a parent is to have a family outing, your job is to budget and create a *proactive plan* prior to going. It is still an opportunity to teach life skills without interfering with the Star Chart or backtracking. You allot $20 for each of your three children. They will receive $20 because they have engaged in the **Star Chart** and have *earned* a Fun Family Night. If they desire extra money, they would have earned it ahead of time through the **Star Chart**. Remember how cool the **Star Chart** is? They checked all the timeframes and stickers and all the details are worked out BEFORE the event.

When you arrive and before you go in, you pre-frame. Simple. "Okay, you have each earned $20. Now, the things that you can do are..." Remember, this is where you have to do a little planning. *Pre-framing* means that you have chosen all the **Parent-approved Decisions** and are now having the **Children Make their own Choices.**

"Planning a game of bowling is definitely one of the items on the list you might want to do. Laser Tag is another option. You may want to go on some of the rides, play some of the games, or order pizza with some beverages." There. You have pre-framed all of their options and their parent-approved choices. All of them. Therefore, you can say, "Look, here's the $20 that you earned. Here are the three different items: bowling, laser tag and games."

One of the most essential steps is to speak to them before you give them the $20. You say, "Excellent. What is your game plan? How do you choose to do all three?"

Remember the formula:

Goal — Plan — Take Action — Perseverance.

You see them begin to chat it out with each other. Finally, one of the kids says, "Okay, one of you guys go find out how much bowling is. One of you can find out how much laser tag is. I'll go see how much each game is." Allow them to collect all of that information independently.

Believe they can learn.

Once they gather all their information, have a pow-wow and discuss the options. This is the time to teach a *life skill* called planning and organizing. Call it what you like. It's the same thing as deciding in a "yes, yes" mode.

The kids can put two and two together because they are smart. They can see that a bowling game costs $3, plus the cost of the shoes, $5 for this game, and $7 for the food. All of it totals $60. They are using all the great math skills they learned in school. If they require and ask for some help, you are there as their *trusted advisor.*

They have a Plan.

"When you spend all of your money, you'll be done. You can spend some and save some, or you can spend it all. But, then, we are all done. Are there any more resources for funding at that time?" "No." "Exactly."

This *proactively* prevents situations like "Oh, Mom, we almost have enough money for the game, so can I have some more?" This is the power of pre-framing. Having them come up with a plan that makes sense to THEM means you are always saying, "Yes." They will choose to do the fun things in the order THEY picked.

THEY are empowered, YOU are free.

This will make you one of the cool parents. You are hanging out in the Family Fun Center. Your kids are cool, smooth and collected. They have their plan. They execute what is important to them and are involved in what the family does. You experience peace. Your kids experience independence, a strong self-image and personal empowerment. The entire night is all about *THEIR choices*. This is so much fun!

At the end of the evening, nothing will sound like "Why didn't I get to do that?" "So and so got to do...." These complaints will be a thing of the past. You are **Making the Transition** from the old parenting style into this new one.

Congratulations on doing something to make a difference for your children. You are part of a movement by spending time on how to *Learn to Speak Kid.* It is a cause to free the next generation of children from bondage.

Let's put this in perspective when it comes to who they choose for their friends. Maybe there are some friends who you don't wish for your children to hang out with, aka the bad influencers or the troublemakers who are not *parent-approved.* You can find the solution in the *Star Chart.* Using and applying the strategies suggested, your child will earn stickers or signatures on their *Star Chart.*

They can earn part of their Saturday afternoon as playtime. "Well, great. Did you want to play with Susie, Tommy or Billy?" Those friends are *parent-approved decisions.* So, when they want to play with any of these friends, it's an instant "yes, yes." Yes for them and yes for you.

Whenever there is any resistance, you can tie it back into the reward. "Remember, if you play with your friends correctly and follow the guidelines, you get your reward."

What about different types of activities you want them to participate in? I remember being small for my age as a kid. Mom chose to protect me. I wanted to play football. We used to get into big arguments. Mom *pre-framed*: "Do you want to play soccer, basketball or baseball?" "Hmm, I want to play soccer and I want to play baseball." I felt more important and empowered when I got to choose something that was already *parent-approved*. And, yes, you might have to backpedal a little bit. But, doing it now is better than later. Do you agree?

Have you ever been in the car with two kids in the back and Mom and Dad in the front? Literally, every two minutes, it's "Mom, Mom, Mom..." or "Dad, Dad, Dad...." It can get to the point where it's "Mom, watch. Watch, Mom, Mom, watch, Mom watch, Mom, Mom, Mom, Mom, Mom..." and Mom's going, "I have no more hair to pull out. Can you sit down and be quiet?" Yes, you have to admit that this is funny because you see that the *kids are creating that environment*.

On the other hand, if you *pre-frame* before the ride with "Hey, we are going for a ride in the car today. Do you remember what things will EARN you a travel star?"

SEE

1. **Self-control:** "I am in control of my body and my actions. I will sit quietly and be cooperative." "I like that. So, when we actually get to the park, you will have earned all of the playtime in the park from when you sat quietly and cooperatively in the car." "Excellent."

KNOW

2. **Responsibility:** "I am responsible for my actions and my belongings. I will use my quiet voice when I am in the car. I will use my loud one when I am outside." "Yes."

DO

3. **Self-discipline:** "I will do what I am supposed to do by being asked only once, which means following what we have planned prior to getting in the car." "Perfect."

BE

4. **Focus:** "I will keep my attention on the task at hand. This allows me to focus on what it is that we are supposed to be doing in the car." "Look how smart you are."

S.K.D.B.

I understand this is an entirely new language and you will have to teach them the words and definitions, but it will be worth it.

Give the kids a *pre-framed* point and perspective that they will be in the car for 20 minutes and that you, Mom and Dad, will have conversations during this time and will be enjoying the ride. Give them one, two or three opportunities for "Mom or Dad." "Would you like to use one, two or three Moms or Dads during the car ride?" "Umm, I'd like two." "Great!" You *pre-frame.* This is where you have something you are pointing out. "In the next 20 minutes, you can have *two* Moms or Dads. We will answer whatever it is you are saying with those two."

Then, when you are talking and they have a question or a comment, they can interrupt and say, "Mom." "Yes, what is it, Susie?" Then they can interact, after which you say, "Okay, you have one more Mom or Dad until we get there."

When this plan is executed correctly, you can be in the right position to enjoy your ride. Whatever it is that the kids are going to interact with you about is already *parent-approved.* You gave them permission during your *pre-framing.* The kids get to make a *choice,* which is really a *decision* for them, though we know it's not. Using this principle, you will discover that you love taking your kids for a ride in the car! Ah, automatically, "yes, yes" rather than "yes, no. "

Another time you may encounter opposition from your kids is bedtime. You know the time is between 8:30 and 9:00 because you have already *pre-framed* it. Going to bed on time contributes to the stars they can earn during that segment. Can you see that?

What do you currently like to do at bedtime with your kids? Is it reading them a story, tucking them in, or letting them watch their favorite show? If what you are doing right now is working, great! If it's not, it's time to use principle seven: **Parents Make Decisions, Children Make Choices.** Doing so will end the power struggle because your child will feel like they have some control over bedtime.

You ask, "Would you like to go to bed now *with a story* or 10 minutes from now *all by yourself*?" "10 minutes all by myself." Now is an opportunity to SHOW them how the clock works and hand over another notch of *Responsibility*." Do you know what 10 minutes on the clock looks like?" "No." Take them over to a clock and SHOW them exactly what to look for.

"Right now, the clock says 8:20. When the time looks like this (SHOW them how the 2 turns into a 3), then it's 8:30 and time for bed." You will be pleasantly surprised when

8:30 comes and off they go to bed with no power struggle because they feel THEY made the *decision*. But, really it was a *choice* that was already *parent-approved.*

You could play this scenario: "Would you like to watch the rest of the show and then go to bed, or would you like to stop the show now, and we will go to bed with a story?" These are already *parent-approved decisions*. They get to make the *choice,* which allows them to have the illusion that they are making decisions. Can you see how powerful this is?

Here's the last one we will cover as we prepare to wrap up. Let's say that you are out and about and, hypothetically, have trained your kid to be a spoiled brat for the last five years. Any time they wanted something, they threw a temper tantrum and you quickly gave it to them so they didn't embarrass you in the store.

I know some people are saying, "C'mon, give them whatever they want. They're just kids," which you now understand doesn't work. It's easy to be impulsive and give them things. That's where we started off in **Making the Transition** from "feeding them fish" to "producing fishermen."

Let's say you are going to the grocery store one evening. You are in the aisle and all of a sudden, you hear, "Mom, can I have this cereal?" And you run through some "yes,

yes" answers in your head. Anything that they ask for gets your answer of "Gosh, I would love for you to have that. That's called a **Goal**." Their new response will be "What can I do to earn it?"

Or, "I would love for you to have that. What are you proposing that you could do to earn it?" Once the *transition* begins, you'll see that they're still going to have impulses. "Can I have this?" "Can I have that?" You always respond with "Yes, I would love for you to have that."

This is a perfect opportunity to teach your kids the value of *parent-approved* nutrition when selecting food such as cereal. You and I know that the marketing of cereal is not in our children's best interest.

If they want a particular cereal, ask if it's one of the three healthy *parent-approved* cereals. If you are still in the training process, you say, "Go and find any cereal with no sugar, chemicals or artificial colors." Start with those three items, while SHOWING them where to find the label on the box.

"Oh, can I have this one?" "Excellent, what are the three key things we always look to avoid being on the label?" "Oh, this one has sugar." "So, what's your best guess?" "Umm, no." "Ah, look how smart you are. You are figuring this out on your own."

As you follow the principle of **Parents Make Decisions, Children Make Choices** your children's requests of can I have will be replaced by two things:

1. **Goal — Plan — Take Action — Perseverance.**

2. *"Yes, yes "* rather than a *"yes, no"* mode.

When you guide your children with those two building blocks, you are **Making the Transition** using this principle of **Parents Make Decisions, Children Make Choices.**

What we have covered here in depth is what you will experience even more practically in life. Think of the *three transitions of how things will happen:*

1. When you implement this program, you are supposed to be *ridiculed.* That lets you know that you are on track.
2. You will get *violently opposed.* Things will always worsen before they improve, just like during a kitchen renovation.
3. Finally, you will be *accepted by self-evidence* as your children begin to create success in their lives without you.

I urge you to read the chapters, invest in the program, listen and engage repetitively until you are living the life of your parenting dreams with healthy, happy and cooperative kids.

Repetition is the second law of learning.

Final Thoughts by Bonnie:

Pre-framing with *parent-approved* decisions makes life between my children and myself so much more peaceful, fun and smooth.

The night we took our kids to the bowling alley was proof in the pudding of how smart kids really are. It took them 15 minutes to devise a plan and pool their money so they could fit in laser tag, bowling and snacks. You could see how empowered they were while making *parent-approved choices!*

In the past, I ordered enough food for the table and then listened to them beg for one more game until we left with them whining and unhappy. This time, they created a plan and worked as a team and I didn't hear one complaint, whine or question about how to get something else. They had fun. We had fun. The night was a humongous success for all, just like Thomas described in this lesson.

I now *pre-frame* before every outing, drive and walk to the store. They know how they can *earn their rewards* by following through with *self-control, responsibility, self-discipline and focus.*

They step up to the occasion every time the **Right Environment** is set. Every time. The result is self-confident children and teenagers who are more helpful, grateful and happy.

1. Why would you never allow your child to make decisions on their own?

_____

_____

_____

_____

_____

2. What is abstract thinking? Does your child have the ability to think abstractly?

_____

_____

_____

_____

_____

3. What is the best way to structure a question to give your child the ability to make parent-approved choices?

_____

_____

_____

_____

_____

4. How does it make a child feel when they have the ability to make choices which, to them, are decisions?

_____

_____

_____

_____

_____

5. What is pre-framing? Why is it important?

_____

_____

_____

_____

Chapter 8

Asking Questions vs. Dictating

~ Asking Questions promotes empowerment;
Dictating promotes insecurity. ~
Thomas C. Liotta

Bonnie: Have you ever received a really ugly sweater or some other useless gift for Christmas from someone special in your life? At every family function, they want you to wear it or show it off. In your mind, you're thinking, "Yeah, where is that thing again?"

How often have you brought home gifts, taken your children on an outing, or gone on a vacation to have them pull attitude with you, act ungrateful and disengage? It's like "What the heck?"

Imagine spending three months planning and spending $10,000 of your hard-earned money for an extravagant family vacation. Your heart feels so good. You are really excited to spoil your family and have a time of togetherness. After everything is said and done, the kids are crabby and a drag to be around. Everyone is stressed, tired and unhappy. It hurts my heart and makes me want to cry right now just thinking about how much I used to do for my children who would end up being ungrateful, feeling unloved and possessing low self-esteem. How does this happen?

Asking Questions vs. Dictating is another principle in *Learn to Speak Kid* that will help bridge the communication gap between you and your children. Read on as Thomas takes you through the lesson.

Thomas: What is **Asking Questions vs. Dictating**? Let's take a moment to relax, go back in time and think: do you remember the magical age when you asked that very simple question? It was a three-letter word for your parents and a very confusing word for you. Today, it's a three-letter word to you and a confusing word for your child.

In this chapter, we will lay the foundation for how, when questions are asked, the answers naturally create a way to make more answers show up in your children's lives. You will also see the value in asking your children questions to motivate them to act rather than just giving them the answers and telling them what to do.

I have previously mentioned that to *Learn to Speak Kid* is like learning a new language. Once you figure out the language, everything else will fall into place. You will see cooperation, harmony and happiness in your home.

Asking Questions vs. Dictating is an interaction with your children. It allows them to get answers to that magical three-letter word and to the many other questions they are yearning to get the answers to. When any person is *dictated* to, their questions NEVER get answered. In the case of *dictation*, the questions are avoided by the parent and answered by someone else. So, what is that three-letter word? Go back to when you were two years old or to a time when you received an answer to a question that was important to you.

Maybe you were helping Mom with something or you were watching Dad do something. They did a thing in a certain way; do you remember what it was that you asked? When they explained a little bit, you asked it again. You asked it again, and you asked it again. It was your favorite word of creativity. You were mesmerized by the word. You were questioning and you were choosing to find more knowledge. You were open. Everything was amazing. "Wow, give me more."

Have you figured out that three-letter word yet? If you have a little two-year-old, tell them something and they will ask, "**WHY**?" In the majority of cases, the answer will be "Because that's what we do." "Why?" "Because I said so." "Why?"

When your child asks, "Why?" it puts you at a crossroads: either you say, "Wow, let me just explore that again and find out why," or you shut it off by saying, "Stop asking questions. Just do it!" All of a sudden, *your child's learning is interrupted*. For the child, it was a special time: "Why?" He or she was exploring.

It reminds me of the Christmas ham story. In this story, there were four generations of ladies. The youngest of these generations was little Julie. She was five years old. She was watching Mom cut the end off of the Christmas ham before putting it into the pot. What does little Julie do? "Why do you do that, Mom?" Mom didn't have an answer. She pawned it off and said, "That's how my mom did it."

That was little Julie's grandma. So, for little Julie, that answer wasn't good enough. She was looking for a real answer. She went to Grandma. "Grandma, why did you cut the end off of the ham before putting it in the pot?" "That's what my mom did."

Great-Grandma was still alive, so little Julie asked Great-Grandma the same question. Great-Grandma answered Julie, "When I was your age, we only had one pot in the house. It was too small for the ham to fit. So, we cut the end off.

When did we stop answering questions or even find out what the question "Why?" was all about? Our grandparents taught our parents, our parents taught us, and now we are teaching our children our methods, beliefs and habits. It falls into the same category as: "Do as I tell you to do; don't do as I do." When we peer under that three-letter word "Why," it is easy to see that there are other unanswered questions disguised as "Why."

When the answers begin to manifest, we can re-evaluate how to cook the Christmas ham. Obviously, our pot is big enough to fit the whole thing now. Why would anyone have cut the ends off a ham? Everybody knows the end is the best part. As we explore the patterns that we used to follow and habits that had been developed, it is apparent that many "Whys" never received answers.

It is not a matter of blame. We are identifying some of the solutions you are beginning to discover and choosing to mend. The "Why" became suppressed and people became *dictated* to. You know and I know that never feels loving. **Dictation** feels like a hate or anger relationship, whereas a **Questioning** relationship allows the child and parent to feel joy, love and happiness.

Asking questions will help them flourish!

When you are *Learning to Speak Kid*, *questions* are open for answering. They get answered and your child will feel heard and loved. When you are operating in traditional punishment mode, where kids are to be *seen and not heard*, *questions* are NOT open for answering. They are ignored and the child is left feeling unloved. All of a sudden, things begin to develop in the wrong direction and the parents are left wondering what has gone wrong and why their children have begun to rebel. Can we correct it? Absolutely! That's what this principle is all about.

What do we mean by the term "**dictating**"? We briefly mentioned it in Chapter 4, **Making the Transition.** Imagine *dictating* to your kids when you must hurry up to get them to school. "Come on." "Get your shoes on." "Get your jacket on." "Get out to the car." "Sit down." "Shut up." "Get your seatbelt on." "Hurry up." "Run to class."

You love them and do the best you can with what you have been taught. Failure to prepare on your child's part does not constitute an emergency on yours, but we find ourselves in situations where we default to *dictating*. Good or bad? It just is. This is how parenting has been executed for the last several decades because we have become a product of our environment. We mold our actions, behaviors and habits based on how we were parented.

Would you like your kids to be able to think? Well, open up your mind, swallow your pride and do something about it.

"I'm afraid to do anything because you always yell at me, no matter what I do. So, I'll sit here and wait for you to *dictate* to me what I'm supposed to do." This is how your child or teenager feels when they are yelled at and *dictated* to for any length of time. If you wish for your children to be completely dependent on you, then continue to *dictate*. But, make sure you leave a place in the basement. Don't ever let them leave the house or, better yet, go off to college with them and tell them exactly what to do there, too. "Go to class." "Do your homework." "Do your laundry."

When the children experience a *transitional* period, you are helping them grow into adults. As they grow older, they will begin to take on more *responsibility.*

Telling them what to do is like feeding them fish. When you are in a hurry and are tempted to tell them what to do, STOP. Start pre-framing instead. You know they require shoes and a jacket; they must get out to the car, and put their seat belts on in order to get to school on time.

Begin **Asking Questions vs Dictating.** Understand and identify when you are *dictating*. Then, begin to re-form the sentences into *questions*. Allow them to answer your questions while you answer their "Whys."

"Okay, we are getting ready for school. What would be best to wear when it's cold outside?" This simple strategy will *camouflage the dictation and* dialogue will begin to commence between you and your child. This dialogue will give your child a greater self-image, increased self-discipline and an improved relationship with you.

It will be awkward if you have never had a conversation like this with your children. Their neurological pathways have not yet been developed, so they will look at you like a deer in the headlights. It is definitely a slow progression. From Chapter 1, **Knowing Your Role as a Parent,** we know that your role is to *teach life skills* to your children. When ARE you going to do it? Or are you just going to write your kids off? Pick one. It's one or the other.

As we go back into this dialogue, now it's "Well, what do you mean?" "It might be cold, or it might be warm. What would be some good things to bring when you go to school today? What kind of clothes?" "Oh! A jacket!" "Ah, excellent. Then, as far as the shoes go?" "Hmm, it's raining outside." "What would be the best shoes to wear?" "Oh, my rubber boots!"

Asking Questions vs. Dictating allows them to come up with the correct answers. Give them the opportunity to create and feel the idea of becoming their own boss. They become *empowered*. You get to praise them and be their hero. "Ah, look at you. You are a smart little guy." "Ah, look at you, little princess. Aren't you just the little smart one today? Great job! You understand what to do."

Then, you get in the car. "Hey, what's the best thing to do to be safe while traveling?" "Oh! Put on my seatbelt!" It's this rather than "Sit down." "Shut up." "Put your seatbelt on." "I'm not going anywhere until...." You know what I mean.

We all had a mom, dad, grandma or grandpa. These are the statements that we may have heard our entire lives. Are you with me? You and I parent how we were parented. This is all we know. You must consciously change your approach if you choose to change your circumstances. Shift into **Asking Questions vs. Dictating.**

At first, you may ask them, "What are you doing?" And you hear back, "Uh, I don't know." They have been *dictated* to for so long that they don't even know how to think. **Questions** may short-circuit them.

Let's say there's a specific task that has to be done. Ask them, "What do you think is the best way to do that?" If they respond with "I don't know," teach them this *jingle jangle*: "*I am a genius. I figure things out easily and elegantly because I know I'm a genius.*"

Now, you can ask your child, "What would a genius do to figure out the puzzle or where the milk goes?" This will allow your child to be creative. Then they can answer, "Oh, well, if I were smart and knew where things went, I would make sure the milk went in the refrigerator." "Awesome. Where's the best place in the refrigerator for it to go?" "Well, I don't know." Remember that sub-category is a life skill? Maybe they have never been taught that the milk goes in the door part of the fridge. So, you SHOW them.

Imagine a time when you used to be *dictated* to or when you used to *dictate* to your kids. "Pick that up." "Put that away." Oh, my gosh. They would walk around the whole house on eggshells. Growing up where *dictation* was accepted as the norm, chances are that your child has never had any opportunity to be creative. They grew up thinking, "I didn't get in trouble today, so it must be a good day." To solve this issue for your child, shift to **Asking Questions vs. Dictating.**

Track interactions with your child by writing down everything you do and say to each other during any given day or week. Translating negative statements is as simple as the game of opposites. What's the opposite of up? Down. Forward? Back. *Dictating*? *Questions*.

You have the right to choose between *dictating* and offering the ability to make a choice. "Pick that up." There's the *Dictation*. Keep track of it by writing the statement down. Now, translate it to "Where's the best place for that to be?" There's a *question*. You are still *dictating*, however you want to look at it, but with this approach, your child or teenager will feel like "Hey, somebody's on my team. Somebody's here to help me learn or gently remind me."

Here is a scenario to help you understand the importance of **Asking Questions vs. Dictating.** You are sitting at a red light in traffic. The light turns green, but you don't notice right away. The driver in the car behind you has two ways to handle the situation. One way is with a light horn tap: "Beep, beep." You look in your rearview mirror and wave, "Oh, thank you," and you go.

Another way is if the car behind you were to honk the horn with a loud long "Beep," accompanied by giving you the finger, telling you that you're number one. You think and angrily yell, "What a jerk!"

What type of demeanor do you naturally fall into? "Oh, cool, thanks," or "Geez, man, these people are rude"? It's the same scenario with a different message. One reacts, speaks and thinks in a *higher vibration.* The other reacts, speaks and thinks in a *lower vibration.*

Asking Questions vs. Dictating. What vibration do you wish for your kids to oscillate in? Is it fear, panic, hate, anger and distrust? Is it love, joy, happiness, gratitude, pleasure and openness? You truly have the ability to decide. I love that! Do you?

You will begin to catch yourself saying, "Put things away." "You aren't putting that away." "You aren't getting this." Write those down on the list of *dictations*. Begin to ask yourself questions like "Hmm, let's see what a good substitution for that one is." You are *thinking*. You're going through the process. You're beginning to **ask questions**: "Oh, hey. What are some of the things that you have to complete before you come to dinner?" "What things need to be done before you play baseball (play with your friends or make a phone call)?"

You find yourself going through a long list of items like "Hurry up and shower." "I've been waiting." "You've wasted your whole day." Another *Dictation* comes up. Write it on your list and translate it to: "Hey, what 's the best way to practice great hygiene?" "Take a shower every day?" "Look how smart you are, yes, taking a shower or a bath. That's what I like about you. You're a genius."

Sometimes, you will go into a room. You see them watching TV or doing something that's not what you wanted them to do because they haven't done their homework. You act in a *dictation* mode as soon as you come in. You shut the TV off and you start yelling at them. What if this was happening at your work? You have a boss who shows up to yell and never tells you anything that you've done right. He only yells at you when you do something wrong. It wouldn't feel good, would it? It is not a healthy vibrant environment for you, your child or anyone else.

Here is a great solution. Ask them, "Before you watch TV or earn the privilege to watch a movie, what must you complete first?" Now, this takes a lot of patience and *pre-framing.* You will witness the results when you practice it and have been around it long enough. Oh my gosh, why would you ever operate your family or live with your kids any other way? It feels good. It will continue to feel good.

Every.

Single.

Day.

Here's a popular statement, especially if you have multiple kids: "Why can't you be more like your brother and get better grades in school?" "Why can't you be more like your sister and do your homework or eat everything off your plate?" The list goes on with all of the possibilities for comparisons. How can something like that ever feel good for a child? Children should only compete with themselves. "What could you learn today that would make you better than who you were yesterday?"

Let's say we did a physical education class with them. They could do jumping jacks, push-ups, or anything that's a physical activity. Let's say they can only do three push-ups. They're a *Champion* right then. Even if their back end is in the air and they look like a mountain. Or, they do the cool little seal thing, pushing up their hands while their hips are still on the ground, not straight like a board. When you instill in your child that the best thing they can do is *compete with themselves*, they will focus their energy on being the best person they can be.

When you shift into **Asking Questions vs. Dictating** and ask these outstanding questions, your child will begin to think and see: "Oh, that's who I was yesterday or last week. Now, I see that I am only in competition with myself."

There is no reason to ever *dictate* or compare your child to anybody else. When you think about it, how is anyone going to win when they compare themselves to someone else? No matter what the topic is — to make more money, be prettier, or be faster — there will always be someone stronger, prettier or faster than you. It makes as much sense as watching the dog run around chasing its tail. Even if he catches it and bites it, it hurts. So, how do you win that battle? How do you win in that environment?

When you compare your children to others, I know you intend to motivate them, but what happens is that your children are being set up for ultimate failures. Even if they were somehow resilient and able to survive in that environment, like the dog, they bite their tail and it hurts. They begin to think that no matter what they do, it is never going to be good enough. Eventually, they refuse to even engage in any effort.

When you begin **Asking Questions**, their hearts open up. That's when their creativity begins to go all the way back to when they were two. And they begin asking more questions. With renewed interest in the world and the desire to ask that three-letter word, what a great place it is to be here.

The word "Why?" and the answers it brings are a great secret of achievement. So many times, you and I were taught that if we didn't know how to figure something out or make something happen, we couldn't do it. "Why?" is their motivator! Do you see?

Why would we continue to repeat the *Christmas ham story* in our lives? Are we all a bunch of lemmings just walking and not understanding where we are going? Sometimes, we don't know why and we keep following, at times even noticing, "Oh, they're just walking off a cliff. Well, I'll keep walking with them." And we keep on keeping on surviving somehow.

I even had one lady tell me, "We survived our parents and our kids will survive us." Great! This is true of everything — religion, schooling and, yes, even parenting. If the purpose of doing something doesn't make a lot of sense, then always entertain the question, "Why?" You may find yourself saying, "That's the way my dad punished me. He beat me with a belt, so I'm going to beat my son with a belt." "Why did he do that?" "I don't know. It's just what he did."

Do you know how genius we really are? Wayne Dyer discussed the topic of being a genius perfectly: *"We were all born magnificent, genius and perfect in every way, but we have been beaten and conditioned into mediocrity."*

The people in our lives who loved us the most and wanted to protect us licked the red off our lollipop and stole our "Why." They made us feel that our creativity doesn't matter and it's not worthy. You don't want to do that to your kids, do you?

If you were born in an environment of ignorance, that's okay. Maybe they didn't understand their genius, or your genius in one of the eight intelligences. This is the idea presented by Howard Gardner in 1983. He suggested that intelligence can be divided into specific intelligences instead of one main ability. So, that was then. This is now. Now you understand that you are either creating an unproductive child who is miserable inside, or you are creating and providing an environment that will allow your child to rise up to their own intelligence and full potential.

Are we going to continue, generation after generation, with the erroneous action of cutting the end off of the Christmas ham? No, we're not. This chapter will open your heart and mind to say, "Let's begin **Asking Questions vs. Dictating."** Ask the right question to entice them to THINK and to have them UNDERSTAND what to do.

"I would love for you to do this." "I would love for you to earn that. What has to happen for that to show up?" Or, even better yet, "What do we have to do to make that work?"

You now understand how important it is to explore and engage with your child's "Why?" I love the "Why?" so much because the truth is that one doesn't know how one will accomplish anything in life. Every great success in the history of mankind was acted upon because someone's "Why?" was so important. They acted on what they knew and continued to act on what they knew until the "how" was figured out. We may never know how to do things, but when we ask, "Why?" then we will figure it out.

At best, if you continue to *dictate* to your children, they will *dodge you* by knowing the minimum they must do to avoid getting yelled at or into trouble. Consequently, they'll be *deceptive* towards you for their entire lives. They will never open up to you.

When you begin Asking Questions vs. Dictating to them, they know they can explore and open up their hearts to you.

They will begin to feel they can come up to you and say, "Hey, Dad, Mom, what can I do to earn this?" "I'd like to be able to do that." "What could I do to earn it?" What a vast magical place to live when your children sit beside you and ask, "What's the best way I can do this?" And, let's say they're 16. "I've got a hot date. What can I do to earn the privilege of your trust so I can borrow the family car?"

This might be a far stretch for some of you right now. That's like a major, magical, make-believe miracle for some people. Seriously, it could be the opposite reaction to what *dictating* will bring and it always exists.

Let's go back to what we just talked about. The first law of learning is to "recognize" or be aware of what needs to be learned. If you are *Dictating*, and most parents do this on some level, then simply "recognizing" that you are *Dictating* is huge. Yes, I am talking to you. You could be as positive and happy as you want, or think you are, but we have all **dictated** to some degree.

The more you shift to **Asking Questions,** the more productive you will become in your relationships. Nobody ever likes to be dictated to, but we sure do like to feel important when our creativity comes into play. It feels really good.

It is okay to relate to your children. Show them your faults. Show how you chose to become a *victor* instead of a *victim*. We will all make goofy mistakes when practicing the new strategies and principles outlined in these chapters.

Remember:

Focus. "I keep my attention on a task at hand."

Responsibility. "I am responsible for my actions and my belongings."

It would be funny to chuckle with your kid and say, "I went to the airport the other day. I was going to get on a flight and head down to Vegas. The funny thing was that I lost my focus. I showed up a day early." Relate to them. Let them know that you're human.

Don't get on this fake facade and *dictate* to them that you're Superman, Wonder Woman, Master of the Universe, and perfect. Therefore, you're going to tell them what to do. Get off that soapbox. Relate to them. Let them know that you mess up.

They exhibit faults all the time. Relate to them. The key here is not to take things so seriously. When you make a mistake, tell them, "Oh, my gosh, how hilarious. If I had maintained a sharper focus, I could have had more time to complete this correctly. But, I missed it. Okay. That's what happens."

Show them that you choose to be a *victor* instead of a *victim.*

There was one time I didn't prepare enough when I took our kids to the library. I didn't have a library card and I thought I could use any library. The library said, "It will cost you $100 to get books here because you don't live in this area." "Wow, okay." The kids said, "I want this and I want that." I told the gentleman at the library, "Hey, you know what? Thank you so much. Today, I learned something about how this library system works."

I was joyful and grateful. The kids saw that. I could have mistakenly blamed someone: "Oh, this is stupid. I can't believe these people." But, then they would have seen how I could become a *victim* instead of a *victor*.

Nine times out of 10, when people first explore anything in life, they will not do it perfectly right the first time — riding a bike, going to the store, learning how to open a checking account, whatever it is. The growing and transitioning part allows them to ask, *"What could I have done to prepare myself better?"*

Do you see the valuable life skills you will teach your children as they encounter these things that will happen for the rest of their lives? The rest of their lives!

Have fun! Explore the creative thinking process and communication with your children. Begin to *guide* your children's behavior lovingly rather than using traditional punishment. **Asking Questions is Guiding Behavior.** *Dictating* can feel a lot like *punishment*. You, too, will rise to the top. Enjoy this chapter. I highly recommend that you go through and answer the questions asked of you throughout this chapter and complete the exercises. Remember, recognizing is the first law and repetition is the second law of learning.

Great job making it this far as you continue on your *Learning to Speak Kid* process.

Final Thoughts by Bonnie:

Before this lesson, all I did was *dictate* to my children. No wonder I ended up with rebellious, lazy and unproductive teenagers! As I began to track the words I would use with my children, it became extremely apparent where I could change and use the language of **Asking Questions**.

It surprised me that they always knew the correct answer. I was also shocked when they would do what I wanted them to do right away when I asked the right questions.

This lesson on **Asking Questions vs. Dictating** is amazing for building a better relationship between you and your child or teenager. It feels so good, as a parent, to ask my children questions. There are no more power struggles or arguing because my children get to *choose* more and more of what is important to them.

I know they are empowered because they feel a part of a conversation where what they say matters.

1. What do we mean by the term "dictating"?

_____

_____

_____

_____

_____

2. Explain the importance of answering your child or teenager's questions.

_____

_____

_____

_____

_____

3. What are the key benefits to asking your child properly formed questions for motivation?

_____

_____

_____

_____

4. Who are the people from whom you learned your parenting skills? There are probably more than just your parents.

_____

_____

_____

_____

_____

5. Describe the emotions you wish your child to learn life skills in.

_____

_____

_____

_____

_____

Chapter 9

Question and Quantify

~ Give them many opportunities to be right by asking the right questions to set them up for success. ~
Thomas C. Liotta

Bonnie: In the movie *Cast Away*, Tom Hanks plays a character, Chuck Nolan. He ended up stranded on an island after a plane crash. He was forced to reside on that island for a few years all by himself. During his stay there, he created a fictitious character named Wilson out of a volleyball. He painted a face on it. He added hair to it. Over time, Wilson became a real character for Chuck to talk to. In fact, Wilson and Chuck became best friends. Chuck could tell Wilson what to do and how he felt.

He could also share when he was frustrated or angry. Wilson always just listened. He didn't talk back, run away, or become sidetracked with anything other than what Chuck chose to discuss with him. In the end, Wilson is lost at sea and Chuck becomes extremely emotional and heartbroken.

Wouldn't it be nice to have a friend whom you could yell at, cry with and share all your secrets with? You could say whatever you wanted without hurting anyone's feelings or worrying about how they would react. Unfortunately, communicating with our children is quite different.

They definitely talk back, get hurt feelings and sometimes get sidetracked by the world around them. You can't share your secrets with them quite yet. When you are frustrated or angry, walking away is better. Take a time-out yourself and then come back when you feel calm.

Thomas will share this lesson, **Question and Quantify**, with you. This chapter will take you another step forward and add a new angle to the previous chapter, **Asking Questions vs. Dictating.**

Thomas: What is **Question and Quantify**? This is a valuable two-way communication tool. Much of the emphasis of these particular techniques is focused on the child. As we are becoming able to harmonize with the children, we are also coming to understand that many of these principles are for self-teaching, self-reflection, stepping up your own game, and becoming more aware of what truly is going on with your child or teen.

This chapter covers a few strategies, such as *show me*, *echo back*, *re-explain for clarification,* and ensuring the child **understands the proper procedures**.

I know you are getting a firm grasp of the four basic building blocks.

SEE

1. **Self-control:** "I am in control of my body and my actions." Your child begins to take on ownership of their life.

KNOW

2. **Responsibility:** "I am responsible for my actions and my belongings." Stories filled with excuses are all gone now.

DO

3. **Self-discipline:** "I do what I'm supposed to do by being asked only once." There will be no need for nagging or begging.

BE

4. **Focus:** "I keep my attention on the task at hand." Tasks, homework and chores will be completed in a timely manner.

S.K.D.B.

Question and Quantify utilizes many of what I call sub-tools. It's a great way to understand *two-way communication.* You will use it with your child to understand THEM on a deeper level and to ensure that your child has understood YOU on a deeper level.

Do you remember your role from Chapter 1, **Know Your Role as a Parent?** You discovered that your role is not to make them happy or do things for them, but to teach them life skills and to guide them up to age 18 and beyond. It could be communication, mathematics or social skills. You understand that. There is a certain standard that they should have as basic abilities. They should be encouraged to rise up to a certain proficiency. By the time your child is an adult, you want them to be productive, efficient and able to do everything independently and in a certain manner. Yes?

Let's proceed with your life skill standards; you are using **Question and Quantify** to clarify that standard with your child.

Do you remember how frustrating it was to ask, "Hey, did you clean out your room, Timmy?" "Yes, I did." And you say, "Okay," while inside, in the back of your mind, or in your heart, you're thinking, "You know what? I bet those socks are still underneath the bed," or "The clothes have not been put away," or "The blanket wasn't quite folded the way it's supposed to be."

And so, you go inside the bedroom and it's *kind* of done. Remember what our parents used to say? "Yeah, you are doing stuff half-assed." We get what that means now.

Now, they say, "I did clean my room." "No, you didn't." "Yes, I did." "No, you didn't." "Yes, I did." This friction is a key moment in proceeding to **Question and Quantify.**

At the beginning of this chapter, I mentioned a few things, like *show me*, *echo back*, *re-explain for clarity,* and ensure that the child *understands the proper procedure*. It's all about empowering your child so they can accomplish a task to YOUR standard by being asked only once.

Whenever you receive any friction from your child, use strategy for a solution. Take a few minutes and think about what you have learned so far. There was **Know Your Role as a Parent, Parent's Brain vs. Kid's Brain, Asking Questions vs. Dictating,** and…okay, let's say that the information they are basing their answer on, "Yes, I did clean my room!" is 100% correct in their mind.

They believe they are 100% correct as they are being very adamant. They've told you, "Yes, I did clean my room," once, twice, three, four, maybe five times. They really believe that they did it. It could be easily understood that they're being disrespectful, arrogant or rude. It may seem like they are being argumentative.

However, when you pause and say, "Hmm. Okay, Timmy. Let's take a look. *Show me* what you did to make sure the room was clean." The *show me* part here is to allow them to present their case and what is important to them from the kid's brain point of view.

Remember, the adult can see both the kid's and the adult's point of view. The child does not yet understand the adult side of things. If they could, they would say, "Oh, I know what you are saying. I raise kids, too." But, they are not there yet. By having your child use the *show me* strategy, they show you what they did to clean their room. NOW, you are going to be observant rather than judgmental.

This is **Question and Quantify.**

So, they take you into their room and say something along the lines of "See? I put all the books in a straight line. All of the titles are facing the same way. See how neat the bookshelf is? My toys are inside the toy box." They are so proud of themselves. But, the adult brain sees socks under the bed, the blanket that wasn't quite folded right, yada yada, which had nothing to do with this validation.

Use a very simple **Question and Quantify** strategy and you will automatically say, "Oh, my gosh. Timmy, you are absolutely correct. You did a great job cleaning your room with the books and putting the toys in their proper place inside the toy box. Great job! Excellent!"

From the previous chapters, you should already have the expectation part of the *Star Chart* posted on the refrigerator. You know what you expect them to do to clean their room. You have three, four or five minimum requirements already pre-framed, written out and displayed, and they are being recognized on a *Star Chart*. Right, Mom? Right, Dad? If you're a teacher, your expectations are posted in your classroom.

Here is the **Question and Quantify** part: "Excellent, Timmy! I like what you did here. What are the three requirements to make sure the room is clean?" *Ask questions*! Use this exact dialogue and you will *Learn to Speak Kid*. Once again, to whose standards is this? Not theirs. That's right. It's YOURS!

To achieve faster success, begin to recognize and honor what your child has done. You don't want to gloss over and reply, "Yeah, yeah, that's great, but you didn't do this other thing." A better answer is "Great! How good does that feel?"

Think about this: When you've done a great thing for your boss, when you did this, this, and this, and he replies, "Yeah, well, you were late," how do you feel? You tell your boss, "I just got you a $10,000 account and now you are complaining because I was three minutes late? Okay, fine." That's the same thing that most parents have been taught to communicate with their children. Kids reflect on what's been shared with them in the same context.

"Excellent! You did a great job here. This right here would be part of what we have to do." **Question and Quantify.** They say, "Well, I did do it." You walk to the refrigerator or to where your *Star Chart* is posted in the bedroom. See that it shows the three, four or five requirements for completing the job.

Your reply could be something as simple as "Well, the bed was made, clothes are put away, all the shelves and toys are as they are supposed to be, and the carpet is clean." So, you have the basic requirements and now you can *echo back.* "*Show me.* What is the best way for this to be? *Show me* how your room is clean. Where do we check?" "I don't know." "Oh, okay, remember the list we made?" "Oh, yeah." And you have them share with you what's on that list. Now, they go through it and read it. "Oh. Bed, covered. Pillows stacked. Got it. The carpet is completely clean. Clothes, put away. Toys are organized. Books, looking sharp." "Excellent."

Now, you **Question and Quantify** the proper procedure. "Excellent. How many of those have we done to MY standard?" "Oh, I did three of them." "Awesome! How exciting is that? You are so amazing!" *Praise! Praise! Praise!*

You are lovingly guiding your children's behavior and you never have to punish them; this is what makes these principles so great! Can you see it?

So, to complete the task and have them earn their star, you ask, "How many more steps do we need to do to make your room **outstanding**?" "Two." "Excellent! That's what I like about you. You're such a smart person. You know exactly what to do."

You may get a complaint at this point, which you will learn more about in the next chapter, but, basically, when you hear a complaint it's because they either **don't know how to** do what you want them to or they don't want to do it.

I know it has been mentioned many times, but I'll say it again: maybe they don't know how to put their clothes away or ensure the carpet has been cleaned to your standard.

Everything you wish for them to be or do is a life skill that must be taught. Yes?

If you show them your exact expectations and standards while teaching them life skills, and they have been proficient in them, then you have your bases covered. That means that they *don't want to do it*. Excellent! Then, you know it goes back to **Knowing the Reward** for your child. Remember?

If they really want the reward, they know what they must do to earn it.

When it's time to hand out the reward, look at all the stars on the *Star Chart* and see how many they have; they add all the stars up and it's simple. They earn the correct proportion of what they DID do.

How great is it now when it comes to *Friday Fun Day*? Let's say you're going to go swimming, to go to a movie or to go rollerblading. It could be paintballing, bowling or camping, whatever it is. Set it up in proportion to what they accomplished during the week.

Let's say they can earn seven stars a day, five times a week, Monday through Friday: seven times five equals 35. You can break it down as follows. Of the 35 total available stars to earn, 90% would be 31 stars. And 31 out of 35 earns the whole big, whatever it is, the whole event. This is considered *outstanding*. Let's pick swimming. At the pool where we take the kids swimming, the public swim time is 90 minutes.

If they earn 31-35 stars in a week, "Oh, my gosh, YOU did it! You accomplished *outstanding* results and you earned the entire 90 minutes. Great job!" They get free entrance and they can swim for 90 minutes.

Average would be 20-30 stars which is about 70%. Then, you say, "My gosh, look at you. You did really well. That will earn you 60 minutes of swim time."

Bare minimum would be 20 or fewer stars, which is about 55%, just barely passing. "Excellent! You earned 30 minutes of swimming! Let's go!" Notice you congratulate them on what they DID do. Be happy and acknowledge their accomplishment.

There is no punishment by saying something like "You only earned this much" or "You didn't earn outstanding, so you don't get to go for 90 minutes." That would be a different parenting program.

THE Creating Champions For Life (CCFL) philosophy ALWAYS Guides them. THIS IS THE MAGIC.

They *always* earn the right to go and receive a reward for work well done. There is NEVER a *punishment*. We are going to the activity; they are invited to come. They are informed exactly what is required of them to participate, so the plan has been *pre-framed.* THEY KNOW EXACTLY WHAT TO DO. Right?

If they have earned three stars out of 35, this would be called *extreme bare minimum.* In this scenario, you would say, "You get to join us. Congratulations on coming! You did great. How many stars did you earn? You need this many for 30 minutes, this many for 60 minutes and this many for 90 minutes."

What ends up happening is that your child will comprehend what goes on in the real world of being a human. You know they are going to go to school and they are going to have to survive in the world. Yes?

"Oh, I want to go swimming the whole time!" That's the reward! "I would love for you to go swimming the whole time. How much time would you like to earn?" "I want to go all 90 minutes." "What has to happen?" You bring the *Star Chart* with you. "Well, I have to earn all my stars." "That's what I love about you. You are so smart. How many stars do you have to earn?" "I've got to earn 31 of them." "Excellent! How many have you earned?" "Three." "Okay, how many more do you need to earn so that you can go all 90 minutes?" "I need 28 more." "Oh, my gosh, look how smart you are!" You are consistently operating in *praise* rather than traditional disciplinary techniques or punishment.

Then, it comes down to learning life skills. Either they *don't know how* to earn the stars, happy faces, stamps or whatever you use, in which case you work together as a team to *teach and show them*.

The other reason is that they *don't want to* earn them and they're not earning their rewards yet. Kids need a motivator. *Knowing the Reward* for your child or teen is KEY here. The reward is what *fills their fuel tank.* From a previous chapter, *Know the Reward*, you've identified the rewards that they are working towards. That is what gets them through this process.

Echo back is an incredibly powerful technique that allows them to SHOW or TELL you that they know the expectations. You know what the reward is for them. The life skill is then executed to a standard that makes sense to you.

Here is an example of *two-way communication*: They are having difficulties with their homework (but this will work with whatever activity you are doing). Now that you understand more about how a child thinks, you can approach your child with a better understanding of what's going on. Use the *echo back* strategy.

"Hey, what are we doing here?" "Well, I'm still working on my math." "Excellent!" "I need help on this particular problem." "Great. Show me what you did." He does, and you reply, "Okay, let me echo back. I see that you are doing this and this, but somehow the numbers aren't making sense over here." "Yes?"

No matter the scenario, when you *echo back* what it is to your child, you can confirm that you are talking about the same thing. If you begin to *assume* you know what they are having trouble with, you both will become frustrated and they will come back at you with a complaint: "So and so is doing this, or so and so is doing that." Use the strategy of **Question and Quantify** to understand where THEY are coming from.

"I heard what you said." Then, you repeat it, *echoing back*, to ensure you heard them correctly before you offer any solution. When you get a chance to *echo back*, it allows you to grasp where they are coming from and where the limitations are so you can guide them appropriately.

"So and so is doing this to me and I am getting frustrated." "Let me understand if I heard you correctly. They are doing this and it doesn't make you feel good?" "Yeah." "Okay."

Then, you always *quantify.* Maybe there are more things to it. "Anything else?" "Well, he does call me names, too." "Okay. He's calling you names, making you feel bad. Anything else?" "Well, sometimes he throws things at me too." "Okay."

Then, you continue to *Quantify*. "Anything else?" "No." "Okay." Continue in this way until they have been able to share ALL of their struggle. Assume nothing.

Every day, they will ask you for something. "I want to go do this." "I would like to have that." "Can I do this?" "Can I have that?" There's the question. They're ready for your next step. You know what to ask.

We enjoy teaching home economics to our kids. Jennie loves to bake the best cookies in the world. I look forward to seeing what she does with her talent in the kitchen as she matures. The chocolate chip and oatmeal cookies she bakes at our home are 100% organic. The chocolate chip cookies represent a *reward for outstanding* actions, behavior and effort throughout the day. As long as you *pre-frame* with your children the fact that the cookies are a *reward*, they will perform better and happily!

Whether you are planning for Christmas, a wedding or a graduation, the most joy is felt during the time *leading up* to the event. This is true for any deadline or goal. I know you know what I'm talking about. When you choose to create a reward for yourself, you are willing to do things you wouldn't do otherwise.

For instance, what would happen if the goal is for you to prepare Christmas dinner and you forgot to order a turkey? It's Christmas Eve. You would drive around in stop and go traffic and possibly have to buy a frozen turkey instead of a fresh one. You would have to stand in line at the grocery store on the year's busiest day. But, you do it, right? The point is that there are certain things we are willing to do when we have a *goal* or the reward of cooking the best Christmas dinner ever!

When your child is working towards whatever it is that's important to them, as discussed thoroughly in **Know the Reward,** they feel worthy. When you do everything for them, even though they think they like the easy life, underneath it all, they feel as if you don't trust them to do a good enough job. When they do nothing for something they want and don't get it, they feel like they aren't worth $10 or $20. Does this make sense?

Once your child, and yes, even your teen, gets the feeling in their heart that they can do stuff on their own, they will begin to excel in all areas of their life. This is powerful information for all parents.

They will begin to ask the question "What can I do to earn a cookie?" "I would love for you to have a cookie. What do you have to do in order to earn a cookie?" Now, I am asking the **Question** and I am **Quantifying.** Using the *echo back* strategy, you are communicating to your child that you heard what they said correctly. Acknowledge it and give them a chance to *understand the proper procedure*. In no context is it necessary to ever say NO.

The *Creating Champions For Life* philosophy always operates in a "yes, yes" mode. The "yes, yes" mode makes this so beautiful.

"I don't know." Okay. This is awesome! Here is another opportunity for you to teach and show them proper communication. "Little Timmy, I know you don't know, but if you had to guess what you would need to do, what would the answer be?" "Umm, I would have to do something outstanding." They will go from "I don't know" to exactly the correct answer.

Every.

Single.

Time.

Give them many opportunities to be right by asking the right questions to set them up for success.

Let's go back to the "I don't know" answer for a moment. You have all of your home expectations, life skills and chores lists written out. You have the Star Chart set up for them to look at. If you love this program and want more help mastering it, consider joining us. Visit the *CreatingChampionsForLife.com* website to learn more.

Repetition is the second law of learning and the charts and worksheets created for you in the Quick Study Guides are priceless. I congratulate you on reading the book this far and implementing everything you can!

They said, "I don't know." "Okay, let's go over here to the chart again. We can look at the entire list of all the things that are outstanding to do. When you do any of these outstanding things, you can earn a cookie," or whatever it is that is on the outstanding list that you have already created and *pre-framed* with them. Then, they say, "Well, I've got to do something outstanding."

"Excellent!" Now, *echo back*. "I would love for you to earn a cookie. I am completely on your side, cheering you on! What kind of things can you do that will be outstanding?" Give them a chance to explain. "I can vacuum the living room; it's outstanding." "I can sweep the kitchen floor; that's outstanding." "I can sweep off the deck; it's outstanding."

Now, you **Question *and* Quantify** by *re-explaining and clarifying* so there is complete confidence that you and your child are on the same page. For your child to have the best chance to succeed in life, it is important for you to teach your child *proper procedures* as part of their life skill training.

Question and Quantify is a wonderful tool to bridge the gap of *two-way communication,* especially when the parent's brain thinks completely differently than the child's. When this strategy is executed correctly, the results you see will be phenomenal, beyond your wildest imagination!

It takes practice, practice and more practice. Read, read, read. Watch the video, watch the video, watch the video.

This is so important to your success because of the transition, the *waffling* and the *violent opposition* from your kids. Daily practice will ensure your success and everything will work out very well. It is essential that the child truly understands what is important to you and that you understand what is important to your child. They wish to please you, so it is imperative that they know exactly what is important to you.

I remember when my little brother was 13. He used to phone me and complain about Mom, and Mom used to phone me and complain about him. He would say, "Mom doesn't even care about me. I could hang out in my room by myself every day and she wouldn't even notice."

At the same time, Mom called me and complained, "He doesn't even want to hang out with me. All he ever does is sit up in his room. I always ask him to hang out with me, but he doesn't want to."

What a frustrating scenario. I now know exactly how my mom felt when my brother or I would say hateful mean things to her. She actually DID care and she cared plenty. It broke her heart when she began to lose control of her kids.

Out of all the reasons for a breakdown in the relationship between a child and a parent, the number one reason is that the parents usually pick something that THEY would like to do. They never used the **Question and Quantify** *principle.* If you want a closer connection with your child, use the *echo back, show me and re-explain strategies* to clarify what your child would love to do.

Parents using this technique will have better, more fulfilling and bonding relationships with their children.

When a parent says, "We're going to spend some quality time together," and they roll their eyes, they mean, "Yeah, great. Here we go with the library again. Mom loves to read. I thought we were going to spend some time together doing what I wanted to do. But, she never hears me." The parent is left thinking, "What's going on? I totally wanted to hang out with you and here we are. Gosh, you never appreciate anything."

Here's another story to solidify the importance of *echo back.* Little Timmy told his dad, Dave, how much he loves paintballing. So, what did Dave do?

"Okay, little Timmy. We are going paintballing!" Dave drew his own conclusion about what it meant when little Timmy told him he liked paintballing. Dave did what his dad always did. He said, "Come on, son. We're going to suit up and go out in the field..." The entire circumstance and event were dictated by Dad! He intended to bond with his son and the same intention was present from the child to bond with his father.

Afterward, Dad asked, "How was that?" "Well, it was okay." "What do you mean, okay? I bought all the equipment, including brand new guns. Geez, what an ungrateful kid. That's the last time I'm going to do something like that."

The art of **Question and Quantify,** which is such a simple and great principle, was missed because Dad did not know any better. When it is implemented into the parent child relationship, the effectiveness of *show me, echo back* and *re-explaining proper procedure* will be beneficial on all levels.

Here is how the scenario could play out when you implement **Question and Quantify**. "Oh, okay. Paintballing, huh?" Dad began to **Quantify**. "Timmy, show me what your idea of paintballing is all about." Timmy replied, "Oh, yeah. There is a gun," and he got really excited. "What they do is go through this obstacle course, and they have these men positioned over here; they are sharpshooters, and they use paintballs because they don't want to use real bullets, Dad. Then, they shoot at each other as they go through the obstacle course in slow motion. They snake through the tunnels and other barriers as they go across and get to the other side to win." Timmy didn't want to *shoot* the guns. He liked *watching* the programs that he saw on TV and playing video games, which were gladiator-type events.

Dad answered in the original scenario without using the **Question and Quantify** principle: "Alright, little Timmy, we are going paintballing," instead of learning what was important to his son. Can you see how powerful this is? How will **Question and Quantify** make a difference in your family's life?

Asking Questions and Quantifying creates a bridge of communication where both parties are 100% correct.

You will have fun moving forward with self-discipline as you choose to implement more and more **Questions and Quantifying.** You will begin to see your kids doing what they are supposed to do by being asked only once. You can often provide a great deal of value to your family and in other places in your life as you execute this.

After Dave learned the art of **Question and Quantify,** he told me one day, "You know, I took some of these techniques and put them to use in my business." "Ah, what kind of business?" I used the same subtle technique with him: *show me, talk to me* and *echo back*. "Oh, so you are having fun with this?" "Yes, I am." "Well, show me what you mean," I asked him. **Question and Quantify**.

"Well, I did a job once and figured out how I thought it should be done. I continued to ask questions until the last questions had to come down to colors. I saved myself thousands of dollars on this because the guy who did it before me did an amazing job. But, you know what he did? He didn't quantify the color. That's the unsatisfactory feeling you get when you're not heard. When I went in and saw the job, I **Quantified.** I asked which color he wanted. I got the contract for the next job and the following job for our company because I understood exactly what the customer wanted."

Regarding the kids, it's not a matter of what *you* want to do with them. You get the most *empowerment* and best results when you know what's important to THEM *and* you do that with them on their level. That's when the bond strengthens in the relationship. It fuses, locks and begins building a "**Plus 1**" moving forward.

Many parents feel there is a strong and necessary requirement to assist their teenagers when they are introduced to new responsibilities, such as driving a car, dating and spending more time away from home. It's also important to help them learn about all of the key things in life: drinking, smoking, drugs and sex. Your children are going to learn about these issues one way or another. Would you like them to learn from you in a very positive, more informed environment? Or would it be better if they learned about this stuff out in the world with people who don't know or care about your child's best interests?

Question and Quantify: by fusing the relationship into an even stronger one, you'll be certain that you are on the right track and using the correct strategies.

For the next phase of **Question and Quantify,** let's put this in a more practical reactionary environment. In this example, the kids are older — they're teenagers. They're skipping school. You catch them drinking, smoking, having sex, or doing something that evokes a response like "Okay, I just got a call from the police. Timmy and all his friends just got caught shoplifting. Honey, what are we going to do?"

Now, anytime I did something wrong, I was punished with *corporal punishment.* I had my own paddle in school when I went to visit the principal. The minute I got home, there was yelling, followed by punishment. Is this really the loving, guiding behavior thing to do?

Let's say you find out that your 14-year-old daughter or son has snuck out of the house. They have gone to a party. You found out they were drinking wine coolers. Here's the **Question and Quantify** principle to use before you automatically go into the gung-ho assault. "What intrigued you about the coolers?" "What was it about the environment that encouraged you to go?" Gather as much information about it as you can, **Quantifying.** Ensure that you *allow them to explain* what they were going through. *Listen* in a very calm manner.

Traditional punishment would be more like: "What the hell are you doing?" "You don't ever do that!" If you still believe this will work for you, you are missing the point of the entire philosophy. Take what Dad and Grandpa taught you and throw it out.

"What was it about doing this that got your attention?" "Seems like a cool thing to do." "Are all the other kids doing it?" "Well, most of them." "Okay. Would you say some of the kids, most of the kids, or all the kids?" "No, just some." "Alright, what was it all about?"

Break it down and gather as much information as you can to understand what made them act out so you can see it from THEIR perspective — not yours. This goes back to the chapter on **Parent's Brain vs. Kid's Brain**. What intrigued them? What got them there? Then, *echo everything back.*

"Okay, let me see if I got this straight. So and so has an older brother, 18 or 19, and they drink all the time. I got it. They usually do it when their parents are not around and the other kids like to meet at their house to drink." You gather all of the things and you say, "Okay."

You can ask them very simple questions: "Is doing what you did a good thing for you?" "Is that the best decision to make?" When you **Quantify** and *echo back*, nine times out of 10, they'll say, "No, it's not okay, but we did it anyway."

This can be a major turning point in their life. *Punishment* mode in these circumstances would set them up for lying to you. *Guiding behavior* through **Question and Quantify** will set them up to embrace you. Punishment doesn't work. All punishment does is encourage your child to find a way to limit the information they give you, or, better yet, they will find ways to make sure you don't find out about it at all. They are still going to do it. *Guiding their behavior* is so important.

I remember being little and my dad smoked cigarettes. I was about four or five years old at the time when I said, "Hey, Dad, I want to do that." He asked me, "You know these are no good for you, right?" "Why do you do it?" I don't remember much about what he might have said.

The point is that I learned so much from my dad. Dad and I had this great relationship. We were like best friends even though we were father and son. "These are no good for you. It's going to cause a specific problem." But, he also asked me, "Why?" "What's the interest?" "What's the intrigue?" "Well, I just want to be cool." I had some thought in my head that it was cool.

Dad handed me a package. So, I had a little packet with three cigarettes in it rolled in my sleeve and I said, "Check me out." I remember seeing it in the early '70s. The men had stylish hair, a white t-shirt and a cigarette pack rolled up in their sleeves, with muscles showing. There was something about that, I do recall. It wasn't the cigarettes; I wasn't even smoking them. The cool image I saw gave me the desire to be a smoker and my dad knew it. He could see that it was because he smoked. I can remember him talking to me three days later when I gave him the pack of cigarettes back. He asked, "What are you doing?" "These aren't cool."

He was **Creating the Right Environment.** He used the **Questions and Quantify** principle and found out that it had nothing to do with smoking cigarettes. Any other family member who saw that would have said, "Give me those!" "What are you doing?" Then they would have smacked me.

Without **Questioning and Quantifying,** there is confusion. Kids are learning all sorts of different things — drinking, sex, partying, stealing — everything! However, when you **Create** *the Right Environment,* you will set your kids up for success for the rest of their lives.

How often is it that a mother is protective of her daughter when it comes to dating? "You are not going out there dressed like that!" "You will not talk to boys until you are 18." She says that because she has her own powerful thoughts and fears. Rather than simply asking her child, "What is it about dating that intrigues you?" "I just think it's fun to go to the movies with a boy." "And...?" "That's it."

If the mother had known the principle of **Question and Quantify** and *echoed back* and *quantified,* then she could have understood her daughter's purpose for wanting to go on the date and hang out with a boy. The ability to see from her daughter's point of view would have grown a deeper connection and trust. Instead, she told her daughter, "No. There's no way you are going on any dates." Then, her daughter is forced to lie to make what is important to her SHOW up. "Well, I'm going to spend the night with so and so." Kids will sneak out and do what they want anyway. The next thing you know, two years later, teenage pregnancy...X, Y and Z.

Do you see how fun and powerful Question and Quantify is? Use it everywhere in your life. Most importantly, use it with all of your children and teenagers.

I find it disturbing that children get *labeled* into groups or categories. This one is the jock, this one is the rocker, the nerd, lazy, loud, mean. Some *labels* go into the learning process: smart, not as smart, ADHD, ODD, conduct disorder and more. There are so many labels that mentioning them here would take all day for you to read.

Many kids I've worked with have told me how stupid they think they are. I remember one time I was working on a simple math assignment with a child when he said something that went like this: "You can't expect the same from me as from other kids. My brain is broken."

I took a moment and thought about this. "Let me make sure I'm hearing you correctly." *Echo back.* "Somebody told you that your brain doesn't work or it's broken?" "Uh huh." "Did I hear you correctly?" "Yep." "Okay, where did you hear that?" "I don't know." "I know you don't know, but if you had to guess, who would you guess?" We will not necessarily get complete answers because kids often internalize the labels they are given and believe something is wrong with them. Have you ever heard of a self-fulfilling prophecy?

"Would you like to carry that *label* for the rest of your life, or would you like to have a different one?" "What if you could *label* yourself anything you like?" "What would you like to call it?" "Well, I want to have a smart brain." "Excellent! Show me, what would a smart brain do?"

Every child is a genius when you embrace their own uniqueness.

Can you see why releasing the labels and accepting and loving your child for exactly who they are is so important?

The smart brain says, "Ummmm...it's not about being good at math. It's about memory?" "Great! Let's get some flashcards and practice some memory techniques. What is your name?" "My name is Timmy." "Excellent, somebody who is smart remembers their name. What are the names of some of your friends?" "Tommy, Sally and Joe." "Great."

You always praise your child's smart brain. Before we can practice math, we need to encourage belief in himself with a few questions we know he can answer. "Remember what books are on the bookshelf and what toys are inside the toy box?" "Yes." "See, that's what a smart Timmy would know? He would know exactly where to put those books and memorize which box to put all his toys in. That's my smart little Timmy!"

I am positive that you see the benefits of **Question and Quantify.** When you don't have a clear understanding of how your child sees things, there are times when action is being taken on things before it is time to. It's like randomly driving around in a car. "Where do we want to go?" "Just around." "Okay. Great!" You are successful. You are driving around. But you aren't going anywhere; it's not **Quantified**.

Begin to use this strategy on yourself and *echo back* that which allows you to *quantify*: *What should I be doing with the kids? Should I buy them things to pacify them, or am I going through each step systematically, putting things together into a cohesive manner?*

This is a fun chapter to play with. You literally have unlimited amounts of potential. When you find yourself at a crossroads, being confused, or not feeling like you're understanding your kids, then using **Question and Quantify** is going to help. It will bridge two-way communication and let things flow with more harmony. It can be used at any stage of the game.

Utilize these techniques of *show me, echo back and re-explain* for clarity to ensure that your child understands the proper procedures for doing something. When your children embrace this, their self-discipline strengthens and they do everything they are supposed to do by being asked only once.

This works in so many ways. The more you use it, the happier you will be.

Final Thoughts by Bonnie:

I have definitely used this lesson in more areas of my life Beyond my children. The tools I learned here help me figure out exactly what my daughter means when she says, "Making out." Or what my son means by "I wish I were dead." These are a few things they have said, which are still not the most horrible things. As you continue to go through the process of breaking them off of the "give me" welfare system, they may say things to you like, "You are a crazy B--CH!"

After **Question and Quantify** I have been able to understand where they are coming from without taking it personally. I have discovered that making out is *holding hands*, NOT *kissing*. *I wish I were dead* means *I don't like today*. A day later, after some discussion, they act like nothing happened.

I am using the most dramatic of expressions presented by my young teenagers. You and I see these statements in our minds as the most horrible ones someone can say. It does not mean the same thing when THEY say them. They are fighting for their life as they knew it before *Learn to Speak Kid* came along, when I just gave them things.

Not taking their statements personally and having the knowledge to ask the right questions will lead your kids on the path of open communication. They can describe what they mean. This is beginning to allow me to engage more deeply in my relationships with my children.

They share more information with me now than ever before. They are open to being honest and telling me their stories. Best of all, I am gaining their respect, not by demanding it but by earning it! If I can take it and move forward with the things they have thrown at me, you definitely can!

Rowan counted $40 in his wallet and declared, "I am rich, I am rich! Take a picture and send it to Thomas."

1. What is **Question and Quantify?**

_____

_____

_____

_____

2. What are the four methods used to implement this positive parenting strategy efficiently?

_____

_____

_____

_____

3. Explain how you can always say yes to your child while teaching them life skills to be successful now and later.

_____

_____

_____

_____

4. How do you give your child the best opportunities to be right and receive praise?

_____

_____

_____

_____

5. In times of trouble, what is the best way to get your child to embrace and trust you?

_____

_____

_____

_____

6. Explain a scenario where action is being taken prematurely.

_____

_____

_____

_____

Chapter 10

Complaining

~ A child's complaint can be your greatest ally. ~
Thomas C. Liotta

Bonnie: Ah, complaining! All my four children seemed to do was complain. They didn't have enough of this, didn't get enough of that and never got to do anything. Seriously, we could be on the way home from an entire day at the water park, and they would whine because I didn't choose to buy them McDonald's meals.

Looking back, this almost seems funny to me now.

This lesson taught me how to avoid temper tantrums, whining and pouting. I learned how to help my children realize the value of the things they were receiving. I went back to Chapter 1 and made sure that everything I was doing was thought out, organized and written down on paper.

Understanding **Complaining** really made sense to me. I realize that my youngest child's classroom temper tantrum was caused by his lack of inner belief in himself. The thought that they wanted to diagnose him with the worst case of *ODD, oppositional defiant disorder,* the school physiologist had ever seen and medicate him is horrifying to me now. I have seen what he is capable of. He is an amazing character with pure potential when he is in the correct environment. Here is Thomas with his lesson on **Complaining**.

Thomas: There is a hidden code locked inside the act of **Complaining.** When you understand what a complaint is, you'll see how a complaint from your children can be your greatest ally. If everybody is **Complaining** about something, there must be some benefit to this communication strategy.

We will go through several lessons and apply the principle of **Complaining** to each one. You are going to learn about *non-confronts.* These are typical behaviors a child displays that will automatically show up to help you understand that a complaint is around the corner. More specifically, this is another, more subtle form of **Complaining.** You will learn one of the best, simplest and easiest to use strategies to help you identify the issue with your child. Then, you can *re-explain* yourself and move things back on track.

What do you see when you close your eyes and ask yourself the question, "What is **Complaining**?" Most people would respond: I don't like it when people complain; I like to keep everybody happy; I feel like I'm doing something wrong when someone complains. **Complaining** means something isn't working right. Most of the time, people who work in the customer service department only hear *complaints*.

But, **Complaining** is a very basic aspect of our vocabulary. It is a foundational piece of the personality for how the majority of our population speaks; it's the way most people have been taught to perceive things; it's the way the people who are doing the teaching have been taught to perceive things; it's the way we see how things have worked and the way we see how things will work. Most people will worry and fret about things that are outside their scope of what exists or about the future, those things that have not happened yet.

When you learn to speak a language that will better serve you and teach that language to your child, you will see there are solutions to every issue. You will have an extra set of eyes that will give you a better chance to consider another way of doing something.

What is your best guess as to what it really means when someone *complains* to you? It might be at your job, your kids or your partner. When your kids begin to *complain*, "I don't want to do that." "That is not fun for me." This is an opportunity to find out what is *really* going on with them, find out what is important to them, and then teach them the necessary related life skills.

The *Creating Champions For Life philosophy* was developed and then anchored by implementing the program with over 2,000 children. When it comes to **Complaining**, the reason for the complaint comes down to two main categories. I welcome someone who might be able to offer a suggestion here, but in my experience, it boils down to two categories.

When a child complains:

1. They **don't know how** to do something. They have not been taught the life skill.

2. They **don't want to** do it. There is not enough fuel in their tank to get the job done.

We are going to repeat that again because **Complaining** typically involves somebody saying, "I don't know how to do that," or "If I complain enough, somebody will do it for me and I'll get out of having to do my chores."

Complaining begins at the baby stage when neurological thought patterns or pathways are being developed in the brain. The baby has one form of communication, which is to cry. That's it. They want something, don't know how to do something, can't reach something, and they *cry*. The crying says, "I'm not happy." "I'm hungry," or whatever it might be. Your job as a parent is to decipher what they are **Complaining** about. "Oh, it was this help they were looking for; their diaper wasn't changed."

Complaining is part of a natural process of how things work. They express nothing more than their one way of communicating with you, such as, "I don't know how to do this." What it comes down to is "Hey, could somebody teach me that life skill?" But, children don't know how to ask for it in that way because they have not yet been exposed to **Know Your Role as a Parent.** You are now aware that you have *life skills* to teach and are communicating them to your child.

Children will take the path of least resistance. Parents are *feeding them fish and* the children rarely have a chance to step up and be the *fisherman*. "If I complain a little bit, they will just do it for me." This is when you hear, "Mom, where's my jacket?" or "Mom, I can't find my socks," or "Mom, I need five bucks!" And when this becomes a habit, it will be, "Mom, Mom, Mom...Dad, Dad, Dad...." forever!

Again, here is **Complaining**. Either they *don't know how* to do something because they have not been taught that life skill yet, or they *do not want to* do it.

When you encounter resistance, the reason will always fall into those two categories. The simple one-two-three strategy makes this so much fun to use:

1. Whatever the complaint is, whether it's I don't know how to do it, I'm frustrated, it's outside my radar, or maybe I gave it a go and it takes a little time to get the hang of something, so I don't want to, whichever it is, always agree. **ALWAYS AGREE.** For example, "I don't want to do that." "I don't want to go over there." "Well, I understand you don't want to go."

2. **RE-EXPLAIN** the task at hand, the lesson to be learned, or the message being communicated.

3. Go right back into asking for the offer — **ASK FOR THE ORIGINAL INTENTION.**

A great example is the difference between a loud and quiet voice. The loud voice is an outdoor behavior. You never have to tell your child "No" for any reasonable level of yelling outside. We help them create the right environment for yelling by *showing* them that yelling is an outdoor activity.

"If you choose to yell, I encourage that. Let's get you into the right environment to yell; you'll be outside." "I don't want to go outside." "I understand you don't want to go outside and I would love to have you inside also, but where is the best place to use your yelling voice? Remember, we agreed." "Outside." "Excellent! Let's go ahead and ensure you get to the right spot because I wish you to be successful in yelling as a healthy part of your development. When you have control of your body, you have a choice to be inside or outside. That's even more of a great success. You have a choice now of which one of those two areas to be in."

It's always a positive "**yes, yes**" mode.

Complaining comes in so many different forms. When the strategies you are learning here are implemented correctly, it can be so much fun.

In the first chapter, **Know Your Role as a Parent,** you learn that you have a set of life skills to teach to your children. That was a huge paradigm shift for you if you always thought your job was to make them happy. Did you really decide to have children so that you could make them happy and do everything for them? They are going to have to learn those life skills eventually. They can be learned easily now with you or the hard way later with someone else.

Here's a scenario of a student named Brandon, whom I had in school many years ago. We were on a trip to the library. We were taking what was supposed to be a fun field trip to find any book they liked. They would spend some time reading before they would get a chance to share one of the things they liked best about what they read.

However, on the way, and completely out of the blue, and as we approached the library, he said, "I don't want to go there. It's stupid." We proceeded to go anyway. As we reached the parking lot, he cursed, threw things around and acted like we were throwing him off a cliff. It was as if he was fighting for his life.

Brandon began to do what I call a *"non-confront."* This is where kids come up with a great **Complaining** "dodge." They say, "I've got to go to the bathroom." "My stomach hurts." Or they would pretend not to pay attention by using a distraction, "Oh, what is that outside?" Or they begin to get in trouble or act out.

Why would they go so far as to throw things around, curse, or do something really dramatic? We got down to where the *complaints* were coming from. Remember, it was either that he *didn't want to* go to the library or that he *didn't know how to* do something there.

Most of the time, parents will look at a child's complaint and say, "Well, he's just misbehaving." "He needs a time-out." "He needs to be talked to." "He needs medication."

When we looked at the situation, we said, "It's obviously something about reading. I guess he wants to do it but doesn't know how." THERE'S his *missing life skill!*

Since Brandon was a student in my program, I said, "Let's get him tested for reading." Sure enough, he was in the fifth grade and reading at a first-grade level. Here's a student whose parents brought him to me and said, "Hey, my kid is acting out. Fix him. Do something." He was merely missing a life skill. The child used *non-confrontations* strategically to avoid admitting that he couldn't read.

Complaining is a deep-rooted program running inside their minds. They don't know how to say, "Hey, you didn't show me how to read four years ago and I've been getting in trouble on purpose and causing mischief, so I don't have to admit it." Brandon did not know how to ask for help.

As you study this program and *Learn to Speak Kid,* it will ensure you see the best results with your children. You will begin to decipher and understand *"I don't know how"* as the indicator that they are really saying, "Could you please *teach me that life skill*?" It's that, or *they don't want to* and, as you now know, the *motivator is missing.* There is no reward.

You will get complaints when it's time to teach your kids a life skill. "I can't do that." "I know you can't do that. The whole purpose of my job as a parent is to teach you these life skills. You are seven years old and we have 11 years to develop them. When would you like to learn if you don't know how to read now? If not now, you are going to need to learn it later in life. When would you like to get started? How about NOW? Now or soon would be a really great choice." You are **Guiding Their Behavior**.

Embrace **Complaining** *because it's a gateway, an open door that will allow you to begin developing life skills with and for your child.*

As soon as they *complain*, you have to think, "Either they don't know how, or they don't want to." If *they don't want to,* then you have to understand what the reward is, **Know the Reward.** What is important to them? *Fill their tank* so they can have enough energy to learn.

Like breakfast, dinner is a fantastic fuel tank filler. Make sure things are completed before mealtimes. Their tank fills up pretty quickly when they get hungry. This is a perfect opportunity for *checks and balances* in terms of receiving stars on the *Star Chart* (or signatures for older kids). We talked about this in depth in Chapter 6, **Know the Reward.**

I love this story as an illustrator. A tribe of people was recently found on a remote island. They had been completely isolated and didn't have access to or knowledge of modern technology. It was deserted and mysterious. They were so far behind all advances around the world that they didn't even know what a ship was.

When people came to visit, they left the ship out in the water, and because the water was shallow, they took small canoes inland. The native people there could not SEE the ships. Even though the visitors could describe them (big, masts, sails, floats, etc.), the native people were confused. "Huh? You are speaking a completely foreign language."

How can you relate if you have never seen a thing before? Einstein's description of the universal law of relativity is that there must be two reference points in order to understand what anything is.

It is critical to understand this relativity point when you ask your child to do something and they say, "Well, I don't know how." "I can't do it, nor do I want to." While they go through their *non-confront* and start **Complaining,** understand that the complaint is like the tribe's situation in which they've never seen a boat before. The child will complain rather than tell you they don't understand what you just said or that they don't know how to do what you have asked them to do.

As strange as that might seem to you, this is the reality for the kids. Their Kid's Brain has never seen what you are referring to.

When you receive *complaints*, get excited to explore something with your child that is going to be completely routine for you. It may seem like "Oh, gosh, I learned that 25 years ago. Everyone knows that. It should be common knowledge." The kids are now beginning to see the word, action or idea for the FIRST time. It could be something as simple as learning how to multiply in math class at school. If they have never multiplied something before, they have no concept of what that would be.

Realizing the root cause of the complaint will alleviate much stress and miscommunication, such as "You should know this," "I think you have ADHD," or "Maybe they are just stupid or slow, or they have a brain deficiency." When you think about it, if you were to switch it around, they would be speaking a different language to you, too. Have you heard of the natural law of cause and effect? Change the cause. You will change the effect.

Another life skill is communication. "I'd love to learn this, but I've never done it before, so it's scary to me." This is where the person teaching the life skill, the parent, the teacher or the coach, has to break down the task and teach the basics of every individual step. "I know you are in fifth grade, but we are going all the way back to the basics of kindergarten steps to get started.

First, I'm going to do it to *show you*. Then, I am going to take it all apart and *you are going to do it*. To fold a blanket, first lay it flat on the floor. The next step is to grab one corner, fold it over and match it to the opposite corner. Then, grab this corner at the other end of the blanket, fold it over and match it to the opposite corner. Make sure it's even on all sides, like this. Then, you fold it in half this way and continue to fold it in half until it is small, flat and even. Do you see what I mean here?" The child will answer, "Yes," usually with an eye roll.

"Great! Okay, so now I am going to unfold it and *you can show me* that you know how to fold a blanket. This life skill will be important when you have sleepovers at your friend's house. Your friend's mom will be grateful for your behavior and skills and you will be invited over for more sleepovers."

Chapter 3 is all about **Creating the Right Environment** for your child to succeed. While you are implementing change and working on your new environment so that your child can become a champion, you will hear many Complaints. "I can't do this." "I don't want to do this." "Can't we go back to the way things were?" Remember, when they say this, it translates to "*Please teach me.*" They are telling you, "You're the parent, you're the life skill coach, come on now, do your job. Be the parent and show me what to do."

"*I haven't been able to ask correctly, but I need you to SHOW me what to do.*"

Creating the Right Environment will help you lovingly guide your child's behavior rather than being frustrated and defaulting to traditional punishment. "Well, I show you all the time; you just don't want to do it," and then you shift into punishment mode by saying, "If you don't do it, you are not getting this reward." Instead, show, explain and work with them to complete the requested task.

You will often hear, "I can't do it." The complaint has come because they *don't know how* to do something, or it's because they *don't want to* do it. Maybe they don't want to because they can't find what they need in order to complete the task. For instance, if your child takes guitar lessons and one day when you push them, they don't want to play anymore, it could be because they broke the guitar.

Ask yourself these questions: Has he done this task before? Is it possible something he requires has been lost or broken? What is the life skill that I have the opportunity to work on with my child with this complaint? Once you've answered these questions, solve the issue. *Show* them what to do, *re-explain* and *ask for the agreed intention* to be done again.

Let's tie some of this together with a few examples. **Let's Create the Right Environment**. You know and I know from going through these chapters, that the *environment always wins.* The water will eventually erode away the rock. It's a matter of time. Even casinos are **Creating the Right Environment** to manifest cash flow. They are designed to make money as long as people are going through them. When you **Create the Right Environment** to develop success in your house so that your children can excel, they will.

Every.

Single.

Time.

Remember that great *attention stance* game where they stand straight up, hands at the sides and eyes looking straight forward? "Show me your best statue that you can do. Remember, statues 1. stay still 2. remain silent and 3. keep strong eye contact until acknowledged. You start off on successions of 10 seconds, then 20. "Gosh, you are going to make it a full 30 seconds; holy toledo, you are at a minute!" They are practicing their will and *self-control*. When your child has the *self-control* to hold their attention stance for five minutes easily, there is now a life skill in place for them to succeed.

When you hear the number one *complaint*, "I can't do it," always add the word "YET." "I know you can't do it, YET." In the final chapter, we'll get into **Linguistics** and introduce you to a principle that will open doors for your child, leading them to greater success, now and forever.

In Chapter 4, *Making the Transition*, you became aware that you did so much for your children for so long; you fed them fish. It's time to tell your children, "You guys need to learn how to catch *your own fish*." As you grow in this philosophy, there will be times when it can be quite taxing; it can feel that you are off the mark when you are actually right on track. *Persevere.*

If you have more than one child and only one of them is catching on quickly and is doing well with the new lifestyle, that is, they earn a bike, a bedroom, a bed, clothes and activities, what is the other child going to say? He is used to *receiving fish.* "How come I can't go?" "How come they get to go?" "I always used to be able to go." "You always did everything for me." "Why don't I get to go if I made my bed?"

Here is an opportunity to teach a life skill. "I know. I want you to have one of those." "I would love for you to go to the movies."

Do you remember the strategy?

1. *Agree.*
2. *Re-explain.*
3. *Ask again for the offer or for what is being taught.*

"I would love for you to go to the movies. Now, what did your brother or sister do in order to be able to go?" "Uh, I don't know." They will usually play a *non-confront* because that's what they are accustomed to doing. You walk them over to the refrigerator. "Remember, there was a list of things for you all to do on the *Star Chart?*" "They had to have their room cleaned, the dishes done and to make sure they had their chores done." Then, praise them, "That's what I like best about you. You are so smart. You knew exactly what to do."

Remember, the whole basis for **Complaining** is that they *don't know how* to do something or they *don't want to* do it. If they don't want to do it and they DO know how, you just saved yourself a lot of grief, time and expense instead of spending an extra $20 to see a movie they didn't have an interest in seeing. If you bring them with you, they won't develop any life skills. Leaving them behind is counterintuitive, but it will put them one step further along the development chain to becoming more successful.

"I'm hungry." "Here's a fish." They feed. A couple of hours later or half a day later, "I'm hungry again." This clearly describes a child who is NOT developing into an *independent* fisherman and you know this because the *complaint* keeps coming back.

How awesome is it that you get to agree with them? "I want to go." "Well, I would love for you to go. What did you have to do that your brother and sister also had to do to be able to go?" Now, when they say they know and they will, it allows you to **Create the Right Environment** for authentic growth. This is how we take the "*dis*" out of behavior *dis*orders to create order.

"We don't promote any laziness anymore. We're weaning you off the welfare system, where you get rewarded for just having a pulse. Just because you are my child, do you think I have to give you something? No. I'm not going to spend the rest of my life, even when you are 40, still making your bed." Ask your child, *"Would you like to*

*learn the **life skill** now, the easy way, or would you like to learn it the hard way later? It is going to happen. By doing it now, it's the easy way, the 'fun-ER' way versus later when it's going to be the 'hard-ER' way."*

I've often seen kids whose parents were so successful that their kids never really had to work for anything. The parents paid for their car, electronics, events and everything else. If this is you, STOP. You're training them for the welfare system.

If you need more convincing, I heard of another case recently where the kid moved out and then came back to live with his parents again. "I'm having a tough time. I don't know where to stay." The parents lined up a car for him, secured a place for him and paid for everything. Once again, they *fed him fish*; they didn't teach him *life skills.*

Later on, the adult kid had the audacity to say, "Well, this isn't a really nice place and that car is old," instead of having any gratitude like "Gosh, I'm happy to have a car. Thank you so much."

Your children will continue to ask for more and more until you **Make the Transition** from feeding them fish to making them a fisherman. "How come I don't have a nice house like you do?" "How come I don't have a fancy car like you do?" "I would love for you to have a car like mine.

What are some of the things that I did or learned to make this car appear?" "I don't know." This opens the door to **life skills**. "This is what it takes to earn a nice home and a fancy car. Now that you do know, I would love for you to have one, too. If you don't know how to do these things, there is a life skill for earning these things. Whenever you are ready to have a car like this, I would love to help you."

Automatically shift into the "yes, yes" mode. You are always on their side. It's up to them to step up. You never have to say no or deny anything.

Here is another really common complaint you will get when **Making the Transition.** "How come I didn't get one?" "How come I can't go?" "How come so and so got that?" "How come I can't have it when they did?" Now that you have the right tools, you know how to break down the *complaint.* "Excellent! Does this mean you *don't know how* or *don't want to*? Oh, you don't know how. We can handle that."

There's a life skill. Again, always:

1. *Agree.*
2. *Re-explain.*
3. *Ask again for the offer or for what is being taught.*

Become aware and visualize the two types of parents: One is lovingly **Guiding Behavior**, where they say, "Oh, wow, I love seeing you clean up the house and clean your room or help with the dishes," or "Oh, my gosh, I saw my car was washed and I didn't even ask for it." POSITIVE ATTENTION!

The second type of parent will say, "If you don't get your stuff done, I'm going to have to *take this away* from you." "If you don't do this, you won't get that." "I'm seeing something I don't like and you will need **punishment.**" NEGATIVE ATTENTION.

We are social creatures. Studies show that humans need social interaction to survive. When a baby is born, it has a certain window of time to bond with its mother or another human being. If it is separated for any great length of time, the baby is gone. It checks out. It experiences *Happy Transition Day*; it dies. We must have social interaction, ATTENTION, to survive.

Whether your kids seem to be misbehaving or going out of their way to please you, they are saying, "I require some attention." It is imperative to validate when they are doing what they are supposed to be doing. They need pats on the back and recognition for their greatness. "Recognize some things that I did." When we miss those windows and operate in punishment mode, "I do good things and don't get recognition, but I do bad things and get acknowledged by being yelled at." "Good or bad, it doesn't matter. Either way, I'm still operating under the survival of attention. I'm getting attention."

Visualize this: You have a garden hose. Do you water your favorite *flowers,* or do you water the *weeds*? Which one will grow?

Over here, you have good behavior. You focus and turn to it; *the water is being poured on your favorite flower*, the good behavior. The thing you like best is being nurtured. Just like flowers require water, fertilizer and sunlight to survive, so does your little genius offspring.

When you focus on the things you don't like, you're over there watering the weeds. The more attention you give to things you don't like or things that annoy you, the more that behavior will grow.

You can choose how you share your love, which, in this analogy, is water.

"If my attention was a hose, would I be watering the weeds or the rose?"

Choose to be proactive. I will give attention to the child who shows these behaviors: kindness, cooperation, respect, hands-to-self and whatever you like. The other negative behaviors will receive no attention.

"You're never paying attention to me." "I agree with you. I do not pay attention to certain behaviors. However, there are many things that I will pay attention to. You know exactly where they are; they are right on the refrigerator (bedroom wall or wherever you posted them)." If you have not taken the time to proactively share the behaviors and expectations you would like to see, do it NOW.

I have worked with thousands of children, and 99.999999989% of them came from homes with a *punishment* mentality. "Well, I better do that so I don't get in trouble," versus "Hey, if I do this, I'll get extra hugs." It's the same message on a much higher vibration. The first one is from a vibration of fear and the second is from a vibration of love. It's miraculously simple and extremely effective.

Remember, in **Know the Reward,** the reward is like the fuel in a vehicle. Pick any car or truck. It uses gas to *take action.* When it's empty, the car will not go anywhere, no matter how well or fast you choose to get there. When you ask these future champions in your life to do something and they say, "Well, I don't want to," nine times out of 10, they don't know how to tell you, "I'd love to get it done, but the tank is empty."

When their tank is full, the task will be done immediately. When their tank is empty, that is their **Complaint.** *When* *you interpret and decipher the code of the* **Complaining,** *YOU KNOW your child's reward.*

Your greatest asset when using the **Know the Reward** principle is *patience*. As mentioned earlier, using a *good sense of timing* with the reward is as important as dropping the punch line at the end of a joke. This is imperative for your success.

You know by now that your job or role as a parent is to provide the three rights of life: clothes, food and shelter. Never deny your child these things. Many parents have been duped into believing that they owe their kids cell phones, computers and their first automobile. They don't.

There are three different levels of basic rights:

1. *Bare minimum*
2. *Average*
3. *Outstanding*

Chapter 6, **Knowing the Reward,** describes this in detail. These three levels will be scored in every segment on the *Star Chart*. The accumulation of stars will average out at the end of every day or every week, depending on how deep and detailed your family plan is. Remember, if you desire further explanation on the *Star Chart* or need help implementing some of these ideas, take the time to come find us at *CreatingChampionsForLife.com*

Your child will begin with a small tank, which will need to be "trained" as you and they grow. Start small and expand. "You're right. You did the bare minimum. Great job! You have earned the bare minimum meal (video game time, swim time)." Once again, they are going to complain, "Well, I want to have more." Get excited. They just filled their tank! This is what you are looking for. Now, go back to the strategy.

"I would love for you to have an outstanding dinner. What would you have to do?" "Well, do the outstanding on my *Star Chart*?" "Excellent! That's awesome! That's what I like best about you. You know exactly what to do. When you are ready to finish your homework, I'm here to help, teach and assist you in being successful along the way. It is 100% up to YOU."

When their tank is empty, that's where all the complaints are. You have to stay consistent on this. Give zero credit.

"Okay, I'll get you the really great, organic pizza that we made from scratch and I know that you will do better next time or later." NO!

I will say it again and again. *Never give credit. They have not earned it.* You will never have to give credit when you complete the program correctly. Your kids will sincerely thank you for this later.

It's all relative. *When their tank is empty, they complain.* That is why they complain. Now, they are ready to eat and their tank is full. "Oh, I'm paying attention to what my parents say now."

If you don't hold them to the agreements you make and the plan you set out, they will feel that it is false when you offer a consequence. "Mom's just kidding. She will forget in a week. She didn't really want me to learn these life skills." But, they sincerely wish for you to hold them to it. When it really comes down to it, there might be those times when you hear them say, "They're cool parents. They do everything for him. Those kids didn't have to clean their rooms and there were always great dinners that weren't even nutritious."

But, as those kids get older, they are going to say, "Wow. I don't think my mom and dad really did care. They just fed us whatever." Eventually, everything is going to click for them. Your children are all going to know and they will think, "How cool is that? Wow, my parents love me. That's why we only drink water and other healthy liquids in the house." **Parents Make Decisions, Children Make Choices.** You are **Creating the Right Environment.**

Once again, **Complaining** is your child *testing the water.* I know that this philosophy makes sense to you, or you would not have gotten this far in the book. You are deciding to *Create a Champion for Life.* Your child will whine, complain and oppose you, but stick to your guns and they will thank you. *Acceptance by self-evidence* will come when you stay on track with what you are choosing to create.

Before we wrap up, be reminded that when the complaints come:

1. *Agree*
2. *Re-explain*
3. *Ask again for the offer or for what is being taught*

"Yes, I *agree* with you. That may not seem fair. However, when you get a chance and understand a little more, you will think I'm one of the coolest parents in the world."

You *re-explain* and *ask for the initial offer*. "Whenever you are ready to make success happen, remember, my role as a parent is to teach you life skills, but it's not my job to make you happy. It's in YOUR power to choose. I am the 'ER' to you, my son, child, daughter, loved one and family."

Enjoy **Complaining** from now on. I know it sounds like a contradiction in terms, but it is a *secret code* for you to learn what's there for you to learn. It's time to step up and be the true champion parent you've always wanted to be. This philosophy empowers you with the tools you need to **Create Champions For Life.**

Final Thoughts by Bonnie:

After discovering this lesson on **Complaining**, I felt so much fresh hope for my children. I told you about Zachary throwing the chairs around in his classroom. I haven't told you yet that three out of four of my children had been diagnosed with ADD. My older son was diagnosed and prescribed a drug called *Concerta*. After six weeks on the drug, he was completely addicted and had a "jonesing-out" experience when he thought he had run out of pills. He was 12.

Paying attention to my children's complaints and understanding where they come from are huge blessings because they help me find solutions that more easily guide their behavior.

Before I *Learned to Speak Kid*, I would close up like a clam and put everything "on ignore" while I did everything for everybody because I did not know what else to do. I gave them everything and bent over backward to make my kids happy. I made horrible mistakes as a mom.

Now, I recognize the complaints early on, make sure they know how to do the job the way I expect them to and ensure they know their reward. I am confident that when you grasp this concept, it will free you from guilt and put you in a powerful position to find real solutions with your child or teenager.

I have to tell you that my kids say, "I like myself," regularly NOW. They tell me how much they love me because I always give them a chance to earn what's important to them. All four of them are no longer "labelled" and are excelling in school. Our home is as harmonious as a finely tuned Swiss watch. The transformation has been absolutely heartwarming and miraculous! It will be for you too.

1. What is the hidden code behind a complaint?

_____

_____

_____

_____

2. What are non-confronts? List at least five.

_____

_____

_____

_____

3. What is the formula, or what are the three steps to take, when you are confronted by a non-confront or complaint?

_____

_____

_____

_____

4. What are the benefits of Complaining?

_____

_____

_____

_____

5. Why is it important to allow your child to step up through a complaint instead of rescuing your child?

_____

_____

_____

_____

6. Why is it important to stick to your guns and follow through on your agreements with your child?

_____

_____

_____

_____

"*I haven't been able to ask correctly, but I need you to SHOW me what to do.*"

Chapter 11

Nutrition

~ There are two things when it comes to food: it's either going to be quality or it's going to be quantity. ~
Thomas C. Liotta

Bonnie: I'm sure you know someone, either directly or indirectly, who has passed away from cancer, diabetes, or heart disease, among the most common, or from other physical body shutdowns.

In the past three years, I have personally attended two funerals for men in their early forties who passed away in their sleep from massive heart attacks. It is at these times one questions, "Why do these things happen? He loved to exercise, worked hard and always had a positive attitude towards life."

Most people do not connect good nutrition with a healthy body. These are physical diseases, but what about mental diseases: ADHD, ODD, anxiety and depression in children? Could **Nutrition** make a difference in the behavior of your child? The answer is an absolute "YES!"

A posting on Facebook has a picture of a tablespoon of margarine and of butter with some ants. The three ants that went near the margarine were dead. The butter had hundreds of ants crawling all over it. Maybe it's disgusting to think about dead ants crawling on your butter, but nature knows best! If the margarine kills the ants, what the heck do you think it does to a human body over a lifetime? Have you ever read the ingredients in margarine? What on earth is all of that stuff?

In an article written by Denis Daneman, MB, BCh, FRCP(C) and Jill Hamilton, MD, FRCPC, it says that overweight and obesity in children and youth are increasing at an astounding rate throughout the world. In 1989, only 2% of youth aged two to 17 were classified as clinically obese; 15 years later, the rate was 10% for boys and 9% for girls. Furthermore, one in four Canadian children is overweight.[1]

1 Denis Daneman, MB, BCh, FRCP(C) and Jill Hamilton, MD, FRCPC, Causes and Consequences of Childhood Obesity, http://AboutKidsHealth.ca/En/News/Columns/PaediatriciansCorner/Pages/Causes-and-consequences-of-childhood-obesity.aspx (2010).

Here are some side effects for overweight children: high blood pressure, raised cholesterol and insulin levels, impaired glucose tolerance, type 2 diabetes, bone and joint problems, obstructive sleep apnea, asthma attacks, nonalcoholic fatty liver disease, kidney problems and polycystic ovary syndrome. Being overweight and obese is also associated with psychosocial problems such as poor self-esteem and depression.

Good proper nutrition can prevent most diseases, whether caused by obesity or not.

We are not here to convince you to switch to organic foods; we are here to encourage you to read the labels on the food you eat and feed your children. Research the side effects now and in the future.

I have watched YouTube videos that brought me to tears because of what I learned about ground beef in fast food restaurants! In switching our diets to mainly organic, I have found that the food tastes better, lasts longer in my body, and makes my children, my spouse and myself feel healthy and vibrant.

This chapter on **Nutrition** will raise your awareness and help you understand its importance. You will see how to assist your children in making great choices for themselves that will enable them to remain healthy, young and vibrant throughout their lives.

Read on to see what Thomas shares with us on **Nutrition**.

Thomas: This is going to be a fun chapter in which you will learn to encourage your children to participate in shopping. We will cover how to incorporate the game of hide-and-go-seek. You will learn to apply strategies from previous chapters, especially **Parents Make Decisions, Children Make Choices.**

We will cover what it means to pre-frame in more detail so you can create success in any Environment. Of course, this chapter will give you the opportunity to become aware of nutrition and teach good nutrition to your children.

When it comes to *Nutrition*, it is important to understand that anything you eat in the store is good if you are starving to death. But, when you add a *"Plus 1,"* meaning that you *add to the sequence,* you *improve* upon that basic level of eating. After you've already gotten out of starvation mode, where you are just looking for anything to eat, you are now beginning to be able to make better choices.

There are three categories for your groceries:

1. *Bare Minimum*
2. *Average*
3. *Outstanding*

Organic is an **outstanding** choice because our body is organic. So, 100% organic is the most obvious and best choice when you really think about it. Any research you do on this will prove to you, beyond a shadow of a doubt, that this is reality.

In this chapter, you will be encouraged to *identify ingredients* and begin to experience major "Ah-Ha" moments. As you execute some of the strategies in this chapter, you will be encouraged to identify certain harmful ingredients listed on the label of the food you're feeding your children.

We will use the example of *high fructose corn syrup*. What if you decided to delete this ingredient from your children's diet? Furthermore, I will guide you to watch for synthetic food coloring and artificial, chemically made, processed foods, which are the furthest thing from organic.

As you research, you will find many shocking ingredients on labels. "Seriously? There's wood pulp in my food as fillers? So, I'm eating wood...wow!" I would give you the answer here, but that is not my job. It is my job to make you **aware** of reading ingredients on your food labels so you can realize what you are putting into your body.

We would never suggest that you stop eating chemicals made from coal tar; we are suggesting that if you are going to eat it, then know that you are eating it and feeding it to your children. This one *life skill* can add years and decades to your and your child's lives. It can also improve the *quality of life* for your family. So, enjoy this chapter and engage as we go into the store and talk about ingredients.

Bread is a basic food in most households. We are now in the bread section in Costco. We hear this from our children: "Can I get the bread?" So, what are your criteria? Remember **Parents Make Decisions, Children Make Choices.**

One key thing you're searching for is any bread with zero sugar and zero glucose-fructose. You're the decision maker. You're the parent. Children develop confidence when they can make *choices*. So, as you make your way through this whole aisle full of all the different types of bread, begin to play a hide-and-go-seek game with them. Tell them, "Pick any bread you like. Just find your favorite with no sugar or glucose-fructose ingredients."

Processed sugar and glucose-fructose, also known as high fructose corn syrup, is a major cause of obesity.

Making these decisions and having your child participate with you will encourage them to ask questions like "What do you mean?" "Why do I have to grab the bread, find the ingredient list and ensure those ingredients are not listed?" "Why is it so important?"

You have the opportunity to teach them a *valuable life skill. Agree, re-explain and* then *ask for the intention again.* It always comes back to this simple formula:

1. *Answer their question.*
2. *Explain what you found in your research.*
3. *Send them off to choose.*

They bring back something that looks nice and colorful, such as eight-grain bread. As you go through the ingredients with them, playing the game of hide-and-go-seek, they look through the list and there it is, both sugar and fructose. This does not meet your criteria. You will always be able to find all organic ingredients in one of the brands available. If you have to, find the organic section and you will find bread with no sugar there.

YOU make the decisions. If eating healthy and organic is important, give them the criteria. You say, "You can find any bread that you like, as long as it has the *cool* organic sticker and there's no processed sugar in it."

Now, the game has begun. They get to search for and find the different brands of bread that contain sugar and ingredients they do not recognize and can't pronounce. They are learning a *life skill* that will become a habit for them to live by with their children: investing in and ingesting organic bread. They will eventually be excited to have found one. "Oh, look at that; this one says organic. Oh, that's the good stuff."

If the bread has sugar, it has organic *cane* sugar, but the bread with no sugar is the best choice. Children like it because they chose it and it's already **parent-approved**.

Going to the grocery store can be a great fun experience versus "Mom, can I have this?" "Mom, can I have that and that?" to which you would have had to say no. Always **pre-frame**. "This is what we're looking for. Pick any specific one you like that has this ingredient or doesn't have that ingredient." That way, whichever one they find, it's already **parent-approved** and everybody wins!

All right, here we are in the **dairy** section. This is where the eggs are, so you send your child off to get eggs. They'll find brown and white ones, big stacks of 60, some in packs of 18, some in packs of 12, some in styrofoam, and some in cardboard.

When you look at the different pricing and packaging, you see five dozen eggs for about $7. Then, you look over there to the left. You see, locally produced, cage-free, meaning they get to run around, 100% organic-fed chickens who laid the eggs; the price is $6 for 24. Now, the essential thing here is that your kids always look for *certified organic-fed, cage-free hens* who laid the eggs. Allow them to pick any eggs that fall in that category.

They will discover that organic eggs are more expensive, at $6 for 24. There are five dozen for $7. When you think about it, you ask, "Why would I buy 24 when I can get 60 for basically the same price, give or take one dollar?" My best guess is that these 60 are NOT free range nor fed good organic meals. If you need to, look up online how hens are raised for mass production. You may be surprised by what you find. Why would we skimp on groceries when what we put in our bodies will determine our health for the rest of our lives?

There are two things when it comes to food: it's either going to be *quality* or it's going to be *quantity*. Something must go down when running a business and negotiating the price or costs. Farmers look at chickens as money. They are forced into cutting corners on what they're feeding them and where they're raising them. This means that the chickens cannot run free. Is it in the farmer's best interest to make decisions based on you and your family or on their business earning a profit? Research here, and you will see that when chickens are mass produced, they are put in boxes about eight cages high and fed on conveyor belts.

Hmm, something for you to research? This may be where the eggs you spend your money on come from. That's something for you to decide, but I always look for those key organic symbols.

Many people like soda pop, especially as a treat for kids. One key factor here is that when your child is arguing about buying pop, you ask them, "Well, what is it that we're supposed to be looking to avoid on the ingredient list? We're looking for things that don't have any sugar, right?"

"If you can find any beverage that doesn't have sugar or glucose-fructose in it, I'll be more than happy to take a look." So, you are always operating in the "yes, yes" mode rather than the "yes, no" mode.

When they find that the second ingredient is almost always sugar, would you ever have to say no to them? No, it's not like that. You ask them, "What ingredients are we looking to avoid in the beverages we buy?" "You can pick any beverage you like, but remember you're looking for one with no sugar or fructose."

So, once again, if they ask you to buy something like soda, you ask, "What are the ingredients we're looking for?" "Oh, yeah, nothing with *sugar* or *fructose*. "Hey, that's what I like about you. You are astonishingly smart. You understand what to look for. Keep your searches going."

Your children can go from soda to soda; the best thing is they are learning to read the ingredients on the food labels they choose. This will become a habit for them. Your child will have fun scanning through the whole ingredient list, looking for one that doesn't have, you guessed it, any sugar! Now, you are making *decisions* about what's important for your child to drink. He or she is excited because they have the ability to *choose*. Plus, they know that what they put in their body will help them remain healthy.

An interesting fact about your body is that it is either alkaline or acidic. It's like the water in a pool or hot tub; if it stays right around the pH level of about 7.0, then everything seems to work well. But, the pool or hot tub gets slimy when the pH gets off.

When you drink beverages high in sugar, your body becomes acidic. Many diseases thrive in an acidic environment. A pH of 2 is 100,000 times more acidic than a pH of 7. One can of soda pop greatly lowers your alkalinity and is 100,000 times more acidic than your natural pH level. A pH of 2 means that a person would have to drink 32 eight-ounce glasses of alkaline water to neutralize the effect of one can of soda.

If a child wishes to drink one of these, you let them know that to have one of these, they also have to drink about 20 times the same amount of water. "Oh, I don't want to do that." "Well, my life skill teaches you how to be healthy, so why would I buy something that would make you unhealthy? Let's find one that will make you healthier."

Now, they understand it, and you are **Creating the Right Environment.** Your child will actually say, "Hmm, maybe I'll just have water because there's no way I can drink 20 or 30 containers of water just to neutralize one pop."

That's a basic fact to share that will help to keep them on track. When kids get to the point where they begin to identify some of the big words on the ingredient list that even I'm not able to pronounce, that is a great start to their lifelong journey of good **Nutrition**. Make it a point to do some research with your child. When you find something like Coca-Cola with phosphoric acid and find that it is used to remove blood stains off the streets, they will most likely choose not to drink it. When they begin to understand some of these things for the first time in their life, they go, "Oh, eww, I didn't know that. I was just mesmerized by the colors."

Your job is to instruct and educate your children so they see both sides of the coin and make better choices.

What about the *junk food aisle?* Are the kids used to eating popcorn during movie night? **Parents Make Decisions, Children Make Choices,** so once again, go ahead and *pre-frame*. You can say, "I'd Love for you to have popcorn. Go ahead and find me popcorn that has just ONE ingredient and a non-GMO stamp (Genetically Modified Organism)." That way, when they find it, you're on the right page and it's already *parent-approved.*

"This one here has two, four, six, eight, 10; there are 12 ingredients in this one." It wouldn't pass. "Let's get this one over here. It just has popping corn!" Allow them to be involved in the process of finding the ingredients. This will plant a seed in their mind. "If this one says just popping corn, what do you need all these other things for?" They'll figure it out; it will start them on a process of questioning and understanding **Nutrition** better for themselves.

Once they begin asking these important questions, you have a perfect communication window: "That's a great question. Let's explore why an ingredient you can't pronounce would be in there. Here we go. It's used for a preservative and to lengthen freshness." You can always operate in that "yes, yes" mode. Empower your *children to make choices* based on YOUR *parent-approved decisions.* That's the best place to be as a parent. Right?

What about *syrup?* "Let's explore some of the syrups and see if we can find something that fits our criteria." Once again, the parent does what? They Make *Decisions.* With that all being said, your job is to *pre-frame* the *acceptable ingredients.* "I would love for you to get syrup.

Go ahead and find me a syrup that has only one ingredient."

"Okay!" Off to the races they go and they look through the entire aisle at the different syrups. When you look at the two extremes of syrups, you'll be able to see the difference. "Oh, I want this one." "Excellent, let me add them up: high-fructose corn syrup, two, three, four, five, six, seven, it contains 10 ingredients. Now, once again, I would love for you to have some syrup." "But, I want this one." "Great, how many ingredients do we look for?" "One." "How many ingredients are in that syrup?" "It has 10." "Great, keep on searching." Eventually, they'll come up with one that has just one ingredient. "Here it is, pure maple syrup." "Excellent! One ingredient that's what maple syrup should be."

Alright, the *cereal* section. Cereal is a favorite food for children. "Mom, can I get that?" "Can I have this?" "Absolutely, I would love for you to have cereal."

You list the prerequisites. "Let's go ahead and quantify a couple of things. I'd like you to find some cereal with zero food coloring and no sugar or *high fructose corn syrup*. You can pick any one you like and it must have at least one or two organic ingredients. Go ahead and find those specific things,"

With whatever criteria you begin to develop, you set the tone. Let your child take off and use their creativity of hide-and-go-seek to find exactly what you're looking for. Their attention will begin to shift *off* of the pretty colors. When I was that age, it was the toy at the bottom of the box that made me convince Mom to buy it. Was it the right choice? No. I didn't have a clue when I was a kid and your children don't have a clue, either.

If you're starting the game, take the simple steps of no high fructose corn syrup, sugar, or any food coloring just to begin the process. If they've been eating only junk for a long time, let me tell you, switching over is not going to be easy. However, you can wean them off, step by step, by removing one or two ingredients each time you **Make a Transition.**

This is a hidden key to success: take the steps slowly.

All right, as you begin the game, remember to start by picking specific criteria for the key ingredients you're looking for or want to *eliminate*. Whatever you come up with for your family's grocery shopping game, that's what's going to be right for you. Here are a couple of suggestions and recommendations on where to start.

We already mentioned *sugar,* so you can start with something like this: "Hey, Mom, Dad, I want this one." "Great, I would love for you to have this one. What's the key thing we're looking for?" *"No sugar."* "Ah, see, you're smart at this." As you explore the ingredients with your children, you count"...one, two, three...oops, there it is, brown sugar. Nope, it doesn't pass. Keep going! You can find it!" *You always give encouragement.* There is a good cereal out there. They will find it. Now, they come up with Cheerios: "Cheerios are good." It doesn't matter what the brand is; go to the ingredients list. "Oh, here we are, whole grain. Uh oh, sugar. Any sugar, fructose, brown sugar, or high fructose corn syrup, yup, doesn't pass. Keep searching."

"Maybe you can even step up your game and find that organic sticker we talked about, little Timmy. You actually grabbed that and it doesn't have any sugar, does it?" They read, "Oh, here you are, evaporated cane juice. There are pumpkin seeds, flax seeds and other seeds." "This is a great choice. Wow, good job, Timmy. You did really well."

When they make their choice and it's been parent-approved, EVERYBODY wins!

How awesome is that? You're now **Creating the Right Environment.** You will not see big temper tantrums or fits. Use the *pre-frame* strategy prior to heading inside the store because when they start coming up to you asking, "Mom, can I have this?" "Mom, can I have that?" chances are, you'll end up backpedaling. But not if you set it up FIRST. *Pre-frame*.

Sometimes, it may be a particular brand you're looking for when you send them on their journey. Let's take Quaker, for example. They have a variety to choose from when it comes to selecting oats. Steel-cut oats, rapid cook oats, instant oatmeal, low sugar oats. You get the picture. Often, you're going to find that the same company has a better version and a starvation version. Remember, any food from any store is awesome if you are starving to death. You send your child: "Go ahead and find the oatmeal with no sugar."

They find a few versions of oats. Have them read the ingredients of each package. You'll hear, "Look at the ingredients right here: sugar, sugar, sugar, it does not pass." However, when you get to another version from the same company and see it has 100% grain oats, it passes. It has no other ingredients. "Excellent choice."

It's important to be aware and think as you teach your children about *Nutrition*. Kids will see many cool flashy colors on different types of products. You know this to be true. Yes?

Country Time and Tang are two great examples. The ingredients in Tang say it's got sugar and fructose and contains 2% of a bunch of other Yellow 5, artificial color, and Yellow 6, and who knows what that stuff is.

Country Time Lemonade is the same thing: sugar, fructose and then 2% of all of these other Yellow 5, artificial colors, and stuff you probably won't even want to know about. It's all sugar and processed synthetic chemicals. These particular products contain *tons* of sugar. Here is a big bag of sugar: add a bunch of things into the bag that don't make any sense to digest and then charge more money for the mixture. This is a fantastic reason to begin to shift from keeping your kids happy with what they *want* to help them to realize what exactly it is that they're drinking and eating.

They would be better off having some water to which you could add some natural fruit, like lemons or blended strawberries. Squeeze some real lemons into the water, add a little maple syrup and have your Country Time drink without any of the unknown ingredients like Yellow 5 and Blue 1. Here is a hint. Would you drink it if I told you that I added some coal tar to your lemonade? Mmm....

When you do your homework, chances are that you will probably never ever drink this product yourself, therefore, you certainly would not wish your children to drink it. It's something to think about. Become aware of the ingredients in the products you feed to your child. If it contains sugar, then that is your choice; have fun. We encourage you to be mindful of what you're doing and to make smart-**ER** *decisions* so your kids can make smart-**ER** *choices*. We're all on the winning team of *Creating Champions For Life*.

Let's talk about gum. There are hundreds of brands and types of gum. You hear this, "Mom, can I have, Mom, can I have, Mom, can I have, Mom, can I have," all the time. Kids love gum. Right? "It's not food, so it doesn't really count. Can I have this one?" They usually pick one that's a favorite color.

Here's a fun way to answer and show your understanding of **Parents Make Decisions, Children Make Choices.** "I would love for you to have some *gum*. Go ahead and find a pack of gum containing no *aspartame*." It's a big word for a child, aspartame. Let the hunting begin.

They look and look and look. "Oh, oh, *aspartame.* Let me go with this one. I bet this one, no. I like this. Where is it? Oh, there it is, aspartame, eww." And they'll go through all the choices of gum. The coolest part is that *repetition* is the second law of learning, so that's what they're going to learn. "Oh, what does this darn aspartame have to do with it? I want some gum."

Then, you can *explore* the fact that *aspartame* is an ingredient that *tames aspirations*. "This is a chemical that makes people go from choosing to make good things happen in their lives to becoming people who go, 'Huh; I really won't do much; not much aspiration going on here. Just relaxing.'"

Peanut butter and jelly is another popular childhood favorite. Decide to commit more and more and you will *look at and research ingredients*. Doing this will become addictive as you discover more and more, side effects from the chemicals that are added to the food you eat. Start looking for *zero sugar*. Look for a jam with just one or two natural ingredients. The same goes for peanut butter; you want just peanuts.

So, whatever your criteria are, give your child a chance to **make a choice** based on what they are looking for and a *choice* of their favorite flavor. As they start looking, they're going to grab whatever they find within their sight. They will see this one, and that one has at least eight different ingredients. Eventually, they will find one or two of them with only the actual jam ingredients. There are some black cherries and some lemon juice in it; it's all natural.

Find two or three different jams to choose from, at most, and let them choose. You will know which one is the best when they make that choice.

We move forward to the *peanut butter*. "Pick any peanut butter you like. Find the one that has just one ingredient." They'll go through, flip over all the labels, look and say,

"Buy this one here. This one here's got, oh, my gosh, about 15 or 20 ingredients on the list." Eventually, they will work their way down and find the right one on the bottom shelf. Ingredients: peanuts.

Summertime is always fun for hamburgers and hotdogs at picnics. Organically grown beef usually has no added antibiotics or growth hormones. When you get a chance, google *"pink slime"* to see what kinds of things are added to mass-produced ground beef. The next time you choose to have a hamburger, remember the pink slime, and we'll leave it at that.

We have just experienced the grocery store. We went through several aisles to raise awareness and create "Ah-Ha" moments for you. In recapping our experience, we've obviously found different cereals and good syrup. You may love fruit juices, milk or meat. You can buy many healthier things wherever you begin your journey; know that it's your *starting point* and it's all good.

Here are some of the things to keep in mind:

One is to **look at the ingredients,** in general. It makes sense to begin removing certain items from the food you feed your children and yourself. When I was running the martial arts after-school program, many parents came to me and said, "Here's little Timmy. He's an eight-year-old who doesn't listen in school. He misbehaves, doesn't do anything around the house and talks back. Here, fix him." And I said, "Excellent, yes, WE can. We, meaning all of us together with this program, can." My FIRST evaluation with them would always be "What does Timmy eat?"

"Well, we always eat good food." "Excellent. Let's go ahead and look at some of the things you eat. Did you, by any chance, notice, or maybe this is the first time anyone brought it to your awareness, any ingredient related to *corn syrups*? Was it a corn syrup solid, a corn syrup, or a *high fructose corn syrup*?"

Many items at the grocery store are subsidized by the government, which makes them available at a much lower price. Instead of using organic evaporated cane juice, which might cost more, these manufacturers get a subsidy for something cheaper, so it's better for their profit margin. Is that right or wrong? No, it's neither. It depends on whether you're a stockholder or a consumer.

Since you're the consumer, you have a *choice to vote with your dollars* on what's important to you. If you don't choose to vote and you buy whatever you happen to see, then you're actually voting: "Yes, please put worse ingredients in the items that I feed my children and myself."

So, you *start eliminating corn syrup* and going more organic. Then, move on to *food colorings.* You'll see natural and artificial colors. You'll start to see things you don't even know how to pronounce, let alone spell on a spelling test. What about Blue 1, Yellow 5 and Red 40? These are chemically synthesized food dyes created from coal tar (petroleum). They are the farthest thing possible from organic. They're put into our food because we like a certain flavor or a certain color that represents a flavor. Today, many of these food dyes are linked to hyperactivity, including ADHD in children.

So, if you have organic ice cream and it's supposed to be chocolate chip mint, the organic chocolate chip mint that I know of is white. It's not green. They add things in there to change the color to green which is not good. I've known this for the last 10 to 15 years. I have seen it work with so many kids. We chose to eliminate these "non-organic" types of items, the chemically synthesized, and all of the artificial colors, Blue 1, Yellow 5, Red 40, fructose, high fructose corn syrups, and anything with aspartame. With all of these things, ask, "From what tree did that grow?"

The more high fructose corn syrups are removed from your diet, the more your kids will move away from being borderline type 2 diabetic (a condition that means there is more sugar in the body than the body can actually balance out) and moving them toward a more restored health. When we discovered the importance of removing food colorings, we removed them. From my observation, when they began to eat better, there was obviously better behavior and health. Our four kids haven't had to see a doctor for over two years.

Your child might be diagnosed with ADHD. I had ADHD when I was a kid. I was extremely active. I noticed that teachers who could "work with me" gave me multiple tasks or extra projects because my mind moved quickly. I was faster than the other groups of kids, so the extra tasks worked out really well. I also know that when I was a kid, I ate unbelievable amounts of garbage types of food. Yes, Mom and Dad served a nice dinner and I got lunch and other things that weren't optimal for my body. At that time, Coca-Cola was a big thing for me. Any candy bar I could get my hands on to eat, I did. Those kinds of things contained ingredients that I now know contributed to that ADHD. I've seen it firsthand.

So, you *vote with your dollars.* Yes, you do. With every dollar you spend, you're voting for what you feel is right for you, your family and your community. When you begin to buy more things that are in the organic category, guess what happens? The money goes to the organic food producers and their prices will decrease because more people are buying them. In the end, the cheap cereal, which has a bunch of garbage in it, will be just as expensive as it is now, while the organic cereals will come down in cost.

I've witnessed directly that many kids who are diagnosed with ADHD will get prescribed medication and help of that nature. I believe that it's all backward; we are putting bad ingredients into their bodies and reacting to them. This is our experience. If you were to eliminate these non-healthy and non-nutritional ingredients, combined with this Learn to Speak Kid language, there is a huge probability for all those misbehaviors to subside or completely go away.

The last thing I would like to share is that when you go to buy *juices*, any type that says *pure*, look at the ingredients. It might say 100% pure juice, but in learning about *pasteurizing*, we found that they raise the temperature to about 160 degrees at a minimum. They say they do this so they can kill the bad bacteria or things that are not healthy. I'm thinking, well, what about all the good things in apple juice? Let's say that we take real apples and juice them, and you drink them right then; that's real **Nutrition**. But, when they juice apples and *pasteurize* the juice, they boil everything off to kill all of the bad which also kills the good. This is so they can put it in a container and have it sit on the shelf for two to three weeks or longer.

Ask yourself, could it all be about the money?

The more organic you choose, the more health you will experience now and in the future. The closer it is to "fresh off the tree" and coming to you with minimal processing, the healthier it is. If you really want to take your nutrition seriously, not only eat organic, but also eat local. Look for *farmers' markets* in your area to get the freshest, most nutritious produce.

I'd like to thank you so much for taking the time to begin the first stage of learning, which is to recognize the importance of good **Nutrition.** Recognize that the ingredients in your food may cause many different effects that are not right for your children, such as behavioral and mental health issues. Recognize that the more you begin to eliminate the causes for poor behavior, the more you replace bad ingredients with good ingredients, the more you'll see better behavior. It will seem like all of a sudden your child is now calm.

Final Thoughts by Bonnie:

I know, I know. **Nutrition**. Geez, I like to eat what I like to eat, too. I love pizza, pop and hamburgers. So do my kids. My waistline also seems to like these types of food, not to mention bugs that cause chest colds, stomach flus and just plain feeling off the mark.

When three out of four of my children were diagnosed with ADHD and my oldest son was prescribed medication, I had to take a look at **Nutrition.** I began to give them fish oil tablets, vitamins and other nutritional supplements. I changed my cereals and began to focus on a few healthy things. I was completely uneducated, or more likely, completely in denial when it came to good **Nutrition**, but I did the best I could with what I knew.

The first time Thomas and I went to the grocery store together, he said nothing until we got to the peanut butter aisle. I picked out a peanut butter. He asked me, "Why did you pick that one?" I looked at him weirdly, like I knew I did something wrong and said, "Because it says creamy on it." He showed me the *ingredients list* which I had never paid attention to before. I had always paid attention to the *cost* of the product. On the ingredients list were about 10 items. He picked up a different kind of peanut butter, Adam's brand, with one ingredient: peanuts. We bought Adam's peanut butter that day and I will tell you right now it is the best peanut butter I have ever eaten and it has *one* ingredient!

Since then, I have checked every label on every item of food that I buy. I do my research on what ingredients are when I do not recognize them. I have discovered that cellulose is derived from wood pulp; it's there to bulk up food. It offers zero nutrients but makes you feel full, so you lose weight. Wow! I also discovered that my favorite candies have coal tar in them and some red colored ice cream treats have bug guts!

Since we changed our diet to all organic, I have noticed a big difference in my children's health, both physically and mentally.

None of my children are on medication now. They are all doing very well in school! I can tell when they have been eating food with chemicals because they usually develop a slight cough or irritability shortly afterward. I found out the other day that the natural immune system also likes to eat sugar. In fact, when you eat more than 100 grams of sugar, your immune antibodies will be tied up eating sugar for up to five hours. This means they are not available to fight off infections.

Do you think it would be important to think twice before taking the lollipop from the doctor's office? As their parent, I must do the best I can to set them up with good habits for life. The food we choose to eat now will be the food we continue to eat in the future. Trust me, when your kids find out the truth about the ingredients you chose to remove from their diets, they will be very grateful.

1. What are the three different categories for your groceries? Describe when you would choose each category.

_____

_____

_____

_____

2. What happens when you decide to remove high fructose corn syrup from your child's diet?

_____

_____

_____

_____

_____

3. Explain the game you can play that will involve your child in the shopping experience.

_____

_____

_____

_____

_____

4. Whose job is it to teach your child the life skill of good Nutrition? Why?

_____

_____

_____

_____

5. Why is it important to shop by the ingredients list, not the price? Describe the difference between alkaline and acidic.

_____

_____

_____

_____

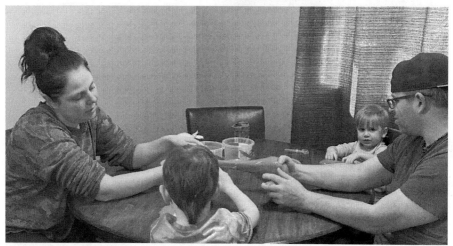

Chapter 12

Linguistics

~ Positive linguistics creates positive opportunities. ~
Thomas C. Liotta

Bonnie: There is a universal law called the *law of polarity*. It is called a universal law because it is *consistent* and *never changing* throughout the *universe*. Gravity is NOT a universal law. It is not consistent throughout the universe. Gravity only exists in this exact form on *this* planet. *The law of polarity* means that you cannot experience good without experiencing bad; you cannot have an up without a down; you cannot have light without dark.

Because this is the final chapter of **Creating Champions For Life's** *Learn to Speak Kid* book, it is important to be aware that you cannot experience good with your kids without experiencing bad. What if there was a way to improve the ratio of good days over bad days with your children by making a simple shift in the words you use?

Linguistics is the *study of language.*

When you study the power of language and words, you become aware that the *law of polarity* means that there is an equal and opposite to everything, including the words used in the language you choose to speak.

You were mainly taught to speak by your parents or whomever you most associated with as a child. If you are from another part of the country, you were even taught how to speak with a different accent.

Successful people speak differently than unsuccessful people. It is a proven fact that the words you use with your child will directly impact their self-esteem. In an article titled "Self-Esteem and 'If...then' Contingencies of Interpersonal Acceptance," Mark W. Baldwin and Lisa Sinclair, University of Winnipeg, write:

"For low self-esteem participants, success and failure contexts facilitated the processing of acceptance and rejection target words, respectively, revealing associations between performance and social outcomes." They conclude the study by stating,

"These results contribute to a social cognitive formulation of the role of relational schemas in the social construction of self-esteem."[2]

Self-esteem is a child's success thermometer in life. They will become what they believe for themselves, no matter what fundamentals they are taught correctly. So, do you agree that the study of language is important for you and for your children? Let's read on to find out what Thomas has to say about words, aka **Linguistics**.

2 Mark W. Baldwin and Lisa Sinclair, Self-Esteem and "If...then" Contingencies of Interpersonal Acceptance, http://SelfEsteemGames.mcgill.ca/research/ baldwinsinclair.pdf (1996).

Thomas: What I love about all of this is that you can change the *momentum of certain behaviors immediately* simply by making a slight shift with the words you use. Consider this question: Do you think a word *before* you speak it? After a moment of thought, I am sure you concluded, "Yes, I think the word before I speak it." That is, of course, the correct answer. You definitely *think* a word *before* you *speak* it. Even if you are one of those "speak your mind" types, you must have the word in your mind before it comes out of your mouth. Some people think the words very rapidly.

Take a moment and place your hand on your throat. Now, say your name. Do you feel a vibration? Keep your hand on your throat and say positive words like joy, happiness and peace. Now, say negative ones like anger, jealousy and hate. You still feel a vibration, whether you say the words loudly or mumble them under your breath. Right? This vibration is an essential piece of the puzzle worth understanding.

ALL sound operates in vibration.

Radio stations are picked up through a vibration frequency. Your words that begin with a thought are first heard by your ears and, more essentially, felt in your heart as vibration. Most people are aware of the term *vibration*. Have you heard the Beach Boys' song, *Good Vibrations*? If not, go listen to it on YouTube. You know what it's like to walk into a room when there's a *sad* person there. You don't even have to talk to them; you know they are sad because you can *feel* it. That is *vibration*.

By learning the basics of Linguistics, you will be able to create positive change for yourself and your child.

If you are driving in your car and continually hold your steering wheel to the left, you will continue moving towards the left. As soon as you make a decision to go in the other direction, you simply turn the wheel in the opposite direction and you head towards the right. Make a shift in language from *un-serving* to *serving*, from *victim* to *victor*, from *bare minimum* to *outstanding,* and, yes, it can be as simple as changing the direction of the steering wheel.

Let's dive into the subject of **Linguistics** where we will discuss some of those un-serving words that you are most likely presently using. Let's see how easy it is to speak *double negatives*. We will help you create an automatic translator so you will be more aware of how to change *any* sentence to cause your message to vibrate on a higher level.

You will become aware of some words that continue to keep people in bondage for their entire lives. You'll soon realize how to create a positive mindset for both your child and yourself by learning to create a new perspective of what's good and what's bad.

For instance, we were taught that blue is for boys and pink is for girls. If you heard the sentence presented in the opposite way, blue is for girls and pink is for boys, that would be perceived as bad or wrong. If everyone in your family uses their right hand and you see someone picking something up and writing with their left hand, that could be *perceived* as wrong or bad.

Your mind will perceive any word you hear as either good or bad. Whichever your perception, someone *taught* you that. Someone along the way taught you that joy, happiness and abundance are positive words and that anger, hate and jealousy are negative words. These words are perceived as negative or positive only relative to another word.

Why is there usually a **challenge** in creating change? What is a challenge to change? Let's look at the word:

CHALLENGE

There are three letters in the word challenge that, when removed, would create or represent change.

C H A L L E N G E

The first "L" stands for **LIES**. These are the lies that your mind will present to you when you encounter any thought of change. You can move forward when you remove self-limiting lies that have stopped you from moving forward in the past. Like learning about the tooth fairy, which turns out to be a lie but seems real to a child.

C H A L L E N G E

The second "L" would represent the word **LIMITATIONS**. *Self-doubt* is a belief that exists in many of our children and adults, such as "I am not good enough" or "he is better than me." Once released, you will be able to move closer to creating authentic change.

C H A L L E N G E

The final letter preventing change is "E," which stands for **EMPTINESS**. "What is this emptiness that I feel inside that is a challenge to change?" There is no passion, pizzazz, drive, nothing. It's just empty.

So, when you remove the **L**IES, **L**IMITATIONS and **E**MPTINESS from the word C H A L L E N G E, what is the automatic transformation of the word? Yes, it is the word:

CHANGE!

I remember a time in my life when learning at school was exciting and fun. I soon learned that there are words in our English language that don't always make sense. Take the word BIG, for instance. The teacher was teaching us how to spell a new word, BIG. "What does the word big mean?" "BIG describes things' size like this building is really BIG or the sun is really BIG.

Right next to the word BIG, they teach us another word. This word is bigger, but it is LITTLE. "What does LITTLE mean?" Little is for things that are small, like an ant. Or, a child is SMALL compared to an adult.

From a child's brain, I remember thinking, "Hey, wait a minute. The word BIG has three letters and the word LITTLE is twice as big with six letters. So, BIG is smaller than little?"

The teacher responded, "That's just the way it is." "Okay. I will accept that because you are my teacher. It just seems weird that something smaller is actually bigger. It's a word; I'll work with that."

As we move forward, I know you are saying, "Yeah, our language is quite strange." You were introduced to multiplication right around grade three, four or five, depending on your aptitude. Shortly after that, you would have been introduced to two types of numbers: negative and positive.

Here, we see the *law of polarity* again: negative and positive numbers, negative and positive words, and negative bad versus positive good.

Here are a couple of facts I was taught about math: If I took a positive number and multiplied it by a positive number, the answer would be a positive number. If I took a negative number and multiplied it by a positive number, the answer would be a negative number. Okay, so the minute you add a negative, the number becomes a negative number. Got it!

So, a negative number multiplied by a negative number should be a negative number, but then I learned that a negative multiplied by a negative is a positive! What? This makes no sense!

"So, what you're saying is positive with negative equals a negative. Positive with positive is positive. But, negative with negative is positive? Okay, you're the teacher. Wow, I'm learning all these great things."

The system's developers found it easy to translate this math formula into the English language. It works like this: the words you use will either empower or disempower you, meaning the successful results you want are moving towards or away from you.

Your words either bring you into a more positive, vibrant vibration, or they bring your vibration down. The words you use either attract people towards you or repel them away from you. This is based on the law of polarity with the law of opposites: up, down; light, dark; front, back.

I found an acronym for the word *GOD*. This has nothing to do with any religious viewpoint. Remember, whatever feeling is associated with the word *GOD* within you was taught to you by someone else. It could be happy, angry or curious. You could have a positive or negative feeling with the word *GOD*. *GOD* is a word.

G Grow
O Or
D Die

From what I observe, the "**G**" stands for GROW. The "**O**" stands for Or. The "**D**" stands for DIE. You are either *growing or dying.* In nature, plants grow, blossom and flourish, or they wither and die. The words you use will help your children grow, blossom and flourish in life, or they will hide all opportunities for success. Again, you choose.

Until now, if you were taught in a manner that caused you to communicate with a language that *taxes* you, meaning it takes away opportunities from you and steals your energy and vitality (hint: you are using it now), would you want to know about it?

Truly, this is YOUR choice. If you understood that words can keep you down, would you work diligently towards correcting this issue? Let's put the words to use in a practical reality. You are out and about and while interacting with the gas attendant, you ask, "How are you?" and he answers you, "Eh...not bad," or "Hey, I can't complain." Think about it. They explained it perfectly to you in mathematical terms. A double negative equals a positive.

Take your hand and place it on your throat. Now, say the word CAN'T. How do you feel? Say the word COMPLAIN. How do you feel? *Every word you speak is attached to a vibe or vibration.* You are creating a low vibration result by speaking two low vibration words in a row. Interesting, huh?

Wow! Most people believe they are being positive when they are really multiplying their negativity by two.

How funny is it, or is it even funny, that people are walking around in their everyday lives answering questions of what they are NOT instead of what they ARE? "How are you?" "I'm *not* bad." I'm not bad? Not bad? Hmm. Get it?

How about "Well, I can't complain." "No Problem." "No worries." The following answers would be the same message with a completely higher vibration. "I'm fantastic!" "Very good." "My pleasure."

Can you see the words we use every day to communicate with or around our children? And can you see how un-serving they are? Is it obvious? Every word you use that has a negative meaning will present a negative vibration, especially if you mix two negative words. These words will disempower you and your child.

Some words sound harmless while stealing our power. TRY is one of these words. It's very disempowering to try. How about "Just give it a try" or "Try harder?" The word try is overused in our vocabulary. It doesn't matter what we are doing, the word try is often used. Whether it is playing a musical instrument, playing a new team sport, or learning to drive a car, the word try is used.

"Try your best."

Try is a unique word because it's a *word of incompletion*. When working with your child to accomplish a new task, they usually say, "I'm trying really hard." In their mind, they are truly doing their best, but the word TRY, a word of incompletion, does not allow them to succeed. This word needs to be transformed into a word of empowerment.

Here is a simple exercise to practice. You can see for yourself what I mean in about 10 seconds. If you can see a pen, bottle or something beside you, TRY to pick it up. Now, you probably picked it up. "Okay, I picked it up." Now, put it back down and TRY to pick it up. It may take a few times, but when picking up the pen or bottle or whatever it is you picked up, you DID pick it up. This is not the same as TRYING to pick it up. Got it?

In the second Star Wars movie, Star Wars V, *The Empire Strikes Back*, Obi-Wan sent Luke to Yoda. Luke's ship crashed and landed in the swamp. When Yoda was teaching Luke how to use THE FORCE to get the ship out of the swamp, Luke kept whining, "I'm trying." Yoda looked at him and said,

"No! Try not. Do...or do not. There is no TRY."

The word incompletion persists as an incompletion even if you *try* really hard; *nothing* will actually manifest. There is no thought of completion being formed in the mind of the person who is trying. Could you imagine trying to go through a door? You either go through it, or you don't.

With the word of incompletion, your mindset is set for incompletion, failure or failure with honor.

There is no more TRY. Now, that word does not exist in your vocabulary! It can be replaced with **do** and **choose**.

Instead of saying, "I will *try* to get my homework done on time," say, "I *choose* to have my homework completed on time."

Another word to go on the negative scale is the word WANT. This may be surprising to you. **WANT** is another **word of incompletion.** To want something means *you do not have it yet,* or it is out of reach, or continuing to remain out of reach. This comes from a "lack mentality" or a "lack vibration." I can see something I like, but I CAN'T have it. I want it. If it were within reach, you would grab it and say, "I don't want it. I **have** it."

Do you remember a time when you were asked, "What do you want to be when you grow up?" Let's phrase that with positive words. "What do you *choose* to be when you grow up?"

Let's say you *want* a new watch. As soon as you get your new watch, what has to happen for you to want it again? Yes, you have to misplace it or break it to fulfill the vibration of want. So, again, it's a **word of incompletion.** Don't *want* to have something. Change it to a **Goal**, create a **Plan, Take Action and Persevere**! The word *shifts* from want to have, to choose, and to create.

The most empowering words you can say to yourself are "**I am.**" Using this technique will add power to your words, actions and gestures. Use "**I am,**" and then add whatever you want behind it. This will allow you to switch your vocabulary from double negatives to double positives! Instead of using *words of incompletion*, use *words of empowerment.* You share the exact same message but on a much higher level of vibration.

An excellent affirmation to share with kids is: "*I am a Genius. I figure things out easily and elegantly because I am a genius.*"

There will be a life skill of **Linguistics** to teach them as they say, "I *can't* open the peanut butter. I'm *trying,*" or "I *don't* know how to turn the hose on." "I wonder what other ways there are to make this work? I know you're smart, little Timmy. You can figure it out. Repeat after me: *I am a Genius. I figure things out easily and elegantly because I am a genius.*"

This will *reset* their mind from an un-serving thought and vocabulary of "I *can't*" to "What I CAN do?" It will set their mind to seek success: "I am a genius..." Their mind is NOW thinking that they are a genius and they will be able to find solutions. And they will find the solution.

Every.

Single.

Time.

What an incredible shift of power we have with a glance at **Linguistics**. We have only touched on a few words out of thousands. This is a language of solution-finding. Now that they know there is a process and a correct answer, even if they don't know the correct answer, they feel more confident that they can find one.

We do not give our children enough credit for what they are capable of most of the time. I have had students say things to me like "My brain doesn't work as well as other people's," or "My brain is broken." I would scratch my head and ask questions. You will learn to ask, "Where did you learn that?" Ask, "Is it serving you now?" Remember, you don't learn a word or thought pattern unless someone has previously taught it to you.

Unless someone tells you it is a broken brain, a brain is a brain. A color is a color until someone teaches you that blue is for boys and pink is for girls. So, ask, "Where did you learn that?" and "Are these self-limiting, brain-damaging beliefs going to serve you now that you are learning the formula of **Goal, Plan, Take Action**, **Perseverance**? Is it truly serving you well on your journey to becoming a *Champion for Life*?"

Do you have the ability to turn a challenge of the "I can't" complaint into a positive? Yes, you do! *Change* happens when you let go of the lies, limitations and emptiness.

There are so many double negatives: no worries, no doubt, can't complain, not bad. It is extremely valuable to understand that children think in absolutes. Remember all that you gained from the entire chapter dedicated to **Parent's Brain vs. Kid's Brain**? What I mean by absolutes is that children will take the meaning of a word and make it real. They see it as absolutely true.

Test this for yourself right now so you can become a believer instead of a non-believer. Think of the first thing that comes to your mind, which is not a pink elephant. If I'm like you and you're like me, you had to think of a pink elephant before you could not think of a pink elephant. You will always see the pink elephant first.

Your brain took the pink elephant as an absolute, so when the question is asked, "How are you?" and the answer is "Not bad." "Can't complain." "No problem!" then the words to focus on are NOT, BAD, CAN'T, COMPLAIN, NO and PROBLEM. The brain will literally believe, "Oh, I am bad. I am a complainer. I am a worry. I am a problem." *The message here is powerful.*

Let's say a child is being teased at school. The bully says, "You're stupid." To protect himself, the child begins to chant, "I'm not stupid. I'm not stupid." Now they are saying, "I'm not." But, what is the brain focused on? Right! The word STUPID!

When it is mentioned to act "as if..." it means to act as if you believe your child is smart; a genius uses good behavior, is helpful and is responsible. Acting "as if..." is a great method for starting a new way of thinking, speaking and responding.

The *Learn to Speak Kid online Self-Study Course* comes with an auto translator in the Quick Study Guide. This is a form that has three different columns in it. They are labeled:

1. *Negative*
2. *Positive*
3. *Neutral*

How amazing is it when you see this for what it really is and begin to use the translator in your home? You will be able to identify the language you are currently using. You will be able to translate your words easily and elegantly as you incorporate the law of polarity. Begin to discover the opposite of negative words.

What is the opposite of bad? Good. What is the opposite of victim? Victor. What is the opposite of worry? Confident. What is the opposite of problem? Solution. As you incorporate the negative to positive translation, you still operate with your child in that "yes, yes" mode. They have not done anything wrong. But, as they use sentences like "I have no doubt..." help them by making them aware and asking them if they can change the sentence into a positive one. They will have a lot of fun playing the game of opposites. "I can't do it. I can do it." "Stupid. Smart." "No problem. My pleasure."

"Little Timmy, what is the opposite of hard?" "Easy." "Wow. You are so smart, little Timmy. That's what I like best about you. You always know the right answer."

The English language we use today is taxing our energy. The majority of people give their energy away every time they speak. Because you are teaching these lessons to your little *Champions*, they will be able to maintain their power through positive **Linguistics.** They will have the ability to choose.

Now that you have had this lesson on **Linguistics,** have your child go through the four basic building blocks and add a little context with the explanation below:

SEE

1. **Self-control:** *I am in control of my body and my actions.* "I am practicing self-control." The translation is "I am choosing self-control."

KNOW

2. **Responsibility:** *I am responsible for my actions and my belongings.* "I will work to keep everything safe," or "I will behave myself." The translation is "I am responsible for my actions and my belongings."

DO

3. **Self-Discipline:** *I do what I am supposed to do by being asked only once.* "I do what I am asked most of the time," or "What am I supposed to do?" The translation is "I will get it done right now."

BE

4. **Focus:** *I keep my attention on the task at hand.* "I heard a noise in the backyard." The translation is "I will complete this task."

S.K.D.B.

These principles or stepping stones go hand in hand, so act as if the child already has Self-Control, Responsibility, Self-Discipline, and Focus. The more these are used and focused upon, the more your child will blossom and flourish.

Remember, what you give energy to will grow.

Do you remember the **GOD** acronym? Growing Or Dying? This is a choice; it is a *mindset.* Are you getting old, or are you becoming wiser? It is all a *choice.* Are your children being nurtured in a loving positive environment, or are they dying inside while searching for the proper **Linguistics** and structure?

You will begin to notice your child running up to you with enthusiasm, beaming, "I finished my homework already!" or "I mowed the lawn for you and you didn't even have to ask me." "Not bad, son." "Not bad, Dad? Did you mean to say, that's REALLY GREAT, son, instead?"

Not bad, negative vibration; really great, positive vibration. Can you see this is the same message, but it puts off a completely different vibration? Once you master **Linguistics**, you will notice negative words and double negatives every day and think, "WOW! "

You will notice on the news that they will only mention things in *negative* terms, like "There was a home invasion earlier this morning." They don't tell about the 99.999999987899999% of the population whose home was safe today. Think about it! If you don't, *someone else* will think about it for you and your family.

The more you grasp the concept of **Linguistics** and operate your auto-translator to create awareness of the positive messages that already exist, the more you and your children will have choices in your lives. Know that there is the law of polarity; every message has an opposite. Begin to drive your vehicle in both directions; learn to speak the other language, the world of positive.

You always have a choice to speak negative or positive words.

Remember the three letters that challenge change. They are "**L** **L** and **E**," which stands for **L**ies, **L**imitations and **E**mptiness. Eliminate lies around and within you, like the tooth fairy. What value does the tooth fairy have in your child's life? What about the confusion that BIG is smaller than LITTLE? Hmm....

Become more aware of the language you are speaking. I believe the more you become aware, the more there will be to become aware of. I congratulate you for completing the entire *Learn to Speak Kid* book! We encourage you to engage fully with the principles presented here, complete the lessons at the end of each chapter, and visit us at CreatingChampionsForLife.com

More than anything, stay consistent with what you choose to continue to create with your Champions! Congratulations!

Final Thoughts by Bonnie:

I am extremely emotional as I sit here thinking about the right things to say. What a powerful program of positive and proactive parenting from beginning to end.

I am emotional because I know this is the secret to creating a successful future for our children and the world, and that the book is about an hour away from being complete.

Since I was introduced to the concept of **Creating Champions For Life**, my life has forever changed. I am making decisions now as a strong, loving and smart parent. I am fighting for the little Champions to come alive more and more all the time. I realize I am not here to be my child's friend, their companion, or the key to their happiness. It is my job to *prepare* them for a successful life.

Before I met Thomas Liotta, I believed that I was the best parent. I always invested both time and money into my children. I did everything for them, but they did not appreciate it. I began to see a fast decline as my children became older. Thomas caught me one day with my *Linguistics*. I mean, he caught me completely off guard! I got upset with him and yelled at him, "I am never negative!" That was a huge eye-opener for me!

I know the lessons provided here are sound.

I know they produce results almost by accident when you execute the strategies.

I know they do!

This is just the beginning of your journey with **Creating Champions For Life.**

It will not be easy at first. I assure you it will be simple and worth the effort it takes to Learn to Speak Kid!

You will see that little Champion inside your child come alive. You will have the best relationship with your children; it will be better and greater than you can even begin to hope for right now. Imagine that every time you have a power struggle with your child, there is a lesson for you. As you listen to them and pass each lesson, your child will rise up and give you the best behavior you have ever seen! It is truly up to YOU.

Visit our website, CreatingChampionsForLife.com, to learn more about us and what we can do to help you become an empowered parent with Champion Kids.

Get our *Learn To Speak Kid Online Self-Study Course and* take what you have learned in this book to a whole new level.

Email us at *support@CreatingChampionsForLife.com* for an invitation to our Facebook group: *Harmonious Parenting: Time-Tested Principles For Cooperation.*

Now that you know we are here to answer your parenting prayers, let's work together to help more families discover proactive parenting using the **Creating Champions For Life** philosophy.

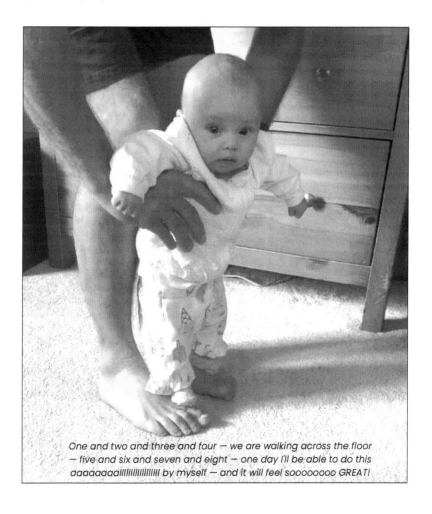

One and two and three and four — we are walking across the floor — five and six and seven and eight — one day I'll be able to do this aaaaaaaaiIIIIIIIIIIIIIIIIIIIIIII by myself — and it will feel soooooooo GREAT!

1. How do the words you use with your child impact them?

_____

_____

_____

_____

_____

2. What are the three letters in the word "challenge" that prevent authentic change?

_____

_____

_____

_____

_____

3. Why do two negative words not equal a positive word?

_____

_____

_____

_____

_____

4. Explain what a word of incompletion is. Share two examples.

_____

_____

_____

_____

5. Explain what vibration is.

_____

_____

_____

_____

Closing Thoughts by Bonnie

I know that it can be hard to believe that you can prevent and reverse ADHD and ODD, oppositional defiant disorder with the principles presented in *Learn to Speak Kid*. I did it with my kids, so I know it's true! It's just as easy to boil water by putting it on the stove as it is to freeze water by putting it in the freezer. It's the same with creating a winning environment for your little ones.

Until now, we have been set up to fail from the beginning as parents. We have been taught to expect terrible twos, horrific threes, rebellion at five and again at age 13. This is off the mark. It's not true. When children rebel, they ask for independence, life skills and acceptance of who they are. Yes, even two-year-olds. When we don't know this, we treat the poor behavior rather than *Learning to Speak Kid.*

All children and teenagers crave attention. The dramatic and steady increase in the diagnosis of child mental and behavioral disorders is astounding and unnecessary. Thomas has worked with thousands of children over 15 years and 15,000 hours to develop this astonishing language of *Kid.* As we explore the parenting methods, including Love and Logic, Positive Parenting Solutions, Peaceful Parent Happy Kids, etc., it is clear they operate from a reaction or response point of view. Every book out there on parenting will teach you how to handle poor behavior.

We are teaching you how to **empower** your children so they don't choose poor behavior; they choose Champion behavior. I have watched my children miraculously transform before my eyes. It has been so incredible that I had to help Thomas duplicate his knowledge for you.

However, it is so different from what society is used to that it will definitely take some repetition, support and time. That is why we created an online *Self-Study Course, Learn to Speak Kid*. If you are having a hard time learning and creating new habits, you may want to consider joining us there.

All my children have been *released* from any ADHD and oppositional defiant disorder diagnosis. In 2014, Jennie and Zachary were tested and did NOT qualify as students with a learning disability. They have also transformed from *Victim* to *Victor*, from defiant to cooperative, from depressed to happy, and from poor grades to fabulous grades.

What is it worth to help your children thrive?

All the answers to transform your parenting life, empower your kids, and eliminate child disruptive behavior disorders like ADHD (attention deficit hyperactive disorder), ODD (oppositional defiant disorder), anxiety, depression and other mental or behavior disorders are within these pages.

Good luck with it. Persevere and send us an email. We would be grateful and love to hear about your miraculous transformations. With the right *Goal* and *Plan* and by *Taking Action* with *Perseverance* to achieve success for you and your family, **YOU CAN DO IT**!

Love and gratitude,

Bonnie@CreatingChampionsForLife.com
Thomas@CreatingChampionsForLIfe.com

Help Us Spread Our Mission

Our mission is to get this information to every parent in the world so that a new generation of parents and children can grow up confident, capable, independent and empowered to become all they have been meant to be.

If you purchased this book from Amazon, please consider giving us a 5-star review. Your positive feedback helps us reach more parents, grandparents, caregivers and teachers.

We are forever grateful for your support!

"Do you have the courage to question anything and everything you think you know about parenting just might be wrong, and examine your parenting approach from a whole new perspective for deeper understanding?"

Final Message from Thomas Liotta

Creating Champions For Life Philosophy allows YOU to be the FIRST in your Family Lineage to create a Hypnotic cure that produces:

HEALING — UNITING — EMPOWERMENT
aka Heaven on E.A.R.T.H.

Great job making it this far as you continue on your journey from a White Belt to a Black Belt Mindset.

0	HOW		WHEN		WHERE			
MINDSET	**0 to 2**	**2 to 4**	**5 to 8**	**9 to 12**	**13 to 17**		**18+**	**EMPOWER**
	JUST SOMETHING DOG	SCONTROL FL	SELF F	FOCUS S	SPEED D	ENDURANCE	TIMING	UNITE	POWER	BALANCE	FLEXIBILITY	POSTURE

Made in the USA
Columbia, SC
08 July 2024

38177660R00248